Animation in Context

Fairchild Books
An imprint of Bloomsbury Publishing Plc

Imprint previously known as AVA Publishing

50 Bedford Square	1385 Broadway
London	New York
WC1B 3DP	NY 10018
UK	USA

www.bloomsbury.com

FAIRCHILD BOOKS, BLOOMSBURY and the Diana logo are trademarks of Bloomsbury Publishing Plc

British Library Cataloguing-in-Publication Data
A catalogue record for this book is available from the British Library.

ISBN:	PB: 978-1-4725-7828-0
ePDF:	978-1-4725-7829-7

Library of Congress Cataloging-in-Publication Data
Names: Collington, Mark, author.
Title: Animation in context : a practical guide to theory and making / By Mark Collington.
Description: New York : Fairchild Books, 2016. | Includes bibliographical references and index.
Identifiers: LCCN 2015043595 (print) | LCCN 2015045783 (ebook) | ISBN 9781472578280 (pbk. : alk. paper) | ISBN 9781472578297 (ePDF)
Subjects: LCSH: Animated films—Philosophy. | Narration (Rhetoric)
Classification: LCC NC1765 .C65 2016 (print) | LCC NC1765 (ebook) | DDC 791.43/34—dc23
LC record available at http://lccn.loc.gov/2015043595

Series: Required Reading Range

Cover image: Looming Marvellous: *Living with Asperger Syndrome*, directed by April Slocombe, London Metropolitan University (2015)

Back Cover image: *Zoi*, directed by Amanda Curl, University of Bedfordshire (2013)

Cover design: Louise Dugdale

Typeset by Roger Fawcett-Tang
Printed and bound in Singapore

Animation in Context
A Practical Guide to Theory and Making

Mark Collington

Fairchild Books
An imprint of Bloomsbury Publishing Plc

B L O O M S B U R Y
LONDON · OXFORD · NEW YORK · NEW DELHI · SYDNEY

CONTENTS

INTRODUCTION

EXPANDING YOUR THINKING ABOUT ANIMATION

Undertaking any media or art and design undergraduate course is a big step in discovering ways of learning, thinking and expressing ideas about the world around us, as well as preparing you to find work in a competitive global job market. Each type of media or art and design subject has certain ways of teaching these things, and animation is one of the most challenging subjects of all to teach and learn.

This is because animation involves a very broad range of time-consuming technical skills, which can often leave little headspace for thinking about much else, aside from copying the visual styles of other work. Therefore, whether given a specific or more open project brief, animation students may sometimes struggle to know how to come up with an idea or develop it into something with a more meaningful narrative and purpose.

Animé is an example of a field of animation that has important things to say about the world we live in and is commercially successful, but is often poorly copied on its visual style alone—in particular the work of Japanese director Hayao Miyazaki and Studio Ghibli. This can limit the career options of enthusiasts to competing with the very best animators of one highly specialized approach to animation production.

This book looks at how reading about animation, film and art theory can help you understand the *deeper* thinking behind different forms of animation such as animé. This enables you to borrow and combine ideas from a broader range of influences to produce other thought provoking, more original and successful projects. Therefore, being able to apply theoretical knowledge to the development of your practical skills can help you to express your ideas more effectively and sustain a more flexible animation career.

WHAT IS MEANT BY THEORY?

Theories are well-established sets of ideas, published by a range of thinkers and philosophers, which can span across different areas of the arts, humanities and social sciences. Theories are used to gain a deeper understanding of the meaning and significance of the work made by other artists, filmmakers and animators.

Theories provide a common framework of terms that can be used to discuss practical methods and more abstract ideas that define certain ways of working. Well-known theories covered in this book include montage and genre theory. Genre theory is used to classify different types of narrative context, such as the Western or science fiction. Montage theory was originally devised to explain and understand how the order, rhythm and duration of shots in a film affect its narrative meaning.

0.1

0.1
The Lady in White, directed by Michael Evans, BA (Hons) Animation, final major project, Cass Faculty, London Metropolitan University, 2015. The style and narrative structure of the animation was influenced by practices used in film noir that play with the standard conventions of film genre (examples of this are covered in chapter three).

INTENDED AIMS & OUTCOMES OF THIS BOOK

This book has been written in attempt to bridge what I have identified as a significant gap between the extensive range of practical animation books and growing number of animation theory books. That is to say, there is little that has been published to help animation students connect often more challenging theoretical ideas with their practical work. However, this book has *not* been written to set out a descriptive history of animation, nor teach essay writing techniques or specific practical animation skills as such.

The main aim of this book is to empower you with the confidence and enthusiasm to engage with theory as an interesting, integral, applied part of the creative process. This book is also intended to help take away the stress often associated with researching, reading, reflecting and writing about animation. Using 'plain English' as far as possible, the book focuses on exploring a core selection of theoretical approaches, which inform animation narrative and visual storytelling.

The main intended outcome of this book is to help you document theoretical ideas from academic books and apply them in a clear structured way to the analysis of any source of inspiration new or old, from an animated short or commercial to a Hollywood blockbuster or famous painting, and be able to think intelligently about how to incorporate ideas from these in the development of your own animation.

INTRODUCING CRITICAL, CULTURAL AND CONTEXTUAL ANALYSIS

Before going any further, I will introduce you to what is meant in this book by critical, cultural and contextual analysis. This will enable you to break down your research and analysis into a manageable set of tasks, so that you can simplify academic jargon, document ideas more easily and apply them directly to a range of practical exercises.

To be critical you will need to able to explore the methods used by a range of animation practitioners, comparing and contrasting their technical working practices and aesthetics with your own. This may be in relation to the cultural analysis of theories and conventions in film, art and design. You will also learn to contextualize where, when or why work was made, exploring how this range of knowledge can be applied to your own practice.

Aesthetic:	A set of principles that guide a particular approach to a style or design
Critical Analysis:	To compare and contrast a range of practioners and working practices
Cultural Analysis:	To understand theories or conventions behind particular ways of thinking
Contextual Analysis:	To analyse where, when and why an animation, film or artwork was made

OUTLINE OF BOOK STRUCTURE, THEMES & SUBJECT MATTER

There are many ways in which the subjects across the chapters of this book could be grouped. What I have tried to do is untangle a complex web of ideas and put them into a simpler linear order. More mainstream and conventional theories are explored first. These are then challenged and questioned by a framework of increasingly abstract ideas. Key theories introduced in this book include structuralism, semiotics, genre, humor, montage, propaganda, psychoanalysis, feminism and post-structuralism.

The book is therefore essentially divided into two parts. The first three chapters explore theories underpinning some of the core narrative methods used in more traditional feature length animation. The following chapters then expand thinking by discussing theories underpinning narrative in more contemporary areas of animation, such as advertising, gaming and animated documentary.

Each chapter includes a range of animation case studies that explore some of these key ideas and concepts, which you should be able to use as starting points to discuss work ranging from Disney and animé to independent artist-filmmakers such as Wendy Tilby, Amanda Forbis and Jerzy Kucia. Analysis is supported by interviews with contemporary industry professionals and student case studies that include 'live projects' made for real clients.

The book also includes pop-up 'key words' lists in certain places to help summarize more complex discussion, as well as more comprehensive key words lists at the end of each chapter. You can then use these terms to search easily for helpful information about selected concepts and topics and work through indexes to quickly find more detailed useful chapters in other sometimes lengthy and challenging books.

All chapters contain a further reading list of both introductory and more advanced texts to help you develop and discuss animation knowledge accurately, in a way others will understand, and pave the way for developing your interests independently after university.

As well as these key words and further reading lists, each chapter is well illustrated with a range of film stills, annotated images (pictures with brief text analysis) and lists of useful films to watch. To pull all of this together, chapters contain research exercises to help you break down analysis of selected animations, related films and artworks, and develop a practical outcome from your research such as a storyboard or set design.

0.2

0.2
De Intus, directed by Gavin Wrench, BA (Hons) Animation, final major project, University of Bedfordshire, 2010. The style and deeply psychological narrative structure of the animation was influenced by conventions used in German expressionist film, which delves deep into our repressed memories and fears (examples of this are covered in chapter four).

The Human Condition

The 'human condition' defines the core narrative theme of this book. This is an idea that has been debated for centuries by many philosophers, writers and artists, and continues to define subject matter in literature, art, film and animation. The human condition itself can be described as the artistic expression of the identity and everyday existence of an individual, society or entire civilization, which is determined by the events of their past, present and future.

Events from the past are often represented as memories, sometimes happy, sometimes sad. There is usually an association with the loss of things once valued. These events from the past define how we respond to and cope with the conditions we live through in the present. Our ability to survive is also driven by a longing for or hope that events in the future will enable us to overcome difficulties in the present, and either let go of or be reconnected with people, places or events from our past.

The human condition therefore is a term that captures the innate survival instinct of mankind to master his own destiny over the constraints and fears imposed upon him by other civilizations, society, individuals or even himself. Ultimately, the human condition is a term that can be applied to the relationship between mankind and the natural environment, that is, the ability of mankind to take control over the natural world and even leave planet Earth altogether in search of an even greater voyage of self-discovery.

0.3

Each chapter explores different forms of artistic expression of the human condition and their historical context. These include fairy tale representations of a child's rite of passage into adulthood; modernist and propagandist representations of the impact of technology and war on the everyman; and interpretations of deeply personal and abstract human experiences using techniques including animated documentary. You should be aware that subject matter is therefore often quite challenging, including discussion of violence and sexuality.

0.3
Production still from *Looming Marvellous: Living with Asperger Syndrome*, directed by April Slocombe, BA (Hons) Animation, final major project, Cass Faculty, London Metropolitan University, 2015. The style and narrative structure of the animation was influenced by more experimental approaches used in animated documentary (examples of these are covered in chapter six).

KEEPING AN ONLINE REFLECTIVE WORKBOOK

Each chapter of the book will help you build on previous exercises, develop ideas and document your practice in your own online reflective workbook. This provides a stimulating way of sharing findings and getting instant feedback on what you are doing from peers and tutors, thus collaborating on an otherwise seemingly daunting research workload. The conclusion to this book will help you consolidate your main influences into a rounded body of research-informed practice to aid future projects and artistic development beyond university.

The screenshot on the facing page (Fig. 0.4) illustrates a suggested format for your online reflective workbook. I recommend that you create a new workbook entry for each part of the book that you might use. For each entry, you might summarize the premise for each chapter and workbook exercise in your own words, as well as upload images, videos and text that you have produced in response to the exercises. There are numerous free blog sites on the Internet and many universities also have their own online learning resources for students to set up e-workbooks.

You may be able to embed video links from other sites of the films and animations that you have referred to in your own critical, cultural and contextual analysis of the case studies from each chapter and that underpin the development of your own work. You must always check the copyright conditions and credit the video source in your online workbook. It is worth setting up an account with some of the main user-generated video hosts to embed video links and upload your own work.

You could type up the list of books (plus chapters or pages) and sources you have referred to from the recommended reading lists, as well as any other books or academic journals you may have found and used. You might also include glossaries of terms and definitions in your online workbook to help you source information in the future. Good examples of online student workbooks and student work covered in this book can be found on the Fairchild Books website, where you will also find links to useful online, professional, international and academic journals: **www.bloomsbury.com/collington -animation-context**

Efforts have been made to be as inclusive as possible of animators, filmmakers and artists from around the world. Case studies explore work by people from Japan, Russia, Iran, Israel, Poland, Britain, Canada, America and more. However, I will admit that this does not extend to all continents. Therefore, while aiming to be inclusive, the book still essentially investigates animation through a western lens.

The exercises in each chapter should help you to think about news stories that may have similarities with subject matter in the case studies covered in this book. By reading about current affairs, as well as reading, thinking and writing about how and why real events have informed the work of others, you will have a better idea of how and why you can express yourself through animation. As an artist, animation can be a way for you to explore the world, understand your place in it and share your own artistic interpretation of world events online with others.

SEMIOTICS & SEMANTICS:
Designing backgrounds to tell a story
20.11.15

Cultural & Contextual Research:

The following workbook entries explore how to create meaning in images through the combination of objects and colours, composition and lighting. I have also researched and referenced how context affects the meaning of images, and grouping of objects within them.

These ideas have been applied to the development of background designs for a 2D project, beat board and production still, to help tell the history of a seaside pier.

I have conducted historical research for my work - into Victorian seaside architecture, and the history of the seaside town of Brighton, to tell the story of its famous West Pier.

Key Words: Indexical, Motif, Paradigm, Symbolic, Synchronic
Key Names: Saussure, Peirce, Lévi-Strauss, Barthes, Vermeer, Hokusai, Hiroshige
Key Books:
Chandler, D. (2007) Semiotics the Basics, Routledge: Abingdon
Hawkes, T. (2003) Structuralism & Semiotics, Routledge: Abingdon

Critical Analysis:

Visually I think my animation has successfully incorporated ideas such as the motifs of Victorian seaside architecture, and use of backgrounds to illustrate the passage of time. But I think that I could have paid more attention to the semantic meaning of objects, particularly towards the end of the film, where the story becomes perhaps a little too abstract for the audience.

Useful Artists & Films:

I have taken inspiration from the work of Japanese Edo artists Hiroshige and Hokusai, whose preparatory images of the 'floating world' are directly suited to my subject matter, and their production methods are similar to the process of animation.

Useful Companies:

I have a keen interest in architecture, and have been looking at how different design and VFX companies visualise projects using animation.

Link to VFX Company
Link to Design Agency
Link to Architecture Firm

MARK COLLINGTON BLOG

0.4
Workbook mock-up.

CHAPTER ONE
LANGUAGE & VISUAL MEANING: PLAYING SHERLOCK HOLMES

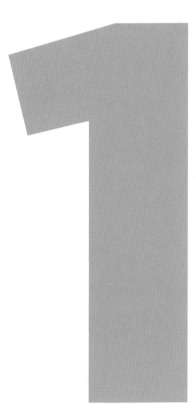

CHAPTER OVERVIEW: DEFINING NARRATIVE & CREATING VISUAL MEANING

In this chapter, you will learn:

- **How animators, artists and filmmakers use narrative methods and visual metaphors to create meaningful images.**

- **How narrative can be presented by combining compositional elements in fine art with the time-based aspects of filmmaking.**

- **The importance of researching the context in which an image is set, and how this affects the meaning we can interpret from it.**

- **How storyboards, layouts and set designs can be used as rich storytelling devices.**

"BE OFF!".

1.1
The chiseled profile of the fictional detective
Sherlock Holmes, with his Deerstalker hat and
Inverness cape, is as instantly recognizable as the
profile of American president Abraham Lincoln or
British Monarch Queen Elizabeth II.

INTRODUCTION

This first chapter asks you to assume the role of the famous detective Sherlock Holmes. You will learn how to visually piece together a story by paying attention to the smallest details in a range of different scenarios. You will investigate the narrative methods through which animators, artists and filmmakers have created images that explore ways of illustrating the underpinning theme of this book, the human condition. This includes analysis of visual metaphors (images of objects that carry meaning) in fairy tale and religion, to how we are defined by our surroundings, work, class, society and personal life experiences.

Narrative is a term commonly used to break down the storytelling process. Storytelling is traditionally used to describe a series of events, held together by a narrative structure with a clear beginning, middle and end. This might be in the form of a short fictional fairy tale or based on real events, from an epic historical drama to a documentary. Paul Wells, who has written extensively on animation, summarizes the essential story and narrative process as follows:

"The idea of a story may be understood as a sequence of events taking place over a particular period of time. These narrative events are informed by a chain of causes and effects, both subtle and explicit, the ultimate outcome of which is a specified moment of resolution.

In animation, what is particularly significant is the *presentation* of these events and, most specifically, how the order, or number, or extent of the events finds unique purchase and execution in the animated form."

Paul Wells (2007), *Understanding Animation*, p. 68

Broadly speaking, this chapter proposes that the term narrative can be applied to the analysis of an *individual* image, interpreting a scene depicted in a painting or photograph and the range of potential backstories or events yet to unfold. It is interesting to consider that the ability to read an image, or series of images, is an instinctive skill we usually take for granted.

But even more surprising is that it is a skill that we all too often forget to use at all. In this chapter we will learn how to see again. We will explore how even the more conventional forms of animation have particular ways of presenting narrative: by combining many of the formal aspects of composition in fine art with some of the time-based aspects of filmmaking.

The chapter begins by introducing structuralism, a school of thought that explores how we use language to construct ideas in our minds and how we express and interpret them through images. We will investigate how abstract symbols, or objects, environments and composition can be used in an image to create narrative meaning. We will also explore the importance of researching the context in which an image is set and how this affects the meaning we can interpret from it.

APPLES: INTRODUCING STRUCTURALISM & SEMIOTICS | WORKBOOK EXERCISE 1.1 | WORKBOOK EXERCISE 1.2 | LOVE LETTERS: SEMANTICS | WORKBOOK EXERCISE 1.3 | TIME TRAVEL: FROM MONOSCENIC TO SYNCHRONIC & DIACHRONIC NARRATIVE | CASE STUDY: SYNCHRONIC LAYOUT DESIGN FROM WEST PIER BY MARK COLLINGTON | CASE STUDY: CREATING A SYNCHRONIC NARRATIVE SET DESIGN | CHAPTER SUMMARY & FURTHER READING | KEY WORDS, NAMES & WORKS

INTRODUCTION

This is illustrated with discussion of the Walt Disney feature animation *Snow White and the Seven Dwarfs*, the film *Nosferatu* directed by F.W. Murnau, the paintings of Johannes Vermeer and Fra Angelico, the film *Vera Drake* directed by Mike Leigh, the Aardman stop motion documentary *Going Equipped* directed by Peter Lord, student stop motion set design work and also my own drawn animation work.

As we explore these theories we will work through a range of exercises to help us understand how to use these concepts in storyboards, layouts and set designs. This will enable you to think about how your animation environments can be used as rich storytelling devices, reducing the labour involved in character animation driving the narrative. However, the important narrative function of the character will be explored in chapter two and in other later chapters.

This chapter will therefore *critically* contrast a range of practices used in art, film and animation. It will look at *cultural* theories and conventions that can be used to understand and depict visual meaning and think beyond the language of the written or spoken word. It will also *contextualize* the time and place in which different images and animations were set and made.

RECOMMENDED VIEWING

Aladdin, directed by Ron Clements & John Musker, Walt Disney Pictures (1992)

Going Equipped, directed by Peter Lord, Aardman Animations (1990)

Nosferatu, directed by F. W. Murnau, Jofa-Atelier Berlin-Johannisthal (1922)

Snow White and the Seven Dwarfs, directed by David Hand, Walt Disney Productions (1937)

Vera Drake, directed by Mike Leigh, Les Films Alain Sarde (2004)

West Pier, directed by Mark Collington, Royal College of Art (2001)

APPLES: INTRODUCING STRUCTURALISM & SEMIOTICS

Like many theoretical paradigms (models of thinking), the essence of structuralism and its influence on fields such as narrative has evolved under a number of thinkers. This chapter introduces a selection of key theories from Ferdinand de Saussure and a series of related ideas from Charles Peirce, Claude Lévi-Strauss, Roland Barthes and Christian Metz.

Ferdinand de Saussure (1857–1913) is largely regarded as the founder of structuralism, through his study of linguistics and literature. But the ideas underpinning structuralism can be traced back to ancient Greek philosophy and were consolidated as a formal set of cultural theories by Claude Lévi-Strauss in the mid-twentieth century.

Saussure determined that language is essential to our perception of the real world. He observed how language is organized by shared abstract rules or conventions and called this langue. He also noted how variations in written or spoken use of these rules altered human perception of actual things, calling this parole.

Structuralism also focuses on the study of myth. Structuralist theorists recognized that despite some superficial differences, the deeper narrative structures found in the literature and visual culture of many different civilizations were essentially the same, and are central to how the human mind makes sense of the world.

Before we explore narrative structures in any detail, it is useful to explore some of the fundamental building blocks of the structuralist linguistic theory. These include semiotics and syntagmatic and paradigmatic analysis, which can also be used to understand how a narrative context can be created in still images.

1.2

1.2
Snow White and the Seven Dwarfs by Walt Disney, 1937. The image of the Wicked Witch presenting a poison apple to Snow White illustrates the concept of semiotic modes of sign.
© 1937 Disney

Semiotics

Saussure broke down language into a system of signs including sounds, words and mental images related to specific things or ideas. This is known as semiotics. He was interested in the seemingly random use of a phonetic symbol (sound of a spoken word) and its linguistic symbol (written word) such as the word 'apple', to represent the concept of the actual fruit. He called the written or spoken word the signifier, the mental concept of the object the signified and the actual object itself the referent.

But what Saussure fundamentally focused on was the importance of the relational structure of language. In other words it is the relationship between words and their written or spoken order that gives language its meaning. That is to say that although the fundamental laws of language follow certain deeper cognitive structures, the actual meanings or associations of words evolve and vary throughout history and in different cultures.

For example, it is only in relatively recent history that the word *apple* has come to mean a specific fruit. Variants of the word in different languages were originally used to describe any round shaped fruit or vegetable. We can see evidence that it was later paired with other words to signify specific types of fruit or vegetable, such as the French name for potato: pomme de terre (apple of the earth). Thus, Saussure observed that the individual meaning of a word is defined by the culture and time within which it exists.

Typology of Signs

Saussure's study of structuralism and semiotics focused on linguistics and literature, i.e., the spoken and written word, but his work did not provide a typology, a system for classifying different types of sign. The American philosopher Charles Peirce (1839–1914) did however map out three main types of signs, each defined by the relationship between the signifier, signified and the referent. This typology is particularly useful for the exploration of semiotics in the *visual* arts, and how we use combinations of simple elements to quickly interpret the meaning, purpose or significance of an individual object or thing in a picture.

Symbol/Symbolic: With reference to Saussure, linguistics and literature, the symbol (signifier) is essentially the random, abstract invention and assignment of a sound, word or colour to represent the mental concept of something real, or an abstract concept such as danger (the signified). The key thing about a symbol is that it is a rule that has to be taught and learned.

Icon/Iconic: An icon (signifier) is an artificially recreated image or sound that directly resembles certain key aspects of the real thing it represents (referent). In very literal terms many cultures' early written languages were formed of icons, simplified images of real objects, often put in sequence to tell the story of an event.

EXAMPLES OF SYMBOLIC SIGNIFIERS:

SIGNIFIER	SIGNIFIED
Word: Danger	Warning
Sound: Alarm Bell	Warning
Colour: Red	Warning

17

1.3

1.3
Peirce's typology—the indexical mode. Footsteps in the snow signify the presence of someone out of shot.

INTRODUCTION | **APPLES: INTRODUCING STRUCTURALISM & SEMIOTICS** | WORKBOOK EXERCISE 1.1 | WORKBOOK EXERCISE 1.2 | LOVE LETTERS: SEMANTICS | WORKBOOK EXERCISE 1.3 | TIME TRAVEL: FROM MONOSCENIC TO SYNCHRONIC & DIACHRONIC NARRATIVE | CASE STUDY: SYNCHRONIC LAYOUT DESIGN FROM *WEST PIER* BY MARK COLLINGTON | CASE STUDY: CREATING A SYNCHRONIC NARRATIVE SET DESIGN | CHAPTER SUMMARY & FURTHER READING | KEY WORDS, NAMES & WORKS

Many cartoons are iconic in their stylized simplification and design of animals, objects and so forth, e.g., Mickey Mouse's stylized ears instantly signify a mouse. Appliance and laundry instructions or mobile phone apps use a set of icons to tell you how to do something or signify a function without using words.

Index/Indexical: Here the signifier is often a 'natural' sign inferring the presence of something real. Footprints in the snow (Fig 1.3) or the sound of a knock on the door (signifier) would prompt the mental concept of the activity or presence of a person not in sight (signified).

A photographer or painter may intentionally focus on a number of real indexical signs to infer a link to something real (referent) that is not directly in the composition of the image itself. This creates a more ambiguous or mysterious image that involves more effort on behalf of the audience to understand what is happening.

Modes of Sign:
Symbolic, Iconic, Indexical

It is also important to note that it is more accurate to describe these three types of sign as *modes* of sign rather than *types*. This is because these *modes* may often be used together or even interchangeably to create meaning, whereas a *type* may wrongly imply that these *signifiers* can only be used separately.

Example of modes used together: The stereotype cartoon devil, for example, is defined by its *iconic* features: horns, tail and trident, and the *symbolic* colour red, which is often used to signify danger in western culture.

Example of modes used interchangeably: The graphic simplification of man and woman to represent each sex is *iconic* in design. But it is also *symbolic* as a learned association for meaning male or female when placed on separate doors of toilets or changing rooms.

WORKBOOK EXERCISE 1.1:
SEMIOTIC ANALYSIS OF *SNOW WHITE*
(DISNEY) & *NOSFERATU* (MURNAU)

For our first exercise we will look at examples of early film and feature length animation to explore some of the main concepts introduced so far. If you type up this exercise in your online workbook (complete with images), it will give you an entry on the analysis of a shot in Walt Disney's *Snow White and the Seven Dwarfs* (1937), and F. W. Murnau's *Nosferatu* (1922), using Saussure's semiotic analysis and Peirce's typology of signs.

Nosferatu is essentially an adaptation of Bram Stoker's *Dracula* (1897), one of the most famous stories about vampires. The film *Nosferatu* is shot using a range of distinctive lighting and compositional techniques closely associated with German Expressionist filmmaking, which is explored later on in chapter four. The folklore origins of the vampire and fairy tale traditions of the wicked witch carry with them many semiotic associations.

Try analyzing the film still from *Snow White* (Fig. 1.2, p.16) using different types of sign:

- The apple itself is an _____ signifier of a real apple

- The ___ colour of the apple is _____, signifying that it is dangerous and _____

Try analyzing the film still from *Nosferatu* (Fig. 1.4, p.21) using different types of sign:

- As with footprints, the shadow of the vampire Count Orlok can be described as an _____ signifier

- This is because the shadow signifies the presence of someone who is ___ / __/ _____

- The shadow can also be described as an _____ signifier, as it simplifies the form of the vampire

- This makes us think of the word 'vampire' in our mind, which is known as the _____ signifier

According to Saussure:

- The word 'vampire' is known as the _____

- The mental concept of the vampire is known as the _____

- The actual vampire itself is known as the _____

Answers in order: iconic, red, symbolic, poisonous, indexical, out of shot, iconic, symbolic, signifier, signified, referent.

INTRODUCTION

APPLES:
INTRODUCING
STRUCTURALISM
& SEMIOTICS

WORKBOOK
EXERCISE 1.1

WORKBOOK
EXERCISE 1.2

LOVE LETTERS:
SEMANTICS

WORKBOOK
EXERCISE 1.3

TIME TRAVEL:
FROM
MONOSCENIC
TO SYNCHRONIC
& DIACHRONIC
NARRATIVE

CASE STUDY:
SYNCHRONIC
LAYOUT DESIGN
FROM WEST
PIER BY MARK
COLLINGTON

CASE STUDY:
CREATING A
SYNCHRONIC
NARRATIVE
SET DESIGN

CHAPTER
SUMMARY
& FURTHER
READING

KEY WORDS,
NAMES &
WORKS

Further work: You could think about trying this exercise again in your workbook, with a number of other shots from different feature length films and fairy tale animations. Such visual codes are often embedded in the moral narratives of western folklore, fairy tale and also religion, with fruit such as the red apple representing poison or temptation, and beings such as vampires or serpents representing death or evil. We are so accustomed to these associations that we may often neglect to use them fully ourselves, so it can be helpful to catalogue them for reference in devising your own scenarios.

Semiotics not only helps us to think about the relational meaning between a particular object and its colour. The preproduction phase of animation also often applies a dominant colour to each thumbnail of the storyboard known as colour keys, and the scenes in the film itself, to signify the mood of a sequence and potentially indicate what is going to happen. In some contexts for example, the colour purple can signify that someone is going to die.

So why not put on your Deerstalker, light your pipe and think about themes of evil, villains, poison and death! Also look for shots where the villainous characters are out of shot but indexically indicated in some way, or where a colour or sound reinforces the dangerous nature of an object or scenario. Useful films could include *Aladdin* (Walt Disney Pictures, 1992) and useful texts for further reading could include *If It's Purple, Someone's Gonna Die: The Power of Color in Visual Storytelling* (see also recommended wider reading at the end of the chapter).

1.4

1.4
Nosferatu, directed by F. W. Murnau, 1922. The terrifying shadow of Count Orlok climbing the stairs is an example of an indexical signifier.

Cowboys: Syntagmatic & Paradigmatic Analysis

1.5

"~~~and you'd better not come outside too soon!"

1250-82

1.5
Roland Barthes' 'garment system' illustrated using the paradigmatic theme of the cowboy.

INTRODUCTION | APPLES: INTRODUCING STRUCTURALISM & SEMIOTICS | **WORKBOOK EXERCISE 1.1** | WORKBOOK EXERCISE 1.2 | LOVE LETTERS: SEMANTICS | WORKBOOK EXERCISE 1.3 | TIME TRAVEL: FROM MONOSCENIC TO SYNCHRONIC & DIACHRONIC NARRATIVE | CASE STUDY: SYNCHRONIC LAYOUT DESIGN FROM *WEST PIER* BY MARK COLLINGTON | CASE STUDY: CREATING A SYNCHRONIC NARRATIVE SET DESIGN | CHAPTER SUMMARY & FURTHER READING | KEY WORDS, NAMES & WORKS

Syntagmatic and paradigmatic analysis was originally used linguistically by Saussure, and was also developed and used by other structuralist theorists, such as Claude Lévi-Strauss and Roland Barthes, to look at the collective meaning of signifiers. This collective meaning takes the use of types and modes of sign a stage further by using another layer of terms to group and classify elements of the image. To illustrate this and make it relevant to your practice we will continue analysis primarily using the term 'object' rather than 'word'.

Put as simply as possible, this section looks at explaining how the combination of several objects or signifiers can be used to create meaning or a narrative context (time and place). The semiotic analysis of the relationship between objects, and their collective meaning, was defined by Saussure using two dimensions known as the syntagmatic and paradigmatic axis.

The Syntagmatic Dimension

This consists of a collective arrangement of individual objects or signifiers known as syntagms. An object or syntagm may or may not signify any specific meaning in itself, but when the object is put together with related objects, it will create a collective meaning. Roland Barthes (1915–1980) outlined this idea using the 'garment system'.

This may essentially be described as a selection of clothes that is typically worn together at the same time, thus forming an outfit relevant to a particular occupation. For example, we might assume from a large brimmed hat, neck scarf, gun holster and boots with spurs that we are looking at a cowboy outfit (Fig. 1.5).

The Paradigmatic Dimension

This forms an axis with the syntagmatic dimension. The paradigmatic dimension is essentially the overarching context that defines a collection of objects, or equally is defined by the collection of objects. The resulting paradigm or context for the group of objects in the case of a cowboy outfit therefore is most likely the American Wild West.

This has an obvious application for character design, but also a room space or environment. In this instance it could be any number of cliché elements from the American Wild West, such as cacti, wagon wheels, wanted posters etc.

WORKBOOK EXERCISE 1.2:
APPLYING SEMIOTICS TO LAYOUT DESIGN

Try creating a sketch of your own bedroom. Then try imposing different paradigmatic contexts on the room. How will the objects and collective modes of sign change if the occupant, such as the stereotype of an adolescent boy, is replaced by the stereotype of an elderly woman, for example?

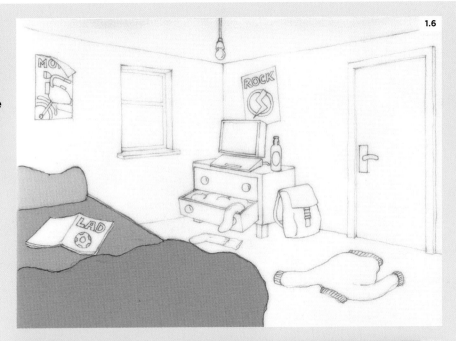

1.6
Quick layout sketch of the room of a teenage boy signified by the variation in the combination of objects and colours (by Mark Collington).

1.7
Quick layout sketch of the room of an elderly woman signified by the variation in the combination of objects and colours (by Mark Collington).

INTRODUCTION | APPLES: INTRODUCING STRUCTURALISM & SEMIOTICS | WORKBOOK EXERCISE 1.1 | WORKBOOK EXERCISE 1.2 | LOVE LETTERS: SEMANTICS | WORKBOOK EXERCISE 1.3 | TIME TRAVEL: FROM MONOSCENIC TO SYNCHRONIC & DIACHRONIC NARRATIVE | CASE STUDY: SYNCHRONIC LAYOUT DESIGN FROM WEST PIER BY MARK COLLINGTON | CASE STUDY: CREATING A SYNCHRONIC NARRATIVE SET DESIGN | CHAPTER SUMMARY & FURTHER READING | KEY WORDS, NAMES & WORKS

Try asking yourself the following questions as you devise a range of different scenarios:

- What is your paradigm or context, i.e., type of place and inhabitant?

- What selection of objects do you need to illustrate this and represent a person?

- How can you use different collective modes of sign to create meaningful relationships between objects, e.g., the indexical signifier of an unmade bed and the symbolic colour blue of the sheets signifying a more typical gender stereotype of a male teenage occupant?

- What does the dominant colour of the overall scene represent to us, if it is the room of an old woman and the colour purple, does it mean she is going to die!?

Summary

Semiotics in many ways states the obvious. But semiotics can be a helpful process to understand how to break down the surprising complexity and detail of the context and components of a scenario in the mind. It is similarly surprisingly difficult to learn how to break down the seemingly obvious process of animating the key frames of a walk cycle for the first time. In other words, there are many processes in animation that we take for granted and therefore often overlook; or do not develop our understanding of them to the extent that we should to create more convincing work.

This is particularly useful if planning involves less familiar combinations of objects and design elements, which need to be accurately researched to make sure you have created an authentic-looking and meaningful background or set design. This is especially important when representing different cultures in your animation work, as the pairing of colours, animals and objects can have very different meanings in different contexts. Semiotics will also help us in future chapters when we look at a range of more complex concepts that build on or contrast with these terms and ideas.

KEY CONCEPTS

- Semiotics: How we represent concepts or things using a range of signifiers such as words or signs

- Typology of signs: How different modes of sign, e.g., iconic colours, symbolic objects or indexical signs, can be interpreted individually or collectively and interchangeably to signify more complex concepts or meanings of individual things

- Syntagmatic and paradigmatic axis: How the relationship between objects/syntagms defines or is defined by a context, and in turn creates meaning.

LOVE LETTERS: SEMANTICS

1.8

1.8
The Love Letter by Johannes Vermeer,
c. 1669–1670: Narrative meaning is created by the
relationship between the combination of different
objects (syntagms) and their semantic context.

The complexity of creating visual meaning, particularly meaning that is culturally dependent, can be seen in the unique combination of elements that form the distinctive outfit of Sherlock Holmes: the Deerstalker, Inverness cape and tobacco pipe. Before the invention of Sherlock Holmes, these items signified their own more obvious purposes quite separate to the identity of the detective— as fashionable hunting headwear in nineteenth century England, nineteenth century Scottish highland dress for protection against bad weather and of course smoking.

However, since the invention of Sherlock Holmes these objects have collectively and even individually come to instantly symbolize the famous detective from Victorian Britain. So we can see how reliant we are on grouping of objects and their context for interpreting their deeper meaning. This is known as semantics, "which deals with the relation of the signs and messages produced by narrative to the larger cultural system which gives it meaning" (Robert Stam et al., 2006, p. 76).

In this section of the chapter we will see how the composition of a collection of a seemingly random set of objects can also affect the deeper semantic meaning of a whole scene. This can often be done accidentally and confuse an audience or be done intentionally to create a particular underlying narrative message or theme.

Reading Meaning in Paintings by Johannes Vermeer

Our ability to read the subtleties of a deeper narrative theme in an image is dependent on the extent of our contextual and historical knowledge of the period in which an image or film is set. Often certain unfamiliar objects may be virtually unidentifiable or even be rendered obsolete in their function and meaning without a certain amount of historical research.

Thus, our ability to understand a narrative, particularly in very old paintings, often requires us to understand the moral codes, customs, beliefs, values and visual metaphors of the given era and culture. We will now explore examples of painting, film and animation, which demonstrate how semantic analysis is important in understanding the deeper narrative messages and themes in an image.

RECOMMENDED VIEWING

Here are three films using strong paradigmatic and semantic composition to explore how we are defined by our surroundings, work, class, society and personal emotional conflict.

Going Equipped, directed by Peter Lord, Aardman Animations (1990)

The Girl With The Pearl Earring, directed by Peter Webber, Archer Street Productions (2003)

Vera Drake, directed by Mike Leigh, Les Films Alain Sarde (2004)

If we look at the paintings of Johannes Vermeer (1632–1675), we can see how his work primarily showed off his technical excellence in his use of light and perspective. This was typical of the Dutch Golden Age of genre painting, which depicted everyday domestic scenes of people working or engaged in leisure activities. Vermeer was able to perfect these skills by often using the same basic composition of a person involved in an activity, taking place at a table next to a window to the left of the image.

Using syntagmatic analysis, we can see how the combination of the kinds of objects and clothes selected by the artist and the related activity of the main subject in the image would signify their status, e.g., rich or poor, master of the house or servant, and also signify their occupation, such as a merchant or cook. From this we can determine the overall paradigm or context of each of Vermeer's paintings.

Using semantic analysis we can often also identify a deeper narrative message or theme in Vermeer's paintings. To do this we must play the detective and piece together the composition of a series of objects that act as visual clues, indicating to us something that has potentially happened outside the immediate image, that may in some way affect the main person in it.

The Love Letter, by Vermeer (c. 1669–1670)

In this painting (Fig. 1.8) the general combination of fashionable clothes, expensive fabrics and objects creates a paradigmatic context roughly identifiable as a wealthy seventeenth century European home. However, the strategic combination of objects, including a letter in the seated lady's hand, the lute on her lap, and the paintings on the wall above her head, were cultural items used repeatedly to create semantic meaning specific to that era.

The lute held by the seated lady was a common symbol for lovers. The painting directly above her on the wall depicts a stormy sea voyage, a popular visual metaphor for a turbulent relationship; the painting above that depicts a man walking into the distance, which suggests a theme of separation. This combination of objects is used to indicate that the letter contains the message that the loved one of the seated lady wished to end their relationship.

Reading Meaning in the Film *Vera Drake*, Directed by Mike Leigh (2005)

The film *Vera Drake* is set around the theme of attitudes towards women, particularly regarding the stigma of unwanted or extra-marital pregnancy, as well as the dangers of abortion in the context of post–World War II Britain. The main character in the film is a cleaner who also carries out illegal abortions for other working class women who 'have got themselves into trouble', and cannot afford to pay a qualified private physician for the procedure.

There is a particular sequence of three scenes in the film that highlights how the objects, lighting and colour of the environments subtly build up the narrative context of the class-ridden society of the era. The sequence begins with a first scene of a well-dressed young woman seeking advice from another lady from high society on abortion. The scene takes place in a well-lit tea room with tiered plates of sandwiches and elegent tea sets.

The film then cuts to a second scene in which Vera Drake is visiting a working class home where she has evidently previously administered an abortion that has resulted in a bed-ridden wife and mother; this then cuts to a third scene featuring the young lady from the first scene dressing herself during a consultation for an abortion in a private doctor's surgery.

The latter two scenes mirror one another in terms of their partitioned compositions, viewing the patients and abortionists in different room spaces through doorways or behind curtains. But more significantly the different scenes contrast with one another in terms of the way the environments reflect the different conditions of working and upper classes. (These scenes are similar to the compositions and subject of class in many seventeenth century Dutch paintings; see the work of Pieter de Hooch in particular, e.g., *The Courtyard of a House in Delft,* 1658.)

In the second scene with Vera Drake, the low lighting, cramped drab décor, tea set and clothing reinforce the conditions typically endured by British working class women in the 1950s. However, the well lit, spacious interiors with elegent or modern furniture in the first and third scenes suggest how wealth is of no more comfort psychologically to upper class women than working class seeking an abortion in that era.

Reading Meaning in the Animation *Going Equipped*, Directed by Peter Lord (1990)

Summary

Going Equipped is a short animated documentary based on an interview with a man describing how the poverty and neglect experienced in his childhood led him into a life of petty crime and time in prison. Pixilated sequences (stop motion animation of real people, objects and spaces) of an untidy and dirty home give a sense of this poverty and neglect.

Numerous scenes set in the childhood home of the interviewee are shot at the eye level of a child. These reveal discarded toys and remnants of meals on the floor, suggestions of insect infestation and cluttered chaotic table surfaces. The general tone and colour of the shots is cold and oppressive, with adults only glimpsed as inactive and uninvolved elements in the sequences. This combination of elements is used to reflect the lack of love and affection experienced during the childhood of the interviewee.

Later images of plain walls, utilitarian furniture and a game of cards signify life in a prison cell. The contrast of a momentary appearance of a toy in the prison cell acts as indexical sign reminding us how the interviewee was essentially still a child during his time in prison and how fleetingly precious childhood can be. Therefore, the living room and prison cell set the context, whilst the transition of objects paired with the narration create the deeper semantic meaning of the film.

Whereas scenes in *Vera Drake* are often conciously intercut to create contrasts of class, *Going Equipped* intercuts between pixiliation of a 'real world' environment and semi-realistic scenes of a stop motion figure in a sparsely furnitured room. This room focuses the audience on the feelings of the interviewee, through sublime acting, well-crafted lighting and sound effects of a wet winter night.

These three examples of semantic imagery demonstrate how our memories of the *past*, the conditions of the *present* time we live in and our fears about the *future* define us. In turn, these different scenerios collectively summarize the key narrative elements that define the human condition outlined in the introduction of this book.

In *Going Equipped*, memories of childhood are depicted by the heavily loaded images of neglected spaces from the childhood home of the adult narrator. In *Vera Drake*, domestic and public spaces are used to illustrate contrasting living conditions, and the pressures of society on working and upper class women in post-war Britain. In the painting *The Love Letter* the semantic composition of objects in the room reveal a woman's fears about the future of her relationship.

1.9

1.9
Going Equipped, directed by Peter Lord, Aardman Animations (1990). Several sequences focus on a hyper-realistic stop motion puppet, which is animated to an original interview with a reformed child offender. This adds intensity to the interview, which is contrasted against real rooms, layered with meaning, that recreate and represent memories from the interviewee's childhood.

WORKBOOK EXERCISE 1.3:
APPLYING SEMANTICS TO SET DESIGN

The exercise below will help you apply the knowledge covered so far to the development of a set design that has a simple historical context. It uses contextual, cultural and critical analysis as a way to help you develop a thorough, well-researched and structured approach to designing and making from research.

Working in reverse to the famous super sleuth Sherlock Holmes, you can now try to structure a scene that provides clues to the identity and recent activity of its absent occupant. This exercise is illustrated using an example of a student animation project. You may however decide to change certain factors such as the location, time period or design era.

1.10

INTRODUCTION

APPLES:
INTRODUCING
STRUCTURALISM
& SEMIOTICS

WORKBOOK
EXERCISE 1.1

WORKBOOK
EXERCISE 1.2

LOVE LETTERS:
SEMANTICS

WORKBOOK
EXERCISE 1.3

TIME TRAVEL:
FROM
MONOSCENIC
TO SYNCHRONIC
& DIACHRONIC
NARRATIVE

CASE STUDY:
SYNCHRONIC
LAYOUT DESIGN
FROM WEST
PIER BY MARK
COLLINGTON

CASE STUDY:
CREATING A
SYNCHRONIC
NARRATIVE
SET DESIGN

CHAPTER
SUMMARY
& FURTHER
READING

KEY WORDS,
NAMES &
WORKS

Part A: Contextual Analysis

- The visual research for the design of the set took place by visiting the Geffrye Museum of the Home in London, which charts the changing use of the 'front room' in the city over several hundred years, using life size mock-ups of the rooms and real artifacts to recreate the spaces.

- The context, current affairs and popular culture from the 1920s period was researched from books and the Internet and is determined by the posters on the walls and gramophone records on the sideboard and shelves.

Part B: Cultural Analysis

- Paradigmatic Analysis: The nature of the apartment and general range of possessions/furniture signify the fashionable status of the young male owner, through the Art Deco interior architecture, expensive 'masculine' designer furniture, and cliché of a drink decanter.

- Semantic Analysis: The long shadows cast by the moonlight, combined with the image of a fashionable Raccoon Coat thrown over a chair, a full glass of whisky and selection of popular records on the table signify that the occupant has recently returned from a night out.

- Adding an anachronism (thing from a time period out of keeping from the time period of everything else) of a laptop computer on the table would completely shift the emphasis of the room, as it would project the time period from the 1920s to the present day, and could instead suggest that the occupant is a collector of Art Deco and 1920s memorabilia.

Part C: Critical Analysis

- Reference to the work of Vermeer inspired the composition, lighting and semantic meaning. The sets are made cheaply using bricolage techniques part inspired by Hans Op de Beeck's film Staging Silence—which incorporates packaging and found objects to create material textures and design structures.

1.10
Semantic composition of a stop motion set design based on a life-sized recreation of an Art Deco apartment at London's Geffrye Museum of the Home. By John Taber, BA (Hons) Animation, Cass Faculty, London Metropolitan University, 2015.

1.11

1.12

You Try

Part A: Contextual Analysis

1. Decide on a general context, i.e., a particular decade, country and urban or rural location.

2. Research current affairs (recognizable key news stories) and popular culture from the place and era.

Part B: Cultural Analysis

1. Visually research the paradigmatic context, e.g., structure, decor and objects specific to your era and location (using primary visual research, drawing from first hand observation visiting a museum or through secondary visual research drawing from books).

2. Use semantic analysis to explore the relationship between the type of room and the main theme or activity taking place within it, from which you will determine the type of occupant or owner: male/female, young/old, rich/poor etc.

1.11 & 1.12
Semantic meaning of the room is changed completely by simply changing an old vinyl record for a laptop computer. By John Taber, BA (Hons) Animation, Cass Faculty, London Metropolitan University, 2015.

INTRODUCTION

APPLES: INTRODUCING STRUCTURALISM & SEMIOTICS

WORKBOOK EXERCISE 1.1

WORKBOOK EXERCISE 1.2

LOVE LETTERS: SEMANTICS

WORKBOOK EXERCISE 1.3

TIME TRAVEL: FROM MONOSCENIC TO SYNCHRONIC & DIACHRONIC NARRATIVE

CASE STUDY: SYNCHRONIC LAYOUT DESIGN FROM *WEST PIER* BY MARK COLLINGTON

CASE STUDY: CREATING A SYNCHRONIC NARRATIVE SET DESIGN

CHAPTER SUMMARY & FURTHER READING

KEY WORDS, NAMES & WORKS

Part C: Critical Analysis

1. Refer to architecture books to devise a floor plan.

2. Look at set design and stop motion books for inspiration on model making techniques.

3. Take a range of photographs of alternative viewpoints of objects, camera angles and lighting to determine the best shot composition with reference to composition in other animations.

4. Compare and contrast your set design with the analysis of the painting *The Love Letter* by Vermeer in the previous section of this chapter.

1.13

1.13
Reverse angle shot of set design by John Taber, BA (Hons) Animation, Cass Faculty, London Metropolitan University, 2015.

TIME TRAVEL: FROM MONOSCENIC TO SYNCHRONIC & DIACHRONIC NARRATIVE

The Synchronic Narrative

'Monoscenic narrative' is a term used in narrative art to classify an individual image, which can contain a basic story or kind of snap shot of a narrative situation at a specific point in time. With the monoscenic narrative we essentially reach an end point to the semantic analysis we have covered so far in reading the narrative meaning in an individual image, such as the paintings by Vermeer, and the narrative set design exercise. It is at this point that we can start to consider how we can make the transition from an individual narrative moment in time to representations of the passage of time using the structuralist terms 'synchronic' and 'diachronic'.

The structuralist Lévi-Strauss referred to the term 'synchronic' to describe the bringing of all narrative elements together at one moment in time. In a visual context synchronic narrative is a term that can be applied to the representation of the passage of time or the unfolding of a series of events in a single image, without any repetition of any of the objects or people in the composition. A synchronic narrative image is able to depict events that happened before and/or follow after what is going on in the present moment of the image. To illustrate this we will briefly look at *The Entombment of Christ*, by Fra Angelico, c. 1450 (Fig. 1.14).

The Entombment of Christ by Fra Angelico, c. 1450

This synchronic narrative image demonstrates advances in perspective painting that enabled the artist to communicate a sense of the passage of time in one composition without any repetition of its individual characters or elements. This was achieved by placing symbolic or indexical signifiers in the distance, such as the empty cross upon which Jesus had been crucified, to show events that had happened in the *past*.

1.14

1.14
The Entombment of Christ by Fra Angelico, c. 1450. An example of a synchronic narrative—an image that uses perspective to create a sense of the passage of time without repeating any of the characters in it.

INTRODUCTION | APPLES: INTRODUCING STRUCTURALISM & SEMIOTICS | WORKBOOK EXERCISE 1.1 | WORKBOOK EXERCISE 1.2 | LOVE LETTERS: SEMANTICS | WORKBOOK EXERCISE 1.3 | TIME TRAVEL: FROM MONOSCENIC TO SYNCHRONIC & DIACHRONIC NARRATIVE | CASE STUDY: SYNCHRONIC LAYOUT DESIGN FROM *WEST PIER* BY MARK COLLINGTON | CASE STUDY: CREATING A SYNCHRONIC NARRATIVE SET DESIGN | CHAPTER SUMMARY & FURTHER READING | KEY WORDS, NAMES & WORKS

CASE STUDY: SYNCHRONIC LAYOUT DESIGN FROM *WEST PIER* BY MARK COLLINGTON

West Pier charts the history and decline of a famous seaside landmark in Brighton, England. The image below shows how a distorted panoramic background design enabled a camera to track through from the floor to the ceiling of the drawn interior of a ballroom. A sense of the passage of time is created by the metamorphosis of the grand ceiling structure into the image of a decaying rib cage that represents how the iconic building fell into a chronic state of disrepair.

The shot is one of many that makes reference to organic structures. Iconic, exotic, organic **motifs** (distinctive and frequently used symbolic decorative patterns or images) were a key feature of Victorian and Edwardian seaside architecture in particular. They were used to create popular themes of oriental exoticism that was imported from the colonies of the British Empire.

1.15
West Pier by Mark Collington, Royal College of Art, 2001. Synchronic narrative layout design that depicts the decay of a building over time.

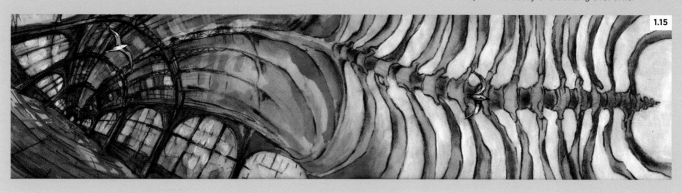

1.15

More recent or *current events* are situated ever closer in the foreground, such as the preparation of Christ's body for his tomb. The composition enables the viewer to read the painting in chronological order from left to right and top to bottom, as with the predominant forms of western writing. This image is also an example of a history painting from Western Europe. History paintings typically illustrated religious or mythological narrative scenes.

Beats, Layouts and Backgrounds
Animation studios often use similar synchronic methods for devising a range of alternatives for a single image to best represent not just a shot, but an overall sequence, scene or even a narrative stage. These images are known as beats and often form the basis of subsequent 2D layout or 3D set designs.

The synchronic narrative image can also essentially be seen throughout many panoramic layouts or backgrounds in more traditional 2D animated feature films. These elaborate winding panoramic landscapes are designed for the camera to zoom in on and pan across, creating the illusion of perspective and a sense of the passage of time in a single image. Such backgrounds often feature in the opening scene of a film to introduce the context or theme for the film narrative.

CASE STUDY: CREATING A SYNCHRONIC NARRATIVE SET DESIGN

We will now consolidate the concepts of semantics and synchronic narrative by looking at another narrative set design student project that builds on the concepts of the previous exercise. Imagine once again that you are the detective Sherlock Holmes. On your travels in Japan you have happened upon the recent disturbance of a now deserted reception room in someone's home. But how can you deduce from clues in the room the nature of a recent tragic event that has taken place?

Part A: Contextual Analysis

• The visual research for the design of the set took place by researching the interior architecture and objects typical of a reception room in a standard Japanese home from the nineteenth century Edo period.

• Strictly observed social codes of behaviour and décor were discovered in reading about the interiors of particular rooms in Japanese culture, which had a significant influence on devising a narrative.

Part B: Cultural Analysis

• Paradigmatic Analysis: The architecture, floor mats, sunken fireplace, teapot, tea set and ornamental feature in the corner of the room reveal the nature and purpose of a nineteenth century domestic tearoom.

• Synchronic Analysis: The dominant shaft of sunlight coming from outside leads the eye from the main entrance left of the shot, up to a Tokonoma (a built-in recess for ornaments) via the teapot, which is boiling over in the middle of the room. Due to the pans scattered about on the floor, our attention is then led across the back wall of the room via a partition to a kitchen. Our eyes come to rest on the macabre sight of some discarded blood-stained towels in the entrance to a doorway leading to the rest of the home. So we are led through a series of actions from the past, through to the present moment.

1.16

1.16
Synchronic narrative and semantic stop motion set design by Elora Aboua, BA (Hons) Animation, Cass Faculty, London Metropolitan University, 2015.

INTRODUCTION

APPLES: INTRODUCING STRUCTURALISM & SEMIOTICS

WORKBOOK EXERCISE 1.1

WORKBOOK EXERCISE 1.2

LOVE LETTERS: SEMANTICS

WORKBOOK EXERCISE 1.3

TIME TRAVEL: FROM MONOSCENIC TO SYNCHRONIC & DIACHRONIC NARRATIVE

CASE STUDY: SYNCHRONIC LAYOUT DESIGN FROM *WEST PIER* BY MARK COLLINGTON

CASE STUDY: CREATING A SYNCHRONIC NARRATIVE SET DESIGN

CHAPTER SUMMARY & FURTHER READING

KEY WORDS, NAMES & WORKS

- Semantic Analysis: The specific configuration of Tatami floor mats signify that important guests were present, and indicate a particular social hierarchy of where people should sit. The guest mat is nearest the guest door (front left) and the host mat nearest the kitchen at the back.

- It is customary for guests to remove shoes upon entering the room, which can be seen by the guest entrance. We can see that the guests arrived in a hurry and seemingly left the room at the back, due to the fact that the order and etiquette of the room has been disturbed, indicated by the shoes left messily at the door, the pot of water left to boil over and pans scattered on the floor. This chaotic environment is uncharacteristic of such a formal society, which with discarded blood stained towels adds a very unsettling feeling to the narrative.

- A Tokonoma usually includes the pairing of a plant and an emakimono (wall hanging picture-scroll). These are usually used to symbolize the spiritual mood of the tea ceremony. The pairing of ornaments in this Tokonoma includes an image of *four* Koi Carp and *three* white Chrysanthemum flowers. The Koi Carp is used as a symbol for 'Boy's Day' in Japan, and white Chrysanthemum flowers symbolize bad luck in Japanese society. The number forty-three is avoided in Japanese culture, as when spoken it sounds like the Japanese word for stillbirth. We are left with the tragic realization that a stillbirth of a baby boy has occurred in the household.

- We can deduce from the unsettled interior that the visitors, potentially the grandparents, entered hurriedly to assist in the birth of their grandchild.

End note: There may well still be a level of cultural inaccuracy here, in the interpretation of the various Japanese cultural visual codes. But the project illustrates how important it is to research and understand every aspect of an image when representing a different culture.

By understanding the natural harmony of a space, whether creating a disturbance within it, or including an anachronism such as a laptop, we are able think about how to use the disruption of a space to develop a narrative that represents events from the past and the impact they have on the present. This powerful scenario also illustrates how animation can be used to represent challenging and emotive subject matter without a more graphic or literal illustration of events.

Triptychs, Beat Boards
& Storyboards

In this final section of the chapter we will briefly discuss how to make the transition from single narrative images to the sequential narrative of the beat board. The diachronic narrative is an overarching term that can be applied to the development of a sequential narrative, which can be the sum of an ordered series of monoscenic or synchronic narrative images.

Historically, the sequential narrative was commonly seen in the triptych. Triptychs are three panels often displayed above an altar in a church, each depicting key stages in a biblical narrative, in much the same way that a modern storyboard depicts key moments in a film. A well-known example of the triptych is *The Nativity, Adoration of the Magi and Presentation in Temple*, by Hans Memling (c. 1470; see Fig. 1.17).

In the same way that syntagmatic analysis can be used to enable us to make sense of logical, accepted combinations of *objects* in individual images, syntagmatic analysis was also applied by French film theorist Christian Metz (1931–1993) to the edited order or grouping of *shots* in a film to form a clear, meaningful, overarching narrative structure. This syntagmatic grouping or ordering of narrative moments became known as syntactics, "the study of the syntagmatic ordering of plot events as a kind of armature of narrative progress and development" (Robert Stam et al., 2006, p. 76).

Metz devised eight syntagmatic types. However, fundamentally we can quickly identify with the idea in relation to the storyboard through his seventh syntagmatic type, the episodic sequence: "A symbolic summary of stages in an implied chronological development, usually entailing a compression of time" (Robert Stam et al., 2006, p. 41).

A visual interpretation of this is known in animation as a beat board, which is the combination of a set or series of beats. Studios such as Pixar use beat boards. These condense a whole film narrative into a much shorter and more manageable storyboard for general preproduction purposes. The beat board is expanded on in more detail in chapter two.

1.17

INTRODUCTION

APPLES: INTRODUCING STRUCTURALISM & SEMIOTICS

WORKBOOK EXERCISE 1.1

WORKBOOK EXERCISE 1.2

LOVE LETTERS: SEMANTICS

WORKBOOK EXERCISE 1.3

TIME TRAVEL: FROM MONOSCENIC TO SYNCHRONIC & DIACHRONIC NARRATIVE

CASE STUDY: SYNCHRONIC LAYOUT DESIGN FROM WEST PIER BY MARK COLLINGTON

CASE STUDY: CREATING A SYNCHRONIC NARRATIVE SET DESIGN

CHAPTER SUMMARY & FURTHER READING

KEY WORDS, NAMES & WORKS

Consolidating Your Research and Practice from This Chapter into a General Preproduction Plan

To summarize all the terminology in this chapter: *Syntactics* (ordering of plot events) is the *syntagmatic* organization (thematic combination of shots) of individual synchronic images or 'beats' (images illustrating passage of time). These contain a *paradigmatic/semantic* organization of *syntagms* (contextual combination and cultural association of objects and their deeper thematic meaning), and modes of iconic and indexical signs (combinations of colours, sounds and specific objects and elements such as red apples, footprints or shadows).

In the future you could use this summary with or without the terminology to structure the research and planning of an initial beat board and set of production stills that are layered with narrative meaning and a sense of the passage of time:

1. Decide on a context: visually research the time and place.

2. Research the cultural environment: research the function of a specific space, the objects within it and the deeper collective cultural meaning of the objects and space.

3. Decide on the nature of the occupants and their activities: think about what individual objects or elements represent and how they indicate the presence of a character.

4. Represent the passage of time: look at how the composition can be used to indicate events both past and present.

5. Think about the relationship between a number of scenarios: place all your scenarios in a narrative order, considering the dominant colour or mood of each scene and how they connect with one another to form a clear, meaningful overarching narrative summary.

1.17
The Nativity, Adoration of the Magi and Presentation in Temple, triptych, by Hans Memling c. 1470.

CHAPTER SUMMARY & FURTHER READING

In this chapter we have used structuralist theories to discover how symbols or objects, environments and composition can be used in an image to create narrative meaning. We have also understood the importance of researching the context in which an image is set. Further, we learned how to represent the passage of time, as a defining aspect of the human condition, in an individual image or series of images.

We have seen how animation has unique ways of presenting narrative. It can combine many of the formal aspects of composition of traditional painting in art, with the properties of camera and editing in the time-based medium of film. We have also developed the cognitive skills to translate all these ideas into layout designs, set designs and beat boards.

Many of the earlier Walt Disney feature films in particular sourced inspiration from European culture and art, from the architecture and folk tales of the Middle Ages to the paintings of the pre-Raphaelites. If you are interested in exploring similar influences in your own work, it is worth referring to the books listed in the further reading list at the end of this chapter.

Overall, this chapter encourages you to start looking outside animation for sources of inspiration to help you develop more layered meaning in visual storytelling. It recommends that you think more carefully about how we represent other cultures by researching them and their visual codes properly. But also it highlights how as animators we can engage in more challenging subject matter about the human condition, without a more graphic or literal illustration of events, and become a more proactive audience in reading the animated image.

The next chapter looks at how to devise more conventional narrative structures in film and animation. It focuses on the narrative formula of the folk tale and myth and how different cultures have used these to understand the world around them. The chapter builds on the narrative function of the environment, but also introduces the symbolism and narrative functions of different types of character, as well as the importance of music in developing narrative meaning.

FURTHER READING

General Animation & Film Texts

Furniss, M. (1998) *Art In Motion, Animation Aesthetics*, John Libbey Publishing: London

Stam, R., (2000) *Film Theory, An Introduction*, Blackwell Publishers Ltd: Oxford

Wells, P. (2007) *Understanding Animation*, Routledge: London

Structuralism & Semiotics

Chandler, D. (2007) *Semiotics: The Basics*, Routledge: Abingdon

Hawkes, T. (2003) *Structuralism & Semiotics*, Routledge: Abingdon

Stam, R., Burgoyne, R. Flitterman-Lewis, S. (2006) *New Vocabularies in Film Semiotics*, Routledge: Abingdon

Fine Art

Brook, T. (2009) *Vermeer's Hat*, Profile Books: London

De Rynck, P. (2009) *How to Read a Painting*, Thames & Hudson: London

Animation/Film Texts on Beat Boards, Colour & Layouts

Allan, R. (1999) *Walt Disney & Europe*, John Libbey Publishing: London

Bellantoni, P. (2005) *If It's Purple, Someone's Gonna Die: The Power of Color in Visual Storytelling*, Focal Press: Oxford

Glebas, F. (2008) *Directing the Story*, Focal Press: Oxford

Johnston, O. and Thomas, F. (1997) *The Illusion of Life*, Hyperion: New York

KEY WORDS

Beat Board
The combination of a set or series of beats, which condenses a whole film narrative into a much shorter and more manageable storyboard

Beats
Synchronic images used to devise a range of alternatives for a single image, that best represents not just a shot, but an overall sequence, scene or even a narrative stage

Bricolage
Making something from a diverse range of found items

Chronological
Events represented in a time-based or historical order starting from the earliest and ending with the most recent

Colour Keys
A storyboard where a dominant colour is applied to each thumbnail to signify the mood of a sequence

Context
The time and place in which something is set and defines its meaning

Diachronic Narrative
The development of a sequential narrative, which can be a series of monoscenic or synchronic narrative images

Dutch Golden Age
A period of genre painting in the Netherlands noted for its quality and level of realism (seventeenth century)

Episodic Sequence
A chronological order of shots that also compress time

Garment System
The overarching context that defines a collection of objects

Genre Painting
Paintings of everyday domestic scenes of people working or engaged in leisure activities

History Painting
Paintings typically illustrating religious or mythological narrative scenes

Icon
An artificially recreated image or sound that directly resembles certain key aspects of the real thing it represents

Indexical
A 'natural' sign inferring the presence of something real

Langue
Structuralist analysis of rules and conventions of language

Linguistic Symbol
A written word

Monoscenic Narrative
An individual image, containing a basic story or kind of snap shot of a narrative situation at a specific point in time

Motifs
Distinctive and frequently used symbolic decorative patterns or images

Narrative
A spoken or written account of a series of events

Narrative Art
Art that tells a story

Paradigms
Models of thinking

Paradigmatic Dimension
The overarching context that defines a collection of objects

Parole
How rules of language alter human perception of actual things

Phonetic Symbol
The sound of a spoken word

Pixilation
Stop motion animation of real people, objects and spaces

Referent
The actual object itself

Semantics
The deeper narrative meaning produced by the grouping of objects and their specific context

Semiotics
The system of signs

Sign
Sounds, words and mental images related to specific things or ideas

Signified
The mental concept of the object that the word represents

Signifier
A written or spoken word

Structuralism
A school of thought on human cognition, linguistics and culture, especially literature

Symbol
The random, abstract invention and assignment of a sound, word or colour to represent the mental concept of something real

Synchronic Narrative
The representation of the passage of time or unfolding of a series of events in a single image without any repetition of any of the objects or people in the composition

Syntactics
The edited order and meaningful grouping of shots

Syntagm
An object or signifier

Syntagmatic Dimension
A collective arrangement of individual objects or signifiers

Triptych
Three panels often displayed above an altar in a church, each depicting key stages in a biblical narrative

Typology of Signs
A system for classifying different types of signs

Visual Metaphors
Images or objects that carry meaning or association with something else, in addition to their immediate appearance or main function

KEY NAMES
Fra Angelico
Roland Barthes
Arthur Conan Doyle
Walt Disney
Mike Leigh
Claude Lévi-Strauss
Peter Lord
Hans Memling
Christian Metz
F. W. Murnau
Hans Op de Beeck
Charles Peirce
Ferdinand de Saussure
Johannes Vermeer

KEY WORKS
Aladdin
Entombment of Christ, The
Going Equipped
Love Letter, The
Nativity, Adoration of the Magi and Presentation in Temple, The
Nosferatu
Sherlock Holmes
Snow White
Vera Drake
West Pier

CHAPTER TWO
CLASSICAL METANARRATIVES:
THE HERO'S JOURNEY

CHAPTER OVERVIEW: DEVELOPING NARRATIVE STRUCTURE & SOUND

In this chapter, you will learn:

- How to develop a complete narrative structure, comparing and contrasting different theoretical approaches to storytelling.

- How music can support the development and narrative function of character.

- To challenge preconceptions about conventional gender roles in animated films.

- How animation directors are able to cultivate a unique voice in their work.

Illustration for the
fairy tale of *Ivan
Tsarevich, the
Firebird, and the Gray
Wolf*, 1902. Artist: Ivan
Yakovlevich Bilibin
(1876–1942).

INTRODUCTION

This chapter will explore the symbolism, function and structure of western fairy tale animation, comparing and contrasting it with the symbolism, function and structure of Japanese animé. This will be illustrated by comparing the historical influence of European and Japanese visual cultures upon one another. In doing so we will begin to unravel the riddles of the otherworldly mythological elements in the films of Hayao Miyazaki and gain a fuller understanding of his recurring deeper themes connected with the human condition. These often include the journey from childhood to adulthood and conflict between mankind, technology and the natural world.

In the first chapter we introduced a range of structuralist theories to explore how to define a narrative context for our work and create a sense of narrative meaning through the visual composition of objects in individual images. We concluded the chapter by discussing how to depict the passage of time in individual images, as well as how to combine the images to develop pictorial narrative sequences such as the beat board.

In this chapter we will explore how to develop a complete narrative structure by comparing and contrasting Russian formalist methods of storytelling with structuralist theories on narrative. We will begin by looking at the Russian formalist Vladimir Propp, who set out a fundamental metanarrative— an overarching narrative structure that could be applied to the analysis of all Russian folk tales and the narrative journey of a hero—as well as subsequent variants of this model that are still used in film and animation.

We will look at the structuralist theories of Claude Lévi-Strauss and Roland Barthes and their analysis of how deeper narrative meaning is created in primitive myths, as well as Strauss' research on the role of music in enhancing the narrative meaning and structure of the myth. We will see how these ideas can be applied to the development and narrative function of a range of characters and other mythical elements.

With reference to feminist theorist Laura Mulvey, we will discover how to become more aware of our audience, looking specifically at challenging our preconceptions about conventional gender roles in animated films. We will also introduce auteur theory, which looks at the ways in which animation directors can find a unique voice and have important influence on the way societies think about the consequences of their actions on others and the world they inhabit.

The chapter will build discussion around a range of examples, in particular the first Studio Ghibli animated feature film *Laputa, Castle in the Sky*, directed by Hayao Miyazaki (1986). The professional case study with Suzie Templeton, director of the Oscar-winning stop motion interpretation of Prokofiev's *Peter and the Wolf*, will also be used to consolidate our understanding of the contextual and cultural discussion of topics covered in this chapter.

The chapter concludes with a student case study that illustrates how some of these narrative theories were applied to a client-led brief for the Museum of London. The project looked at how to tell the story of Thomas Becket, a famous English saint, by developing an animated storyboard that was assembled and exhibited in the form of a 3D zoetrope at the museum.

The workbook exercises covered in this chapter will help you think about how to break down a standard narrative structure with reference to *Laputa* and also how to reinterpret the animé formula of Miyazaki in your own personal way. This will be achieved through the development of a narrative context, theme and structure that is based upon firsthand visual research, awareness of current affairs and an understanding of myth and folklore. In summary, this chapter will look at a range of universal allegorical narrative forms, which are briefly defined below.

INTRODUCTION

HEROES &
TOTEMS:
MORPHOLOGY,
NARRATOLOGY,
MYTHOLOGY

CASTLE IN THE
SKY: MYTHICAL
FORCES,
FLOATING
WORLDS &
FLYING MACHINES

WORKBOOK
EXERCISE 2.1

WORKBOOK
EXERCISE 2.2

CASE STUDY:
*PETER &
THE WOLF*

INTERVIEW
WITH SUZIE
TEMPLETON

CASE STUDY:
SAINT THOMAS
BECKET

CHAPTER
SUMMARY
& FURTHER
READING

KEY WORDS,
NAMES & WORKS

A Definition of Allegory and Some of Its Different Forms

Allegory: A story that can be interpreted to reveal hidden layers of meaning

Myth: A fictional story that explains a natural/social mystery or phenomenon

Folk tale: A fictional moral story, often based on superstition, and passed on by word of mouth

Fairy tale: A more fictional and magical equivalent of the folk tale, usually in written form

RECOMMENDED VIEWING

Aladdin, directed by Ron Clements & John Musker, Walt Disney Pictures (1992)

Laputa, Castle in the Sky, directed by Hayao Miyazaki, Studio Ghibli (1986)

Peter and the Wolf, directed by Suzie Templeton, Breakthru Films (2006)

Ponyo, directed by Hayao Miyazaki, Studio Ghibli (2008)

Snow White and the Seven Dwarfs, directed by David Hand, Walt Disney Productions (1937)

The Hobbit (trilogy), directed by Peter Jackson, New Line Cinema (2012–2014)

The Little Mermaid, directed by Ron Clements & John Musker, Walt Disney Pictures (1989)

ADDITIONAL RECOMMENDED VIEWING

Avatar, directed by James Cameron, Twentieth Century Fox Film Corporation (2009)

My Neighbour Totoro, directed by Hayao Miyazaki, Studio Ghibli (1988)

The Man Who Planted Trees, directed by Frédéric Back, Radio Canada (1987)

Watership Down, directed by Martin Rosen, Nepenthe Productions (1978)

When the Wind Blows, directed by Jimmy T. Murakami, Meltdown Productions (1986)

HEROES & TOTEMS: MORPHOLOGY, NARRATOLOGY, MYTHOLOGY

Morphology

2.2

2.2
A scene from the fairy tale *Little Red Riding Hood*. Engraving by Gustave Dore, 1870.

Russian formalism was a school of literary criticism that studied the structure of literature. Vladimir Propp was one of the leading Russian formalist thinkers. Propp (1895–1970) published the ***Morphology of the Folktale*** in 1928. This morphology (which, simply put, means the study of forms), or generic structure, defined a sequence of thirty-one key 'functions', or narrative stages, that could be applied to the structure of all Russian folk tales. Thus, he took the oral traditions of the folk tale and translated them into the literary or written tradition of the fairy tale.

Before summarizing or paraphrasing these thirty-one stages, it is helpful first to expand on the definition or *function* of the fairy tale in the broader context of child development. Animation author Maureen Furniss explores the nature and purpose of the fairy tale by summarizing the views of American child psychologist Bruno Bettelheim (1903–1990), who saw the fairy tale as a process useful for coping with childhood traumas.

If we consider any number of fairy tales in this context, we often see recurring themes that reflect the rite of passage or growing up, such as learning how to be independent from our parents, knowing how to chart a safe journey through an unknown place, how to deal with strangers and so on. In another of his books, *Historical Origins of the Wondertale*, Vladimir Propp similarly cites rite of passage and death as the key components of the folk tale.

❝Bruno Bettelheim has analysed the functions of fairytales and other forms of traditional literature. He suggests that fairy tales are perfectly suited to helping a child with the traumas of growing up . . . In all their original forms, many traditional stories are violent and fear-producing, yet Bettelheim contends that these elements very much represent the experiences of children. By presenting solutions to these situations, the fairytale provides a child with a model for coping with his or her fears.❞
Maureen Furniss (2012), *Art in Motion, Animation Aesthetics*, p. 115

The rite of passage of a protagonist (the main character in a story) can also be described as a character arc. This illustrates how a series of events shape a character's personality development throughout a story, which can often be the challenges of life faced from childhood into adulthood. In the section below you will see an abridged version of Propp's Morphology.

This abridged version includes a selection of his more easily identifiable narrative stages broken down into three key sections: the beginning, middle and end. The beginning introduces the world that the young protagonist has grown up in. The middle in a sense charts their journey through adolescence, and the end essentially illustrates their passage into adulthood.

ABRIDGED VERSION OF PROPP'S MORPHOLOGY

(Beginning)

1. Absentation: A protagonist intends to go to work or on a journey.

2. Interdiction: An authoritative figure tries preventing this with a warning.

3. Violation of interdiction: The protagonist sets out to disobey the warning and the antagonist (villain or enemy) may be introduced.

9. Misfortune or lack is made known, hero is dispatched with a request: The protagonist is sent on an errand by the authoritative figure.

12. The first donor function: The protagonist is intercepted and 'interrogated' by another character and receives a task and/or 'magical agent' from them.

(Middle)

15. The hero is transferred: The protagonist or 'Hero' goes on an adventure to fulfill the task, travelling 'through the air', 'over water' and 'climbs a stairway' (generic incidents).

16. The hero and villain join in direct combat: The protagonist and antagonist meet properly.

17. The hero is branded: The antagonist in some way injures or alters the protagonist.

18. The villain is defeated: But the protagonist then defeats the antagonist.

(End)

23. The hero, unrecognized, arrives home: The protagonist returns from their adventure but continues to assume an everyday life.

24. False hero presents unfounded claims: Another character claims to have done the work of the protagonist.

25. A difficult task is proposed to the hero: The protagonist is presented with one final challenge that reveals them as the true hero.

30: The villain is punished: The antagonist is killed or banished.

31: The hero is married and ascends the throne: A king rewards the protagonist by granting marriage to a princess, enhancing the protagonist's status, wealth etc.

Seven Archetypes or Dramatis Personae According to Propp

Propp also identified seven typical character types or archetypes that feature across the thirty-one narrative stages of the folk tale. Each archetype is essential to help introduce and explain aspects the plot and the main character's development during their journey or rite of passage. Thus, the archetypes have a syntagmatic purpose—a collective narrative function and meaning that help to define and structure the fairy tale. Propp collectively termed the archetypes and their respective functions as the Dramatis Personae.

We will now briefly outline how these archetypes typically function within a narrative. First, we see the protagonist or Hero introduced at the beginning of the story. The Dispatcher then sends the Hero out with a task during which he is intercepted by a Donor. In turn the Hero embarks on a larger quest set out by the Donor, who gives the Hero a *magical agent* to help him on the quest.

During the quest the Hero receives guidance from a Magical Helper, before being confronted by the antagonist or Villain. Upon ultimately defeating the Villain, a False Hero attempts to claim recognition for the defeat. But the Hero is then revealed to the Princess and her father (the King), who rewards the Hero with his daughter's hand in marriage.

Propp's Morphology in Relation to Other Fairy Tales & Myths

The written folk tale or fairy tale is of course not the unique invention of Propp or Russian culture. The Brothers Grimm (1785–1863 and 1786–1859), for example, were German linguistic and cultural researchers who had compiled many German and Scandinavian oral folk tales over a century before the publication of Propp's Morphology. Their legacy includes a large number of written fairy tales including Snow White and the Seven Dwarfs and Little Red Riding Hood (Fig. 2.2).

What is important to remember about the folk tale or fairy tale however, is the overall function or purpose, which is perhaps less evident in the work of Propp. Although fairy tale essentially documents a 'rite of passage', Propp's model concerns itself primarily with narrative structure. This aspect of Propp's work, though adopted into structuralist narrative theory, was problematic for Claude Lévi-Strauss, whose research was central to structuralist narrative theory.

❝Propp's analysis in short, reinforces the view that narrative is fundamentally syntagmatic in mode. But the major breakthrough represented in his work derives from his insistence that in the fairy tale the all-important and unifying element is found, not on a quasi-'phonetic' level, within the 'characters' who appear in the story, but on a 'phonemic' level, in the characters' *function*; the part they play in the *plot*. ❞
Terence Hawkes (2003), *Structuralism & Semiotics*, pp. 51–52

Mythology & Narratology

Russian formalism developed in parallel with a number of structuralist narrative theories collectively known as narratology, a term introduced by structuralist theorist Tzvetan Todorov. For Lévi-Strauss (1908–2009), the deeper structure or *meaning* of a story was a priority over a more superficial generic narrative structure. Through his anthropological research (study of human societies), he noted how despite various superficial differences, there was a fundamental similarity in how myths operate across a range of primitive civilizations throughout history.

More specifically, Lévi-Strauss looked at the universal way in which the primitive human mind made sense of natural phenomena in the world. In other words, he looked at how combinations of certain things, such as types of animal behaviour related to certain weather patterns, were interpreted by civilizations and used as a means of explaining abstract modes of thought.

Lévi-Strauss noted the similarities between different myths around the world by studying the paradigmatic relationships between the groups of signifiers used in myths and their broader cultural or semantic context. That is to say, he identified the fundamental theme or concept of a myth by looking at the collection of the various signs or objects, e.g., wind (index) or bird (symbol), and how they would assume different meaning depending on the type of landscape, climate and culture of a civilization.

For example, you might be familiar with certain types of animals being attributed to personality traits in Native American Indian culture. These are known as totems (a term also used by Propp), which include the bear (courageous and protective) and thunderbird or eagle (intelligent and divine). Whether found in Native American Indian legend or ancient Greek mythology, throughout history it is this relationship between such signifiers that has been used to educate or morally guide people in different cultures through the social or personal inner conflicts on their journey through life.

2.3

2.3
The mythical thunderbird or eagle, an icon of intelligence and the divine, sits at the top of the Native American totem pole.

❝**Mythical stories are, or seem, arbitrary, meaningless, absurd, yet nevertheless they seem to reappear all over the world. A 'fanciful' creation of the mind in one place would be unique—you would not expect to find the same creation in a completely different place.** ❞
Claude Lévi-Strauss (1989), *Myth & Meaning*, pp. 11–12

Modern Myth

The work of Roland Barthes (whose description of the 'garment system' was covered in chapter one) also centred on the idea of how within a myth, the mystical powers of a particular object can become a metaphor for a set of cultural values or represent conflicting states of being. Barthes, however, was interested in illustrating the power and use of myths in *modern* mass culture. He published these ideas as a collection of essays in his book *Mythologies* (1957). This became one of his most important contributions to structuralism and semiotics.

A clear illustration of the modern myth can be seen in his essay *Wine & Milk*. Here Barthes highlighted how wine has become an important almost spiritual symbol or *totem* of French identity and romanticized aspect of French lifestyle, in a similar way to how the English ceremoniously drink tea. The way in which wine or tea is drunk can also signify the status of a person.

Barthes also highlighted the transformative effect of red wine, and how its blood red colour imbues it with a mystical power. Instead of a good fermented grape drink, wine may become a totem of evil, as it often transforms a person to the opposite of their usual state, e.g., from happy to sad, kind to violent, good to evil, and so on. Thus, wine is another example of how cultural context can change the deeper semantic meaning or function of a word or object.

From red wine to poison apples or frog princes, similar kinds of signifiers are found throughout folklore and fairy tale, and could be applied to a number of characters and objects found in Propp's Morphology. The cultural significance of such symbolic foods or creatures leads us onto one last central theory relevant to our selection of structuralist methods useful in constructing narrative: binary opposites.

Binary opposites

Binary opposites are juxtapositions or meaningful contrasts of signs. These could include good and evil, beautiful and ugly, young and old, or male and female. The concept of difference between signs was first emphasized by Saussure and later developed by Roman Jakobson (1896–1982). Jakobson argued that binary opposites are central to human thought and are used to create order and meaning, to the extent that the use of one sign will immediately conjure up the thought of its opposite, even if the opposite is absent.

The idea of binary opposites can be clearly seen in the titles of fairy tales such as *Beauty and the Beast*, or if not in the title, certainly in the archetypes of almost all fairy tales, which include the *hero* and the *villain*. These contrasts or conflicts also form a key aspect of Lévi-Strauss's theories on cultural myth, which he extended to the organizing principles of culture in general.

"The ultimate function of myth, for Lévi-Strauss, was to represent the apparent resolution of a social conflict."
Robert Stam et al. (2006), *New Vocabularies in Film Semiotics*, p. 19

"Woman, then stands in patriarchal culture as a signifier for the male other, bound by a symbolic order in which man can live out his fantasies and obsessions through linguistic command, by imposing them on the silent image of woman still tied to her place as bearer of meaning not maker of meaning."
Laura Mulvey (2009), *Visual and Other Pleasures*, p. 15

Issues of Representation

It is this binary structure of the fairy tale and the structuralist approach to film narrative that comes under particular scrutiny for very 'black and white' or biased narrative messages. Feminist film theorists such as Laura Mulvey were concerned with how such structures precondition children to generally accept or expect the hero in a fairy tale or film to be a male character, and for fairy tale and film as a whole to be understood from the 'male gaze' (point of view).

Traditionally the female character in fairy tale plays a somewhat submissive or passive role. Snow White, for example, demonstrates a certain vulnerability and helplessness. She is jealously persecuted for her good looks by an ageing evil queen and gets lost in the woods to which she has fled. She ends up keeping the home of the seven dwarfs in order, and then falls into a death-like sleep after eating a poison apple given to her by the evil queen who appears in the form of an old witch. The salvation of Snow White finally comes in the form of a kiss from a dashing prince.

Variations on this narrative can be seen in the many animated renditions of different fairy tales. This does not bode well for female identity, which is formed around the sexist male ideals of beauty, with old women often depicted as sources of evil that only value good looks as a form of female empowerment. In the case of Snow White, we also see notions that women lack a sense of direction, but are keen housewives, and always need a man to bring them back to their senses!

2.4

However, things begin to improve. We see Propp's narrative archetypes applied more interchangeably to the hero and heroine in *Aladdin* (1992) than in earlier fairy tale films. The heroine became a more forthright and less submissive central character, with both Jasmine (Princess) and Aladdin (Hero) defying authority and determining their own rites of passage.

The film follows the parallel journeys of *both* protagonists. Jasmine defies her father's orders by leaving the palace and ultimately decides whom she wishes to marry without sacrificing anything in the end, while Aladdin continually thwarts the attempts of Jafar (antagonist) to capture him and returns to Agrabah in a hero's parade in the hope of winning back the princess.

But such films still fall short of resolving many problematic issues of representation. Gender-biased narrative structures will be explored further through the main case studies in this chapter and consolidated in chapters five and six. Nonetheless, the narrative theories, principles and structures documented by Propp, Lévi-Strauss, Barthes and Jakobson have endured as highly influential narrative conventions. These were largely consolidated, developed and hugely popularized by American author Joseph Campbell (1904–1987).

2.4
Disney's *Aladdin* (1992) represents a significant transition in the studio's maturing approach to the portrayal of the lead female character or heroine.
© 1992 Disney

The Hero's Journey &
the Writer's Journey

Joseph Campbell's work on comparative mythology essentially combines structuralist and formalist approaches to creating narrative structure and meaning. He defined his own set of nineteen narrative stages, based upon his comparison of many of the world's mythic traditions. Fundamentally, Campbell defined the universal recurring motif of the 'hero', his adventure and transformation, as the 'Hero's Journey'.

The success of this formula perhaps lies in how it comes to represent our own ability to survive and master our own destiny in the real world. Typically the 'Hero's Journey' reflects how in real life we learn the ways in which we can overcome deep-rooted traumatic memories from our childhood by confronting and overcoming our fears of the future.

Our memories might also be in the form of a nostalgic longing for a happier time in the past. The fears of the future may represent unfulfilled hopes for restoring harmony to the injustices imposed upon us by the present world we live in. Recognizing these hopes and fears, as well as the 'tests, enemies and allies' we face in real life, in many of the fairy tales and films we enjoy reading or watching provides a means of reflection on, but also escape from, our everyday lives.

Christopher Vogler, a contemporary Hollywood story consultant, writer, producer and teacher, condensed Campbell's narrative formula even further, into the twelve stages of the 'Writer's Journey'. Campbell and Vogler's respective work on mythology and universal narratives continues to influence a broad range of media from filmmaking to game design.

Vogler's work has influenced successful animated features such as *The Lion King* (1994), and studios such as Pixar have devised their own further condensed versions of this model. The narrative stages of the 'Writer's Journey' are particularly useful for helping to devise and connect the visual scenarios for each stage of a beat board and build on the semantic images discussed in the last chapter, such as the work of Vermeer or the student set design of a Japanese tearoom.

2.5

2.5
The idyllic settlement of Hobbiton in the region of Middle Earth called the Shire is home to the hobbit Bilbo Baggins. His call to adventure comes in the form of a visit by the wizard Gandalf and a group of dwarfs who disrupt the tranquility and order of his home and require his help in reclaiming their mountain kingdom of Erebor.

Narrative/Visual Breakdown of the Writer's Journey
(with Part Reference to Disney's *Aladdin* and *The Hobbit* Trilogy, 2012–2014)

1. Ordinary World: An image of the protagonist going about their everyday activities in a particular historical and geographical setting, e.g., Aladdin stealing food in an Arabian market.

2. Call to Adventure: Another image reveals a problem or challenge that the protagonist must resolve. They might, for example, be depicted as being presented with a call for help from a Princess, or as becoming imprisoned and encouraged to escape by an elderly fellow prisoner, e.g., the kidnapping of Jasmine and the imprisonment of Aladdin by Jafar.

3. Refusal of the Call: After an initial refusal by the protagonist to resolve the situation, due to a sense of helplessness or for fear of the unknown, they are prompted into action by a change in circumstances, e.g., Aladdin has given up hope of rescuing Jasmine or saving himself, until another prisoner (Jafar in disguise) reveals to him a secret passageway out of the prison.

4. Meeting with the Mentor: A wise old person, such as a wizard, reveals themselves to the protagonist and imparts important advice to them in preparation for their journey or quest to find something or someone. The mentor also presents them with a magical device that will help them on their journey, e.g., the 10,000-year-old Genie in a magic lamp.

5. Crossing the Threshold: The protagonist is seen setting off to a special new world by travelling over water, climbing up a mountain or flying through the sky, e.g., Aladdin leaves the 'Cave of Wonders' on a magic carpet.

6. Tests, Enemies and Allies: The protagonist learns the ways of the new world, meeting new characters in testing environments who impart important advice and join them for at least part of the journey. Fights or shady dealings in taverns are often used for these introductions, e.g., the hobbit Bilbo Baggins meeting the dwarfs, elves and so on.

7. Approach to the Inmost Cave: The protagonist may literally descend underground towards a cave or the depths of an enemy castle in the special new world, in order to reach the thing or person concealed there needed to vanquish the enemy or restore order, e.g., Bilbo Baggins enters the mines in the dwarf kingdom of Erebor in search of the magical Arkenstone.

8. Ordeal: Upon reaching the inmost cave they may also metaphorically confront their innermost fears or a major challenge, such as being confronted by a giant dragon or navigating a huge fiery precipice, e.g., both, in the case of *The Hobbit* trilogy.

9. Reward (Seizing the Sword): The protagonist finally seizes or regains the object, thing or person they set out for, such as a magical weapon, a map, attaining special knowledge or instructions or being reunited with a special person, such as a parent or loved one who may represent the reconciliation of a deep broken bond, e.g., the Arkenstone or Princess Jasmine.

10. The Road Back: The protagonist is chased out of the cave by the beast, runs from erupting lava or runs from an exploding weapon that they have disturbed upon entering the inmost cave and seizing the reward. This marks the point at which the special world must be left behind ahead of the road home, e.g., Smaug the dragon.

11. Resurrection: The protagonist's soul is cleansed by one last brush with death. They face a last gasp attempt by the enemy to destroy them, which they miraculously survive, or in which they potentially lose one of their closest allies. The humbling moment helps them to rediscover their humanity, e.g., Bilbo Baggins mourns the death of Thorin II Oakenshield, the Mountain King.

12. Return with Elixir: They arrive home with the object, person or knowledge needed to vanquish the original enemy, prevent future attacks or maintain a new way of life, e.g., Bilbo Baggins returns home with gold, a magic ring, knowledge to create a map of Middle Earth and a more worldly outlook on life.

CASTLE IN THE SKY: MYTHICAL FORCES, FLOATING WORLDS & FLYING MACHINES

2.6

2.6
Laputa, Castle in the Sky (1986).
The film narrative is enriched by
references to the mines in South
Wales, the flying machines
such as the Zeppelin from the
interwar period and the meme
of the 'floating world' of the Edo
period in Japan. This results in
a timeless and placeless mix
of cultures that enhances the
deeper meaning of the story
and underpins the universal
appeal of the film.

From Picture Scroll to the Floating World

The classic animé film *Laputa, Castle in the Sky* is a rich example of an animated feature film that reflects many of the formalist and structuralist theories on folk tale and myth, as well as aspects of the human condition covered in the chapter so far. *Laputa* was the first Studio Ghibli film directed by Hayao Miyazaki (1986). This animation illustrates many of the similarities and superficial differences between the visual narrative cultures of the east and west, as well as the fascinating cultural exchange of ideas and artistic practices dating back several centuries between Europe and Japan.

The purpose of this section of the chapter is to highlight some key starting points for thinking about how not just to replicate the visual style of animé but also how understand how to use key features of the medium to create narrative meaning visually in your own work. But before analyzing the structure and meaning of *Laputa, Castle in the Sky*, it is important to understand the cultural symbolism in animé more fully. To do this, it is helpful to examine the evolution of Japanese narrative art through some of the historical periods that shaped the form, subject matter and semantics (deeper symbolic meaning) of Japanese visual culture.

In chapter one we saw how the emakimono picture-scroll is used in the domestic Japanese tearoom to symbolize the spiritual mood to be observed in the room. The emakimono picture-scroll dates back to twelfth-century Japan. These scrolls depicted finely detailed images or scenes reflecting key themes relating to the human condition, from birth and death to love and war. These were approached with subtlety to reveal the spiritual complexity of such subject matter.

These pictorial traditions evolved during the Edo period, from the early seventeenth century to the mid-nineteenth century. Innovations in woodblock printing meant that images could be mass produced by a lead artist, teams of woodcarvers and printers. These images, known as ukiyo-e, had stronger outlines and became bolder in their use of colour. We see cultural echoes of these mass production rendering techniques in modern manga and animé production.

The steady growth in trade with European nations in the seventeenth century also saw the increasing import of European art and culture to Japan. The paintings by Dutch artists (such as Vermeer) in particular fascinated Japanese scholars due to the level of realism in the images and the techniques used to achieve it. This had a significant influence on the level of realism in the development of ukiyo-e art, the legacy of which once again can be seen in the realism in modern animé production.

Dutch and Japanese ukiyo-e artists also shared an interest in the everyday subject matter of genre painting, depicting the everyday lives and activities of ordinary people. In the latter Edo period, images typically depicted subjects ranging from farming, fishing and trading in marketplaces to the theatrical companionship of geishas or courtesans grooming themselves.

❝Contained within the cosmic world of *emakimono* was also the acute effort to recognize particularities and emotional nuances of human conditions. As a result, these picture-scrolls did not only reflect the trends in medieval Japan but also provided a guiding window for us to understand the psychological and ideological perspectives of the artist and his spectatorship's aesthetic expectations.❞
Tze-Yue G.Hu (2010), *Frames of Anime, Culture and Image Building*, p. 27

Tracing Oriental Influences on European Art, Animation and Film

European art and culture was in turn significantly influenced by the import of goods from Japan, especially in the latter half of the nineteenth century. Japanese ukiyo-e woodblock prints in particular influenced French artists known as the Post-Impressionists, who were preoccupied with the use of bold colour and similar subject matter ranging from vaudeville theatre performances to the everyday lives of prostitutes in brothels.

One of the most famous Post-Impressionists, Henri Toulouse Lautrec (1864–1901), emulated many of the techniques of Japanese woodblock printing by creating posters using the latest lithographic printing press techniques in Europe. His images resembled ukiyo-e prints in many ways, right down to the oriental styling of text and his signature.

The legacy of post-impressionist assimilation of Japanese traditions of bold colour, simplified design and subtle observations of everyday life can also be seen in French comic book art and animation. Popular examples include the work of Nicolas de Crécy and Sylvain Chomet (*The Old Lady and the Pigeons*, 1998) and the live action films of Jean-Pierre Jeunet (*Amélie*, 2001).

INTRODUCTION | HEROES & TOTEMS: MORPHOLOGY, NARRATOLOGY, MYTHOLOGY | CASTLE IN THE SKY: MYTHICAL FORCES, FLOATING WORLDS & FLYING MACHINES | WORKBOOK EXERCISE 2.1 | WORKBOOK EXERCISE 2.2 | CASE STUDY: *PETER & THE WOLF* | INTERVIEW WITH SUZIE TEMPLETON | CASE STUDY: SAINT THOMAS BECKET | CHAPTER SUMMARY & FURTHER READING | KEY WORDS, NAMES & WORKS

However, more fundamentally, ukiyo-e also reflected a romanticized ideal of a 'floating world'. Many images by famous Edo artists such as Katsushika Hokusai (1760–1849) and Utagawa Hiroshige (1797–1858) were set against the mountainous backdrops of the Japanese landscape, with volcanoes appearing to float above the level of the clouds. Fishing vessels at sea and bridges linking islands or riverbanks also often featured as the context for the daily routines of the people depicted within these scenes.

Yet by the mid-twentieth century Japanese culture had been radically transformed through rapid industrialization and also the total nuclear atomic destruction of Japanese cities by the Americans, which essentially ended the Second World War. The resulting urban regeneration and expansion into the countryside, as well as a city culture and an economy built on technological innovation, had detached people spiritually from Shinto, the state religion of Japan up until 1945.

The Shinto faith worships deities or souls in the form of abstract natural phenomena such as the wind and sea and inanimate natural forms such as trees, which feature extensively in the Japanese visual culture of ukiyo-e from the Edo period. Culturally inherited behaviours or ideas, such as use of the wind, sea or trees, as symbols of the spiritual world are known as memes.

2.7

These spiritual memes in the form of otherworldly Japanese natural landscapes, contrasted with the mechanization of the modern industrial age, as well as the hand-drawn graphic use of line and colour and a high level of realism have become culturally embedded in animé, the work of Studio Ghibli and Hayao Miyazaki in particular.

2.7
Mount Fuji seen from Nakaharo, Japan. Woodblock print by Katsushika Hokusai (1823–1829). The image is an example of the 'floating world' of the Edo period formed of floating mountains and bridges over water.

Laputa, Castle in the Sky:
Narrative Breakdown

2.8

2.8
Colliery Pit, Rhondda Heritage Park, Rhondda
Valley, South Wales. The mines in the *Laputa,
Castle in the Sky* were largely inspired by
Miyazaki's visit to the coal mines and mining
communities in Wales.

INTRODUCTION

HEROES &
TOTEMS:
MORPHOLOGY,
NARRATOLOGY,
MYTHOLOGY

CASTLE IN THE
SKY: MYTHICAL
FORCES,
FLOATING
WORLDS &
FLYING MACHINES

WORKBOOK
EXERCISE 2.1

WORKBOOK
EXERCISE 2.2

CASE STUDY:
PETER &
THE WOLF

INTERVIEW
WITH SUZIE
TEMPLETON

CASE STUDY:
SAINT THOMAS
BECKET

CHAPTER
SUMMARY
& FURTHER
READING

KEY WORDS,
NAMES & WORKS

Many of Miyazaki's animated feature films are instantly recognizable above all for their narrative contexts, structures and deeper narrative themes. His films invariably look at the relationship between mankind and his exploitation of his natural environment. Like in many folklore traditions, Miyazaki often uses children as symbols of purity venturing into the unknown, where they encounter strange creatures or natural spirits that guide them on their journey to confront and resolve the ills of adulthood and the modern industrial world.

The film *Laputa, Castle in the Sky* begins in the *ordinary world* of a largely abandoned mining town. The male protagonist, a young boy called Pazu, is obsessed with flying machines and the legend of the *floating world* of Laputa, which he believes to be partially revealed behind a giant cloud in a photo taken by his late father during a flight through a great storm.

Pazu's *call to adventure* begins with the appearance of Sheeta, the young female protagonist. Pazu witnesses Sheeta falling down slowly to earth after escaping from her evil captor Muska on a flying military fortress in the sky. She is unharmed by the fall due to the levitating powers of the mystical pendent worn around her neck. This encounter motivates Pazu to prove to himself and others that the floating world his deceased father discovered was real. Pazu's fascination with Laputa clearly demonstrates his adoration for his father and how much he misses him. Sheeta reveals to Pazu that she has a connection with Laputa through her family name. It is later revealed that she is also the heiress to Laputa.

Following a *meeting with the mentor* of Uncle Pom in the mines, who explains the mythical powers of the rocks, the children embark on a journey to solve the mystery of Laputa. The film continues to follow a narrative structure that resembles the standard twelve stages of the 'Writer's Journey' or the *Morphology of the Folktale*.

The story is also interwoven with many of the natural forces and elements common in the Shinto faith—notably the wind and a giant tree at the centre of a floating castle in the sky. The wind features prominently in the flight sequences, while the castle echoes the iconic 'floating' volcanoes, man-made bridges and structures that feature in many ukiyo-e landscapes.

The magical force of a giant mythical Aetherium stone concealed in the depths of the castle—sourced from the mines featured at the beginning of the film—is analogous to nuclear power and nuclear warfare. The Aetherium stone enables the castle in the sky to defy gravity and cause mass destruction on the planet below.

Ultimately, destruction of the floating castle itself is caused by the misuse of the giant mythical Aetherium stone, due to the corrupt obsession with power of Muska (who turns out to be a distant adult relation of Sheeta) and the greed of the military forces that assist him in attempting to take over Laputa.

Muska and the military forces are wiped out in the destruction of Laputa. The children, however, survive in the roots of the giant tree that had overgrown and held together the ancient castle structure until that point—symbolizing perhaps the power of 'mother nature' to reclaim planet Earth from its destruction by mankind.

WORKBOOK EXERCISE 2.1:
APPLYING THE 'WRITER'S JOURNEY' TO *LAPUTA, CASTLE IN THE SKY*

Using the narrative structure of the 'Writer's Journey' below, try completing the narrative breakdown of Laputa. It may help you to reference the summary of Propp's Morphology contained in this chapter. For each stage, try to identify how different character archetypes, objects or natural elements help create deeper narrative meaning. A few tips and narrative stages already covered have been included for you to get started and expand upon:

1. Ordinary World: The mining town where Pazu (hero) lives

2. Call to Adventure: Arrival of Sheeta (princess) and her magical pendant

3. Refusal of the Call: Does Pazu or Sheeta refuse the call?

4. Meeting with the Mentor: Seeing Uncle Pom in the mines

5. Crossing the Threshold: How do Pazu and Sheeta set off into the unknown/ get into the sky?

6. Tests, Enemies and Allies: Re-capture of Sheeta, flying robot, Dola and sky pirate family

7. Approach to the Inmost Cave: What do Sheeta and Pazu find in the depths of the castle?

8. Ordeal: Who or what confronts Sheeta there?

9. Reward (Seizing the Sword): What do the children gain, learn or achieve after the destruction of Laputa?

10. The Road Back: How does Miyazaki condense, combine, twist, avoid or symbolize 10–12?

11. Resurrection: You try

12. Return with Elixir: You try

From Aetherium to the Arkenstone: You could also try comparing and contrasting the many parallels between the narrative structures and symbols in *Laputa* and *The Hobbit* trilogy.

INTRODUCTION

HEROES &
TOTEMS:
MORPHOLOGY,
NARRATOLOGY,
MYTHOLOGY

CASTLE IN THE
SKY: MYTHICAL
FORCES,
FLOATING
WORLDS &
FLYING MACHINES

**WORKBOOK
EXERCISE 2.1**

WORKBOOK
EXERCISE 2.2

CASE STUDY:
*PETER &
THE WOLF*

INTERVIEW
WITH SUZIE
TEMPLETON

CASE STUDY:
SAINT THOMAS
BECKET

CHAPTER
SUMMARY
& FURTHER
READING

KEY WORDS,
NAMES & WORKS

Unique Visions:
Introducing Auteur Theory

Generally speaking, formalist and structuralist theories are not concerned with individual expression or authorship, at least with regard to film and animation. Formalist theories dictate a standard narrative structure that leaves limited scope for invention of new ideas by a director. Structuralist theory, on the other hand, is in a sense more preoccupied with universal or collective authorship—which in the case of large-scale film and animation production would take account of the writers, cameramen and editors—and not just the vision of the director.

The combination of such theories still dominates studio practices in mainstream cinema, mainly in America, but also in other countries, including Japan. In 1951 André Bazin (1918–1958) and a group of other French film critics established a magazine called *Cahiers du Cinéma*. Writers included filmmakers such as François Truffaut (1932–1984), who published a manifesto essay for the magazine in 1954 in reaction against the dominant and more conservative values of the large film studios that imposed limitations on the creativity of filmmakers.

What Truffaut, Bazin and others recognized was that there were certain film directors who were able to work within such dominant narrative conventions of large-scale studios and still find a powerful 'individual' voice. This is because they had particular technical skills, filmmaking styles and interests, which made their films instantly recognizable. Such Hollywood directors included Fritz Lang, Charlie Chaplin and Alfred Hitchcock. In 1957 Bazin summarized the idea of authorship in his article 'La Politique des Auteurs'. Not long after, American film critic Andrew Sarris popularized these ideas, which became known as Auteur Theory.

"For Truffaut, the new film would resemble the person who made it, not so much through autobiographical content but rather through the style, which impregnates the film with the personality of its director. Intrinsically strong directors, auteur theory argued, will exhibit over the years a recognizable stylistic and thematic personality, even when they work in Hollywood studios."
Robert Stam (2000), *Film Theory, An Introduction*, p. 84

63

The Anime Auteur: Research, Memories and Female Protagonists

2.9
Crowds watch the German LZ 129 Hindenburg airship making its first test flight from the Zeppelin dockyards at Friedrichshafen, Germany, March 4, 1936. The Zeppelin and other fantastical aircraft commonly feature as the basis of the narrative components in many of Miyazaki's films.

Hayoa Miyazaki is an example of a filmmaker whose feature length animations bear an instantly recognizable authorship. However, despite the excellence of traditional drawn animation techniques and level of realism in his films, these traits are not uncommon amongst the stylistic Japanese traditions that come together to form the animé genre. Rather, it is the deeper semantic themes, narrative contexts and other narrative elements that define Miyazaki's unique formula.

We have already discussed how Miyazaki's films are underpinned by mankind's diminishing relationship with the spirituality of the natural environment and often contain themes influenced by the closing events of the Second World War. Miyazaki was himself born towards the end of the Second World War. His father was the director of the Miyazaki airplane factory, so flight and war define many of Miyazaki's early memories and can be seen in recurrent narrative components in his films.

But again, even these narrative contexts are not totally unique to his films. Perhaps what defines his storytelling ability is how he creates believable fantasy worlds that have universal appeal. In true Japanese tradition, he is able to blend the cultures of east and west (e.g., borrowing the idea for a floating castle from the European tale *Gulliver's Travels* by Jonathan Swift) and observe a unique level of cultural authenticity by meticulously researching modern European culture.

The mining towns in *Laputa*, for example, were inspired and designed from visiting the impoverished coal mining communities in Wales during the decline of British industry in the 1980s. The resulting artwork was not only visually authentic, but also infused the narrative with an empathy and understanding of how these environments reflected the story and struggles of their real inhabitants. Combined with the mythical symbolism of the Edo floating world, Miyazaki is able to transport us from the real world to a timeless and placeless fantasy one.

But perhaps what defines Miyazaki's films more than anything is how he is able to move beyond a rational text to a more evocative narrative that focuses on nostalgia—re-experiencing fond innocent childhood memories and reconnecting with our hopes for the future. Thus, one of his greatest skills is the ability to achieve a balance between expressive action sequences, with prolonged periods of limited animation and awe-inspiring panoramas that provide the audience with the opportunity for moments of quiet contemplation about the conditions of the human experience.

By researching our subject matter properly and also looking at the work of other filmmakers that relates to our projects, we have the possibility of creating narratives that reflect the events of the world around us. Many great film auteurs are defined by this capacity, the ability to communicate a universal message that captures the concerns of the time in which they live. This ability to remain contemporary and relevant is also reflected by another important aspect of Miyazaki's work: the representation of female characters. From manga and animé to shunga (ukiyo-e erotic art), there is a long tradition of depicting highly eroticized and even pornographic images of submissive young women in Japanese culture.

Not only do Miyazaki's films avoid overtly sexual and sexist depictions, they often also feature a female hero-protagonist or include the platonic (nonsexual) relationship of a male and female protagonist of equal narrative importance. Thus, while Pazu still comes to the rescue of the princess Sheeta on several occasions in *Laputa*, Sheeta is gifted with access to mystical powers and self-determination that extend well beyond the traditional gender roles of western folk tale or sexual identity in Japanese culture.

An interesting cultural contrast in the depiction of gender can be seen in *Ponyo* (2008), Miyzaki's interpretation of the folk tale of *The Little Mermaid*. First, Miyazaki uses the sea to highlight a deeper narrative theme of pollution and global warming. Second, instead of focusing on the story of a more traditional romance, we see the platonic friendship between the girl Ponyo (who is represented as a fish) and the boy Sōsuke, which develops as a symbolic representation of the possibility of a harmonious relationship between nature and mankind.

Furthermore, unlike many folk tales, the relationship between the two children is not determined by a father figure (i.e., mankind); rather it is brokered between the children's mothers. Ponyo's mother is depicted as a sea goddess, which is undoubtedly a reference once again by Miyazaki to the concept of 'mother nature'. Interestingly however, it is worth noting that despite Miyazaki having a much less male-centric worldview in many respects, his popularity also highlights the phenomenal global influence of an entertainment medium still predominantly directed by male filmmakers.

WORKBOOK EXERCISE 2.2:
USING A 'MIYAZAKI FORMULA' TO DEVELOP
YOUR OWN FILM IDEA

This exercise can help you consolidate the ideas covered in the chapter so far into preproduction work for a film idea of your own. I have put together an example of how you might identify a theme based on current affairs, make visual and historical research into a particular context, reinterpret the animé formula of Miyazaki in your own personal way and develop a beat board formed of production stills based on the twelve-stage 'Writer's Journey'.

Narrative Theme: Decide on a universal ecological issue currently featuring in world news, e.g., renewable energy versus fossil fuels, specifically the impact on local communities of minor man-made tremors caused by fracking—the high-pressure injection of liquid into underground rock used to extract oil or gas (circa 2012).

Narrative Context: Visually research and make sketches of a location, e.g., one threatened or affected by fracking, such as Falkirk in Scotland. Look at contrasts between old rural buildings and modern technology, such as the futuristic Falkirk Wheel, which could inspire a *Laputa*-style world of barges and canals leading to the Scottish Highlands, instead of flying machines leading to floating castles in the sky.

Cultural Heritage & Stylistic Influences: Research ancient local cultural heritage and representations of natural phenomena as the basis of your story, e.g., Celtic folklore and Scottish mythical creatures such as the Loch Ness Monster. This could help you develop characters or archetypes that you can pair with the various narrative stages used to tell the story. Research into ancient and more modern indigenous art could also help in an appropriate stylizing of your animation, e.g., Celtic art or the Art Nouveau furniture and the architectural designs of Charles Rennie Mackintosh (1868–1928).

INTRODUCTION

HEROES &
TOTEMS:
MORPHOLOGY,
NARRATOLOGY,
MYTHOLOGY

CASTLE IN THE
SKY: MYTHICAL
FORCES,
FLOATING
WORLDS &
FLYING MACHINES

WORKBOOK
EXERCISE 2.1

**WORKBOOK
EXERCISE 2.2**

CASE STUDY:
*PETER &
THE WOLF*

INTERVIEW
WITH SUZIE
TEMPLETON

CASE STUDY:
SAINT THOMAS
BECKET

CHAPTER
SUMMARY
& FURTHER
READING

KEY WORDS,
NAMES & WORKS

2.10

Potential Narrative Stages

1. Ordinary World: The Scottish town of Falkirk

2. Call to Adventure: A fracking incident destroys part of the town

5. Crossing the Threshold: The *young* protagonist heads off 'over water' via the Falkirk Wheel and canal seeking help to save the town from an international fracking company

7. Approach to the Inmost Cave: The protagonist descends to the bottom of Loch Ness

8. Ordeal: The Loch Ness Monster confronts them

9. Reward (Seizing the Sword): The protagonist learns about hydroelectric power and other renewable energy sources, as the Glendoe Hydro Scheme above Loch Ness discharges water into the loch below

12. Return with Elixir: The older, wiser protagonist returns back to Falkirk, where they educate the local population about renewable energy sources and lead a campaign to close down the local fracking activities

2.10
The Falkirk Wheel in Scotland is an extraordinary architectural feature that lifts canal barges out of the water and connects them with a canal system above. This concept image for workbook exercise 2.2 includes art references to William Morris and Japanese Edo woodblock prints.
By Mark Collington (2016).

CASE STUDY:
PETER & THE WOLF

Peter & the Wolf is a fairy tale that was created as a narrated orchestral piece for a children's theatre in Moscow by Russian composer Sergei Prokofiev (1891–1953). It was designed to introduce children to the structure of the various sections and instruments in the orchestra. The story itself maps out the rite of passage of a boy, Peter, who leaves home and ventures into the woods against the warning of his grandfather. He is met by a series of animals that present him with a set of moral dilemmas before fighting and capturing a wolf. The wolf is a symbol of danger in many cultures due to its illusive and predatory nature. Returning to town with the wolf and deciding its fate signifies Peter's bravery and moral transition into adulthood.

Prokofiev devised *Peter & the Wolf* (1936) during the same Soviet era in which Propp wrote his *Morphology of the Folktale* (1929). Although Prokofiev and Propp had no direct connection to one another, Peter & the Wolf essentially follows the same structure and contains many of magical components of the *Morphology of the Folktale*.

This case study will now apply the narrative methods covered in this chapter to the analysis of Oscar-winning stop motion director Suzie Templeton's interpretation of Prokofiev's *Peter & the Wolf* (2008). Questions and answers from an interview with the director are also used in the analysis as well as her interpretation of the original fairy tale.

This professional case study is particularly useful as it also introduces us to the importance of sound in animation. The use of sound in animation will be explored in a number of ways across all of the chapters. This chapter focuses on *Peter & the Wolf*, as it is a prime example of the relationship between semiotics and sound. The case study and interview may also help you to think about how to use music to plan your work, but develop the contents more intuitively.

2.11

2.11
Peter & the Wolf by Suzie Templeton, 2006. Part eighteen of Vladimir Propp's *Morphology of the Folktale* ('The villain is defeated') illustrated by Peter capturing the wolf.

INTRODUCTION | HEROES & TOTEMS: MORPHOLOGY, NARRATOLOGY, MYTHOLOGY | CASTLE IN THE SKY: MYTHICAL FORCES, FLOATING WORLDS & FLYING MACHINES | WORKBOOK EXERCISE 2.1 | WORKBOOK EXERCISE 2.2 | CASE STUDY: *PETER & THE WOLF* | INTERVIEW WITH SUZIE TEMPLETON | CASE STUDY: SAINT THOMAS BECKET | CHAPTER SUMMARY & FURTHER READING | KEY WORDS, NAMES & WORKS

Suzie Templeton's Adaptation of Prokofiev's *Peter & the Wolf* (2006); Narrative Stages According to Propp's Morphology, Abridged & Illustrated

(Beginnning)

1. Absentation: Peter's desire for independence and going on an adventure into the allure of the clearing in the woods.

2. Interdiction: Grandfather warns and prevents Peter from doing so.

3. Violation of interdiction: Peter sets about making plans, disobeying his grandfather's orders.

9. Misfortune or lack is made known, hero is dispatched with a request: Grandfather sends Peter into town on an errand to keep him out of harm's way.

12. The first donor function: Peter is '*interrogated*' and '*attacked*' by hunters and receives a '*magical agent*' in the form of a balloon from the circus master (the elements in italics are generic incidents outlined by Propp for this stage).

(Middle)

15. The hero is transferred: Peter is inspired by the balloon and his acquaintance with a bird to now escape into the clearing in the woods. Using rope and a tree he travels '*through the air*', he then skates across ice '*over water*' (italics again represent generic incidents).

16. The hero and villain join in direct combat: Peter tries to capture the wolf.

17. The hero is branded: The wolf scratches Peter's face.

18. The villain is defeated: The wolf gets tangled in the net.

(End)

23. The hero, unrecognized, arrives home: Peter arrives in the town atop the caged wolf.

24. False hero presents unfounded claims: The hunters try to convince the crowd that they captured the wolf.

25: A difficult task is proposed to the hero: Peter is faced with a moral dilemma. He witnesses his grandfather negotiating the highest price for the wolf between the circus master, the butcher and the hunting shop owner. In the end Peter takes the initiative to set the wolf free.

Introducing Leitmotifs

In his book *Myth & Meaning*, Lévi-Stauss determined that in general the structure of music was much like the structure of the myth. He argued that meaning was created not by individual notes or even the whole sequential musical score, but by the combination of different musical phrases.

Prokofiev's *Peter & the Wolf* is interesting, as it blends the deeper thematic aspects of myth with the more linear structure of fairy tale.

Prokofiev's original format did this by using music and narration. The narration told the overall story, but the music created the deeper shades of meaning. This was achieved by pairing musical instruments and phrases with the main characters in the story. Each archetype therefore has a distinctive musical sound. The musical phrase associated with each character is known as a leitmotif. The leitmotifs also change tempo and key according to the drama unfolding in the story.

For example, the string section of the orchestra is the leitmotif assigned to Peter. This reinforces the fullness of his role as the hero. We hear his leitmotif in a major key, a higher octave and upbeat tempo in more triumphant moments, or in a minor key, lower octave and slow tempo during more serious moments. This is a principle used in many films and television programmes, including popular American television series such as *Mad Men*.

Prokofiev clearly uses a varying combination of character archetypes to tell the story thematically, as well as following an overall sequential narrative. The characters therefore take on a deeper collective semantic meaning and narrative function according to how and when they appear in the story. The bird, for example, is the primary magical helper, whose flute leitmotif has a light, playful and slightly mystic quality. The bird, duck and cat generally provide comic relief when they appear together.

The leitmotif is the sound equivalent of the motif introduced in chapter one. To expand, a motif is a term similar to the totem or symbol. A motif is an image that is used repeatedly to reinforce an idea or theme associated with something more specific. For example, images of a unicorn or thistle, lion or rose, and cockerel or lily have instant associations with Scotland, England and France, respectively. These are often *learned* mythical associations used to reinforce national ideologies. Motifs regularly feature on flags, coins and the clothing of national sport teams.

We can also be conditioned by leitmotifs. The sounds of the bagpipes or accordion have for example an instant association with Scotland and France, respectively. However, leitmotifs can also be 'hardwired' into the human psyche. In other words, there are many natural and manmade sounds that evoke an instinctive emotional feeling or association in the human mind, such as the wind, sea, chanting or drumming. Leitmotifs can in this way be associated with abstract cultural ideas and evoke spiritual feelings, akin to the memes signified by the wind and sea that often feature in animé, for example.

2.12

2.12
Film still from *Peter & the Wolf*. Peter and the animals, such as the duck and bird, each have their own unique leitmotif—a particular musical phrase and instrumental sound.

INTERVIEW WITH SUZIE TEMPLETON
ON HER ADAPTATION OF PROKOFIEV'S
PETER & THE WOLF

2.13

Cultural and Contextual Analysis on Realism, Time, Setting and Narrative in Set Design

Suzie Templeton's stop motion adaptation of Prokofiev's Peter & the Wolf *has comparable hyper-real animation qualities to the hand drawn animation of directors such as Hayao Miyazaki. It is interesting ask ourselves why such hand-crafted realism seems to be favoured so often in animated representations of myth and folk tale.*

2.13
A photograph of a Russian cottage taken by Suzie Templeton that formed visual research for the development of set designs of Peter and his grandfather's home in *Peter & the Wolf*.

Are there any particular factors that determine your style and approach to stop motion filmmaking?

I always set out to make my films feel real to me. There's a moment in puppet making when making a face for example, when it suddenly feels really alive. But I'm not going for total realism, rather something that might be described as a 'poetic realism'. This is what I am naturally drawn towards from a making perspective—I like to make things in this way—based on reality but taken a little bit beyond, although I do also like watching more stylized work.

It is often important to research the location of story during preproduction. This comes with a whole range of practical implications on how an animation is made, right down to capturing a feeling of authenticity and creating narrative meaning.

To western eyes perhaps, your sets resemble a stereotypically provincial, communist, modern day setting. With this in mind, there are interesting interpretations from the original story, such as where Peter goes through a gate out into a meadow. In your film we have what looks like Peter escaping out of the secure confines of his grandfather's small holding into a small industrial drainage outlet at the edge of the woods. Was a political or geographical context important to you in designing the environment for your film?

Not necessarily political, I wanted to stay away from that entirely, but definitely geographical. I wanted the film to feel Russian, and feel Russian to a Russian person. I wanted it to feel authentic in that way, and to *feel* real, or like it *could* be real. I went to Russia to research these settings, and did a lot of travelling around rural and semi-rural situations. The setting in the film wasn't a real place, but was an amalgamation of real things, with a lot of the architecture being based on photographs I had taken.

Did you look at how each environment could add to the narrative, tell parts of the story and also what it could tell us beyond the characters?

Yes. The environments are all character led. For example the grandfather's house gives a lot of clues to their life beyond the narrative. I find it fascinating how the process of scriptwriting, with its multiple expansions, reductions, edits and revisions, leaves unfathomable residues within a film. They are the residues of rejected and maybe even forgotten ideas. They are often intangible but can be *felt*. They can most clearly be seen in sets and props, and their presence enriches our relationship with the characters, adding to a sense of realism.

INTERVIEW WITH SUZIE TEMPLETON
ON HER ADAPTATION OF PROKOFIEV'S
PETER & THE WOLF (continued)

2.14

Cultural Analysis of Gender Politics & Character Motifs

As a director it is also important to consider our responsibility to the audience and our ability to understand how we as well as our audience may interpret the characters in a story. This is so that we do not unintentionally offend anyone and make sure that the audience can empathize with the characters, but more importantly to realize that our work has the potential to influence the opinions of others.

2.14
Dog by Suzie Templeton, Royal College of Art, 2001. A young boy comes to terms with the death of his mother while grieving for his dying pet.

INTRODUCTION

HEROES & TOTEMS: MORPHOLOGY, NARRATOLOGY, MYTHOLOGY

CASTLE IN THE SKY: MYTHICAL FORCES, FLOATING WORLDS & FLYING MACHINES

WORKBOOK EXERCISE 2.1

WORKBOOK EXERCISE 2.2

CASE STUDY: PETER & THE WOLF

INTERVIEW WITH SUZIE TEMPLETON

CASE STUDY: SAINT THOMAS BECKET

CHAPTER SUMMARY & FURTHER READING

KEY WORDS, NAMES & WORKS

Structuralist or formalist tales, that you could argue include Prokofiev's *Peter & the Wolf*, are often accused of being intrinsically male in their psyche and use of binary opposites. Do you feel that is still true, or are we past that—is this important to you as a female director, and if so, how have you tried to address a male bias in storytelling?

I think that this is definitely being addressed, you can see studios such as Disney really trying to get past it, but I think that we are still in the process of getting past it. It is important to me. So far I have tried to avoid female characters, but the only female character I have ever represented was an evil old woman [laughs].

Suzie Templeton became known for her stop motion work through her BAFTA award-winning film Dog, *2001 (Fig. 2.14). The story uses an analogy of a family's dying pet to help a boy understand the bereavement of his deceased mother. The film was made with the same hyper-real animation qualities as Templeton's subsequent adaptation of Prokofiev's* Peter & the Wolf.

It is interesting to note that as a female director in all your films, from *Stanley* to *Dog* and *Peter & the Wolf*, your main characters tend to be old men and boys. Is this just a coincidence, you say you avoid female characters?

I identify very strongly with my characters. For example in the film *Dog* I identified very strongly with the boy. Of course I did consider making him into a girl character, but I just couldn't be as honest with the representation of the character if it was a girl. But narratively there wouldn't have been any difference. I'm currently writing a new film. Now that I'm a mother I feel I can make the protagonist a girl character—as I feel old enough and distant enough to be able to represent her faithfully without feeling *too* close.

Your film *Dog*, appears to use the analogy of a family's dying pet to help a boy understand the bereavement of his mother. What do you appreciate most about the motif of the animal as a storytelling device?

In *Peter & the Wolf* I wanted each of the animals to represent a part of Peter that he needed to integrate into his own character, and as they played their various roles within the story he could take on those attributes that they were all teaching him.

You mention in another interview on *Peter & the Wolf*, a decision to make the wolf a female character. Why—and how do you feel you signify this as it is perhaps not so obvious?

I wanted those who were animating the wolf to be subtle with the animation, because I think the wolf has such a terrible reputation within storytelling and within folk tales, that it is generally and often represented as a monster, and I wanted it to be represented in a sympathetic way. I thought if the animators knew that it was a female wolf they would animate her in a different way.

75

INTERVIEW WITH SUZIE TEMPLETON ON HER ADAPTATION OF PROKOFIEV'S *PETER & THE WOLF (continued)*

Cultural and Contextual Analysis of Narrative Structure, Sound & Deeper Meaning

Sound is an essential ingredient that can be easily overlooked among all the other technical aspects of production. It is important to consider its relationship with the narrative as well as the visual from the outset. As we have already seen with the use of leitmotifs, it can help determine deeper narrative themes and the semantic or cultural context in which a film is set. It can even affect the technical methods used throughout production.

Were you aware of Vladimir Propp's Morphology during pre-production? If so, how closely would you say it informed your narrative structure? Or was your adaptation made directly from Prokofiev's original story and score?

I was aware of Joseph Campbell's work. But I work quite intuitively, and with this piece I was working just from the music. Prokofiev had already structured it, so I had that already to work with. So the structure came out of the music. We didn't really have storyboards but we did have a previz animatic [rough 3D rendering of film], and it was very detailed and precise down to absolute timings of when things should happen.

We must also be careful when interpreting an existing story that we understand its original cultural context, so that we can make sure that our work has artistic integrity and know how to convey different layers of meaning.

As with all adaptations there are a number of discrepancies between your film and the original story. What was perhaps an underlying theme for *you*, and were you consciously trying to convey your own moral message in your interpretation of the story?

Yes. What I wanted to convey was the idea that the wild, nature, the wild animal, has a value in itself, and intrinsic to itself. Not a monetized value, that is the way of looking at nature at the moment. And I wanted Peter to be moving towards the next level of consciousness.

Are there any particular directors that inspire you, because what you have just described is essentially the essence of many of Hayao Miyazaki's films, most of which have some kind of ecological message? *Ponyo* for example takes the fairy tale *The Little Mermaid* and includes a whole ecological undertone about pollution of the sea and global warming. So are you inspired by any auteurs such as Miyazaki?

I am very inspired by Miyazaki. His work is the benchmark to which I aspire. I aspire to his level of storytelling with the layers he weaves in, which you can watch with a four-year-old and be equally inspired.

2.15

2.15
Ponyo directed by Hayao Miyazaki, Studio Ghibli, 2008. The film has a subtext concerned with pollution of the oceans and global warming.

CASE STUDY:
SAINT THOMAS BECKET

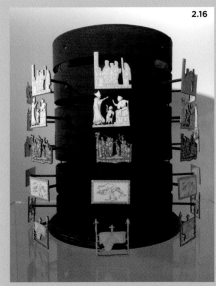

2.16

2.16
3D zoetrope telling the life of Saint Thomas Becket, made for the Museum of London by the BA (Hons) Animation Course, Cass Faculty, London Metropolitan University, 2014.

We close this chapter with a short case study of a 'live project' made for the Museum of London by a group of animators at the Cass School of Art, London Metropolitan University. This project highlights some quick and easy ways of applying the essence of Propp's Morphology to a client-led-brief and considering an innovative animation format for a museum exhibition.

The aim of this brief was to engage visitors with some of the Museum of London's smaller artifacts, animating the life of Thomas Becket using the ancient pilgrim souvenirs from his shrine as the focus for telling his story. Becket was Archbishop of Canterbury from 1162 until his murder in 1170. He is venerated as a saint and martyr.

The ancient pilgrim souvenirs are mostly badges and holy water bottles. They depict various scenes from Becket's life and death, e.g., returning from exile on a ship or horse, being murdered etc. They also commemorate the various relics that you could see in Canterbury Cathedral, where his shrine was.

These pilgrim badges can be laid out in a chronological order much like the images in a beat board. They were paired with a set of historical facts researched about Becket's life and then set loosely against the twelve stages of Christopher Vogler's 'Writer's Journey' to create a clear narrative structure.

2.17

2.17
Saint Thomas Becket pilgrim badges; originals from Museum of London with clay and laser cut replicas by Michael Evans and Emily Pizzey, BA (Hons) Animation, Cass Faculty, London Metropolitan University, 2014.

Students then made laser cut or hand crafted clay reproductions of the pilgrim souvenirs. These were animated as eight frame sequences. The horizontal sequences were then placed in vertical order on the drum of a 3D zoetrope and brought to life by rotating the zoetrope under a strobe. To create a thematic audio backdrop in the exhibition space, a voice artist was recorded reenacting famous quotes by Thomas Becket and King Henry II.

Working with museums is a great way to source narrative material for an animation project. Many artifacts in museums chart out the journeys of historical figures and are interesting totems in themselves that are great for recreating and animating. Museums often look for novel ways to bring their exhibitions to life and engage with their visitors. Such projects also highlight the opportunities for animators to consider alternative formats and venues for their work, serving both commercial and educational outcomes.

Saint Thomas Becket's Story Told Using Vogler's 'Writer's Journey'

1. Ordinary World: Becket was a well-educated man working as a bank clerk in London.

2. Call to Adventure: He then got a job as clerk in the household of Archbishop Theobold.

3. Refusal of the Call: But Becket was ambitious, working his way through the various positions in the household and got appointed as chancellor for the new king, Henry II.

4. Meeting with the Mentor: The King and Becket become friends.

5. Crossing the Threshold: The Archbishop dies and the King appoints Becket in his place.

6. Tests, Enemies and Allies: The King argues with Becket, who takes his new authority and power as Archbishop very seriously.

7. Approach to the Inmost Cave: Becket fears the wrath of the King and flees to France.

8. Ordeal: Becket returns to England and continues to argue with the King.

9. Reward (Seizing the Sword): Four knights overhear the King cursing Becket, but misunderstand his rhetorical question "Not one will deliver me from this low-born priest!"

10. The Road Back: The knights break into the cathedral and kill Becket by slicing off the top of his head with a sword. The knights then flee.

11. Resurrection: The monks collect the blood from Becket's corpse to use as a holy relic.

12. Return with Elixir: Becket becomes a saint three years after his death and his relics a point of pilgrimage for his followers and the sick.

CHAPTER SUMMARY & FURTHER READING

In this chapter we have discussed how formalist and structuralist theories underpin the essence of many classic, mainstream, feature length, animated films. We have learned how to research a narrative context and analyze the narrative structure of a fairy tale; reflect upon the deeper meaning and narrative function of mythical forces, objects and creatures; and consider the role of music and leitmotif in supporting narrative structure and the narrative function of characters.

In doing so we have seen how a range of film and animation directors have explored the universal themes of the rite of passage and hero's journey. Through this we have been introduced to the concept of the auteur. This has helped us become more aware of our audience, looking specifically at issues of representation, as well as how to express more profound moral messages about the world or times that we live in.

We have discussed how the level of realism used by both male and female animation directors actually enables us to escape the real world, re-experience nostalgic memories of the past and visualize our hopes and fears about the future. We have also seen how the effective use of realism is dependent on thorough visual research of the places in which the story is initially set.

2.18

From Miyazaki's films such as *Laputa, Castle in the Sky*, to *The Man Who Planted Trees*, directed by Frédéric Back (1987), or *Avatar*, directed by James Cameron (2009), there have been a range of notable animated (or animation-dependent) films that look at the impact of technology upon civilizations and mankind's ruthless consumption of the resources of his natural environment, but also his capacity for conflict and war.

In many cases the tree has been used as a symbol for the natural world, while mountainous or floating lands and flying machines have been used to signify mankind's obsession with overcoming the natural world. We will continue to explore and expand how these deeper narrative themes and structures can be applied to a range of different yet particular narrative contexts in the next chapter, in order to understand the function and purpose of genre.

2.18
The floating mountains in *Avatar* closely resemble Rock Mountain in Zhangjiajie national forest park of China, a World Nature Heritage Site. Science fiction feature films often use dramatic real landscapes from Earth as inspiration for alien planets.

INTRODUCTION

HEROES &
TOTEMS:
MORPHOLOGY,
NARRATOLOGY,
MYTHOLOGY

CASTLE IN THE
SKY: MYTHICAL
FORCES,
FLOATING
WORLDS &
FLYING MACHINES

WORKBOOK
EXERCISE 2.1

WORKBOOK
EXERCISE 2.2

CASE STUDY:
PETER &
THE WOLF

INTERVIEW
WITH SUZIE
TEMPLETON

CASE STUDY:
SAINT THOMAS
BECKET

CHAPTER
SUMMARY
& FURTHER
READING

KEY WORDS,
NAMES & WORKS

FURTHER READING

Russian Formalism, Structuralism, Fairy Tale & Myth

Barthes, R. (2009) *Mythologies*, Vintage Books: London

Campbell, J. (2008) *The Hero with a Thousand Faces*, New World Library: Novato

Lévi-Strauss, C. (2014) *Myth and Meaning*, Routledge: Abingdon

Propp, V. (2011) *Morphology of the Folktale*, University of Texas Press: Austin

Vogler, C. (2007) *The Writer's Journey*, Michael Wiese Productions: Studio City

Zipes, J. (2011) *The Enchanted Screen*, Routledge: New York

Issues of Representation

Mulvey, R. (2009) *Visual and Other Pleasures*, Palgrave Macmillan: Basingstoke

Wells, P. (2009) *The Animated Bestiary*, Rutgers University Press: London

Auteur Theory

Furniss, M. (1998) *Art In Motion, Animation Aesthetics*, John Libbey Publishing: London

Stam, R. (2000) *Film Theory, An Introduction*, Blackwell Publishers Ltd: Oxford

Wells, P. (2002) *Animation Genre and Authorship*, Wallflower Press: London

Animé

Hu, T.G. (2010) *Frames of Animé, Culture and Image-Building*, Hong Kong University Press

Lamarre, T. (2009) *The Animé Machine: A Media Theory of Animation*, University of Minnesota Press

McCarthy, H. (2002) *Hayao Miyazaki, Master of Japanese Animation*, Stone Bridge Press: Berkeley

KEY WORDS

Allegory
A story that can be interpreted to reveal hidden layers of meaning

Antagonist
The villain, or enemy of the hero

Archetypes
Typical character types

Art Nouveau
Period of decorative art and design taking influence from organic forms (turn of 20th century)

Auteur
A film director able to work within dominant narrative conventions of large-scale studios, yet still find a powerful 'individual' voice

Binary Opposites
Meaningful contrasts of signs

Cahiers du Cinéma
Highly influential French film critics' magazine (est. 1951)

Celtic Art
Ornate stonework and metal work from ancient Celtic peoples

Character Arc
The inner transition of a character's moral values and behaviour during their rite of passage and narrative journey

Dramatis Personae
Archetypes featuring at key narrative stages to help explain moral aspects of the plot

Edo Period
17th–19th century period in Japan famed for Ukiyo-e images

Empathize To fully understand the situation or view of someone else, without necessarily agreeing or disagreeing with it

Fairy Tale
A more fictional and magical equivalent of the folk tale, usually in written form

Folk Tale
A fictional moral story often based on superstition and passed on by word of mouth

Hero's Journey
A combination of formalist and structuralist narrative techniques by Campbell

Leitmotif
A musical phrase associated with a character

Male Gaze
Feminist criticism of mainstream film narrative as it is usually presented from a male point of view

Meme
A culturally inherited behaviour or idea

Metanarrative
A narrative structure and set of values that underpin and dominate mainstream forms of literature, art and culture

Morphology of the Folktale
Formalist narrative structure of 31 stages by Propp that mapped out a universal formula for the folk tale

Myth
A fictional story that explains a natural/social mystery or phenomenon (favoured by structuralist thinkers)

Narratology
Structuralist theories that are more focused on deeper narrative meaning (in myths) than structure (in fairy tale)

Nostalgia
Recalling and re-experiencing fond memories

Post-Impressionism
Predominantly French group of artists (late 19th century) most recognisable for their expressive use of colour

Protagonist
Main character (usually a hero) in a story

Rite of Passage
A ritual transition from one stage of life to another

Russian Formalism
A school of literary criticism that studied the structure of literature

Totem
An object or animal that carries spiritual meaning

Ukiyo-e
Bold, colourful, Japanese wood block images, typically depicting everyday life and 'floating world' landscapes, with stylized perspective and asymmetrical composition

Writer's Journey
A condensed equivalent of the 'Hero's Journey'

Zoetrope
A 19th century optical toy—a series of drawings are animated by viewing them through the slots of a spinning drum

KEY NAMES

Frédéric Back
Roland Barthes
André Bazin
Ivan Bilibin
Bruno Bettelheim
Joseph Campbell
Sylvain Chomet
Nicolas de Crécy
Brothers Grimm
Utagawa Hiroshige
Katsushika Hokusai
Roman Jakobson
Jean-Pierre Jeunet
Claude Lévi-Strauss
Charles Mackintosh
Hayao Miyazaki
Laura Mulvey
Sergei Prokofiev
Vladimir Propp
Andrew Sarris
Suzie Templeton
Tzvetan Todorov
Henri Toulouse-Lautrec
François Truffaut
Christopher Vogler

KEY WORKS

Aladdin
Amélie
Hobbit, The (trilogy)
Ivan Tsarevich, The Firebird and the Gray Wolf
Laputa, Castle in the Sky
Little Mermaid, The
Man Who Planted Trees, The
Old Lady and the Pigeons, The
Peter & the Wolf
Ponyo
Snow White

CHAPTER THREE
GENRE: FROM CLASSICAL HERO TO MODERN EVERYMAN

CHAPTER OVERVIEW: IDENTIFYING NARRATIVE TYPES

In this chapter, you will learn:

- To examine the narrative structure and function of genres including fairy tale, Western, science fiction, comedy and film noir.

- How genre can express issues relating to the human condition and how modern genres have illustrated this through the experiences of the 'everyman' rather than the 'hero'.

- How plot devices specific to film and animation, including the use of mise-en-scène, narration, archetypes and leitmotifs, define different genres.

3.1
The journey into the unknown perils of the forest
often defines the fairy tale genre.

INTRODUCTION

This chapter begins by introducing Genre Theory as an extension of the Russian formalist and structuralist narrative theories of Propp and Lévi-Strauss presented in chapter two. It will explore the narrative structure and function of genre by discussing fairy tale, Western, science fiction, fantasy and comedy, and explaining the historical contexts from which these genres emerged. The chapter will also contrast genre with the distinctive narrative *style* of film noir.

The chapter revisits the theme of mankind and his relationship with the natural world introduced in chapter two, as a defining aspect of *genre* with reference to the famous book *The Human Condition* written by political theorist Hannah Arendt. We will then look at how the human preoccupation with mastering our own destiny can be illustrated by the experiences of the 'everyman' instead of a 'hero', which is another defining element of modern genres.

This chapter will therefore involve even closer, critical, cultural and contextual analysis of the relationship between art, historical events, current affairs and technology. We will also discuss other plot devices more specific to film and animation, including the use of mise-en-scène (filmic composition) and narration, and revisit the concepts of archetypes and the leitmotif in defining different genres.

The range of concepts and theories covered in each of the various sections of this chapter will be illustrated using a range of short case studies of films, including *Star Wars*; *The Good, the Bad and the Ugly*; *Toy Story*; and *Modern Times*. These concepts and theories will then be applied to the analysis of the main case study *WALL•E* (Pixar, 2008), which highlights the fine line between humor and the more serious subject matter that generally defines the human condition.

Once again a student case study (on hybrid genre) and a set of workbook exercises are included with the aim of helping you to incorporate ideas covered by the chapter into your project work. This includes a simple exercise on the contextual analysis and comparison of films from different genres, and a practical exercise that explores genre through the development of a beat board animatic with a soundtrack formed of leitmotifs.

By the end of this chapter you will have consolidated a critical, contextual and cultural knowledge of a core range of conventional narrative techniques. These will form the foundations for comparing and contrasting more contemporary approaches to visualizing narrative in animation, covered in subsequent chapters.

RECOMMENDED VIEWING

Blade Runner, directed by Ridley Scott, The Ladd Company (1982)

Harry Potter series: Parts 1–7, directed by David Yates, Chris Columbus, Alfonso Cuarón & Mike Newell, Warner Bros. (2001–2011)

Modern Times, directed by Charlie Chaplin, United Artists (1936)

Star Wars Trilogy: Episodes IV–VI, directed by George Lucas, Lucasfilm (1977–1983)

The Big Heat, directed by Fritz Lang, Columbia Pictures Corporation (1953)

The Good, the Bad and the Ugly, directed by Sergio Leone, Produzioni Europee Associati (1966)

The Lord of the Rings Trilogy, directed by Peter Jackson, New Line Cinema (2001–2003)

The Matrix, directed by the Wachowskis, Warner Bros. (1999)

Toy Story, directed by John Lasseter, Pixar (1995)

WALL•E, directed by Andrew Stanton, Pixar (2008)

SPACE COWBOYS:
GENRE & CONTEXT

The concept of genre can be traced back to the ancient Greek tragedies and comedies. It is a term commonly used to define different types of narrative context and themes in literature, film and animation. Many narrative art forms have shared or similar genres as well as ones particular to their discipline. Animation has its own very distinct genres including animated documentary, for example, which will be discussed in chapters five and six.

For the purpose of this chapter, we will begin by exploring the concept of narrative genre by comparing and contrasting fairy tale with the Western and also science fiction. What we will see is that the most common genres essentially follow the *same* fundamental pattern of events as the formalist narrative structure of the fairy tale and contain a similar set of universal themes as those identified in structuralist theories on myth.

The Russian philosopher, scholar and semiotician Mikhail Bakhtin (1895–1975) believed that genre should not just be seen as a means of *classifying* narrative structure, general contexts and themes. More specifically, he believed that a genre is a narrative form that helps us *understand* the world around us, defined by the specific time and place in which the genre originated.

As we have seen in chapters one and two, the fairy tale genre formalizes oral traditions of the rural folk tale. In a time *before* industrialization of society and migration of the population from the countryside to the cities, the journey into a forest in the fairy tale was used to map out the fears and obstacles confronting a child on their journey into adulthood.

As we progress through this section of the chapter we will see how the existence or purpose of genre has become more complex, in response to the rapid cultural and technological developments during the twenty-first century; dominant genres evolved and new genres grew out of the existing ones, which then also hybridized with one another at an increasing rate.

"Genres are dependent upon the audiences for both their existence and meaning."
Barry Keith Grant (2011), *Film Genre, from Iconography to Ideology,* **p. 20**

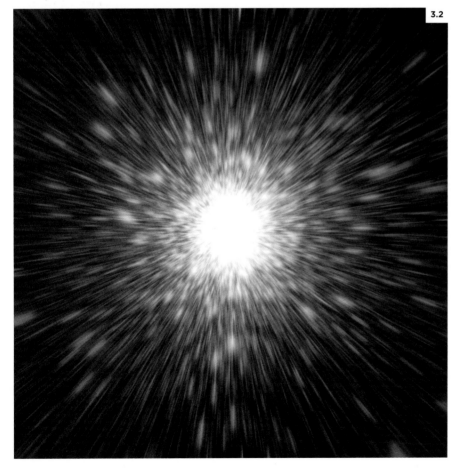

3.2

3.2
Interstellar travel at warp speed to new frontiers is a feature of many science fiction stories.

The Western

The structuralist Lévi-Strauss has made some of the most prominent cultural and contextual analysis of the Western genre. The Western, while set in the very different historical context of the American 'Wild West', has many parallels to the fairy tale and also the myth. In the case of the Western, we see a similar moral narrative journey to the hero in the fairy tale.

A cowboy, lone ranger or bounty hunter replaces the child of the fairy tale, venturing into the unknown and conquering the lawlessness and wilderness of the American frontier lands. Thus, the paradigmatic and also semantic context shifts from the forest of the fairy tale to desert-like settings and rundown single-street wooden settlements, containing iconic objects such as tumbleweed, chuck wagons and saloon bars of the Wild West.

3.3

The concept of the binary opposite in either the Western or fairy tale is one of fear and suspicion between the protagonist and the stranger. In the fairy tale, familiar threats tend to include motifs of animals such as the wolf, whilst in the Western, outlaws and bandits often feature as the archetypal antagonist (stereotypical enemy). But the notion of the binary opposite can extend further to the contrast of one setting with another, i.e., the protagonist's journey from *civilization* to the *wilderness* and back, and also to the protagonist's resulting *individual* identity (his character arc) versus the norms of the *society* to which he returns.

Western *films* in particular also draw upon musical leitmotifs and a theme tune in defining the genre. These include the harmonica, whistling, church bell, Latin American trumpet, guitar, Native American Indian pan flute, drum and chant. These very human sounds reinforce the context and emote a deeper universal sense of raw humanity, getting back in touch with the forces of nature, and evoke a *feeling* of nostalgia in the audience. Famous examples of the Western theme music include the film soundtracks by Ennio Morricone for a series of films known as *The Dollars Trilogy*, directed by Sergio Leone and featuring Clint Eastwood.

3.3
The iconic image of the 'Man With No Name' in *The Good, the Bad and the Ugly* (1966). The character looking into the wilderness and adventure of the desert with gun holster and poncho could just as easily be Luke Skywalker on the desert planet Tatooine in *Star Wars*.

Hybrid Genres & Sub-Genres

At this point we can also use the film Western as an example for considering the evolution or hybridization of genres. Some theorists would describe hybrid genres as the dynamic mixing of genres. A superficial illustration of this would be *Cowboys and Aliens*, directed by John Favreau (2011), where the context and narrative premise of the Western is combined with key components from science fiction, such as alien invasion. This is comparable to the arrival of European settlers in North America and invasion on Native American Indians.

However, a single film does not instantly create a hybrid genre. The concept of the hybrid genre can also be a little more complex than a simple blending of narrative themes and contexts. The Polish formalist scholar Ireneusz Opacki argued that hybrid genres are the result of the influence of a dominant or 'royal genre' on less dominant or secondary genres. Here the narrative structure, but also the deeper semantic codes, of one genre impose certain conventions on another genre.

It could be argued therefore that the Western itself is essentially a hybrid genre of the fairy tale genre. The Western may have initially emerged as a newer and less established genre, as it is more specific in terms of its historical context (time and place in which it is set), whereas the fairy tale reflects more universal and timeless traditions of folklore and oral storytelling. The formalized conventions of the fairy tale may therefore be seen to exert influence on the structuring of Wild West narratives to create the Western genre.

In turn each genre or hybrid genre may also continue to be adapted and reinvented, giving rise to a sub-genre. The earliest Westerns found popularity in the silent film era. The 'Golden Age' of the Western can be located in the 1950s. Earlier Westerns reflected broader themes such as changes to old ways of life, from the impact of European settlers on the Native American Indians to the industrialization of the Wild West through mining and the steam locomotive.

The type of Western with which most of us are probably more familiar is actually a sub-genre from the 1960s known as the 'spaghetti Western'. Spaghetti Westerns involved much more action and gun fighting to entertain the audience than older Westerns. Famous examples include *The Dollars Trilogy* by Sergio Leone. A sub-genre might therefore be viewed as a body of films or books that follow the same narrative format as the texts of a dominant parent genre, but shift the emphasis to the development of a particular aspect of the narrative theme.

It is a resistance to the mechanization or modernization of the world we live in, and a return to 'good old-fashioned values', that often drives an audience's nostalgia for film genres such as the Western. However the growing popularity of the science fiction and fantasy *film* genres also emerged during the 1950s and 1960s, an era defined by the Space Race.

3.4
The journey into the lawlessness and wilderness of the unknown American frontier lands defines many Western genre narratives.

3.4

“ Every literary trend—or phase of it—has underlying it certain defined socio-historical factors, which shape specific attitudes towards the world and a certain sphere of interests and problems. In turn this brings with it the creation of a specific system of poetics, an ensemble of means of expression, of ways of structurally linking them, which— growing out of the 'extraliterary' environment of the trend—carry in them historically specific meanings and functions. **”**
David Duff (2000), *Modern Genre Theory*, p. 119

Science Fiction or Fantasy?

The genres of science fiction and fantasy can be similarly defined as the transferal of present day situations into fictionalized alternative utopian (perfect and idealistic) or dystopian (decaying and dictatorial) worlds. These enable us to explore similar politics and crises central to the human psyche, whilst also momentarily escaping our own troubles. Sci-fi tends to be explored in the context of either theoretically possible or technologically advanced societies, based on experimentation with scientific knowledge. Fantasy, on the other hand, is usually set in more mythical worlds based around adventures with magic and supernatural forces.

Famous early literary science fiction novels that have also been reinterpreted into film and animation include Mary Shelley's *Frankenstein* (1880) and *The War of the Worlds* written by H. G. Wells (1898). Recent animated reinterpretations include *Frankenweenie*, directed by Tim Burton (2012), and *War of the Worlds: Goliath*, directed by Joe Pearson (2012). *The Lord of the Rings* written by J. R. R. Tolkien (1937–1949), and J. K. Rowling's *Harry Potter* books (1997–2007) are clear examples of fantasy novels that have been translated into film.

The *Star Wars* film trilogy, *Episodes IV–VI*, directed by George Lucas (1977–1983), perhaps marks an interesting crossover between the science fiction and fantasy genres and a transition into an era of hybrid and sub-genre *science fiction* or *fantasy action* films such as *The Matrix*, directed by the Wachowskis (1999). Whereas *Star Wars* responds to an era more preoccupied with space travel and the binary relationship between forces of good and evil, *The Matrix* is defined by the binary relationship or conflict between the real world and cyberspace. Increasingly, the two genres challenge human perceptions of reality, time and space.

From the notion of the "Final Frontier" as the premise of the *Star Trek* television and film adventures to the farm boy Luke Skywalker raised on the desert planet Tatooine in *Star Wars*, part of what marks out the success of such science fiction or fantasy genre films is how they essentially relocated key components of the Western, fairy tale and also the myth to outer space. The hero's journey in many but not all cases becomes an intergalactic one full of space cowboys, as well as the quest of human civilization to make sense of its place in the wilderness of the universe.

3.5

3.5
The settlements and moisture farms on Luke Skywalker's home planet Tatooine in *Star Wars* have parallels with the desert settlements of the Wild West. Many of the locations and much of the architecture in *Star Wars* also directly resemble gorfa (granaries) and matmata (underground houses) in the Tataouine desert region of Tunisia.

TO INFINITY & BEYOND:
THE HUMAN CONDITION & GENRE

3.6

3.6
Newspaper Rock, a petroglyph panel etched
on a sandstone wall in southeastern Utah near
Canyonlands National Park, is an example of early
human civilization recording its labour through
semi-permanent images and structures.

**The chief characteristic of this specifically human
life, whose appearance and disappearance constitute
worldly events, is that it is itself always full of events
which can ultimately be told as a story.**
Hannah Arendt (1958), *The Human Condition*, p. 97

INTRODUCTION

SPACE
COWBOYS:
GENRE &
CONTEXT

TO INFINITY
& BEYOND:
THE HUMAN
CONDITION
& GENRE

WORKBOOK
EXERCISES
3.1 & 3.2

CASE STUDY:
FROM *MODERN
TIMES* TO
WALL·E

YOU KANT
BE SERIOUS:
COMEDY GENRE
& THEORIES OF
HUMOR

THE BIG DEBATE:
GENRE OR
STYLE?

CASE STUDY:
DOMESTICATED

CHAPTER
SUMMARY
& FURTHER
READING

KEY WORDS,
NAMES & WORKS

The Vita Activa & Natality

The condition of our existence has seemingly always preoccupied mankind. From the myth and fairy tale to the Western and science fiction, discussion of genre has reinforced how at different periods throughout history, civilizations have reflected on mankind's place in the world, using stories and images to understand and record what defines their society and the human (or hero) within it.

The book *The Human Condition* written by German-American political theorist Hannah Arendt (1906–1975) is one of the most famous modern accounts exploring the complexities of our existence. Though originally published in 1958 and founded on the theories of ancient Greek philosophers such as Plato and Aristotle, many of the concerns covered in her book find as much, if not more, relevance today. The book structures its analysis of the human condition around three key forms of human activity—labour, work and action—collectively defined by Arendt as the 'vita activa'.

Arendt uses the term labour to think about how the existence of mankind, and the individual, is defined by his basic survival of the conditions of any given natural world and the daily tasks needed for our biological survival from birth to death, such as the production and consumption of food and water, cleaning and the removal of waste.

Work is used to think about mankind's ability to artificially transform and overcome his natural environment with the production of 'things', from man-made objects and images to monuments and buildings. Mankind thereby celebrates human conquest over the natural world, and this helps to give us a sense of material permanence or immortality through the creation of the human world. Action is used to describe the laws formed by the government or civilization of the human world to prevent it from falling apart.

The final term Arendt uses, natality, underpins all three forms of human activity. What she means by natality is how a civilization is defined and held together by its own unique combination of labour, work and action, but also how the arrival or 'birth' (and even death) of each new civilization in the world affects other existing civilizations. Further, she uses the concept of natality to explore how *within* each civilization the birth or arrival of new people may in turn change the balance or structure of the civilization itself. It is the relationship between the human world and the natural world, the affect of one civilization upon another, as well as our capacity to think and act as individuals and ability to change the rules of a civilization through our public interaction with others, that for Arendt are the essence of the human condition.

Applying the Vita Activa & Natality
to the Analysis of Genre

LABOUR OF LOVE: APPLYING NATALITY TO A BRIEF ANALYSIS OF *TOY STORY*

The narrative underpinning Pixar's *Toy Story* trilogy is a clever example of how the concepts of the vita activa and natality of two different genres can be used as the basis of the conflict in one animated film. In *Toy Story* we see the lead protagonist Woody, a toy cowboy and his world of the Western genre, threatened by the arrival of a new space hero Buzz Lightyear. The allure of Buzz's world of the science fiction genre threatens to replace the work of the world the toys have built for themselves under the leadership of Woody.

However, this conflict is resolved when the two very different protagonists labour together for the love of their owner Andy, in the fear that as he grows up, the loss of this love will threaten the existence of all the toys and both genres. Thus, what we witness is a conflict between two civilizations, resolved through the action of two characters in response to a common threat and the birth of a new relationship between two heroes.

3.7

3.7
Toy Story 3 (2010). The *Toy Story* series cleverly combines the Western and science fiction genres.
© 2010 Disney·Pixar

What Arendt maps out is essentially an overarching philosophy, which enables us to research any civilization and develop a story around it using the concepts of vita activa and natality. This is illustrated below by applying the vita activa and natality to the analysis of the Western genre:

- The notion of *labour* relates to how the basic existence of the nomadic cowboy, lone ranger or bounty hunter is shaped by him seeking food and shelter from the natural environment of the desert by travelling from one settlement to another.

- The concept of *work* is illustrated by the building of, for example, a wooden township, goldmine and railroad, which give a sense of purpose and permanence to new settlers (over and above basic survival) in an otherwise inhospitable environment.

- The idea of *action* is represented by martial law imposed by a county sheriff upon any violent actions or disputes in townships and settlements by armed bandits or outlaws.

- Finally, *natality* can be demonstrated by the political intervention of the cowboy, lone ranger or bounty hunter at each settlement, challenging the authority of the sheriff and the law by taking on bandits and outlaws himself. The term 'natality' can also be applied to the work and action (building of settlements and introduction of land ownership laws) of the European settlers, which changed the natural world in which the nomadic Native American Indian civilizations had lived and began its transformation into a modern America.

INTRODUCTION

SPACE
COWBOYS:
GENRE &
CONTEXT

TO INFINITY
& BEYOND:
THE HUMAN
CONDITION
& GENRE

WORKBOOK
EXERCISES
3.1 & 3.2

CASE STUDY:
FROM *MODERN
TIMES* TO
WALL·E

YOU KANT
BE SERIOUS:
COMEDY GENRE
& THEORIES OF
HUMOR

THE BIG DEBATE:
GENRE OR
STYLE?

CASE STUDY:
DOMESTICATED

CHAPTER
SUMMARY
& FURTHER
READING

KEY WORDS,
NAMES & WORKS

Summary of What We Have Covered So Far in the Book

For your convenience, whether attempting the simplest animated short, which might be condensed down to a beginning, middle and end, to a manageable but more expanded twelve-stage writer's journey, in this chapter we have now covered two further levels of analysis in structuring a classical metanarrative and *hero's journey*.

First, we have identified some of the dominant *genres* and investigated how they are defined by different *paradigmatic* contexts (types of objects and characters found in a particular setting), *semantic* themes (values and behaviours of a particular time and place), *symbolic* sounds (leitmotifs and soundtracks of a particular time and place) and narrative journey of a protagonist—not just from one place to another, but also his internal moral journey or character arc.

Second, we have developed a deeper understanding of how to interpret or even 'invent' other less familiar genres, by identifying the vita activa and natality of any given culture. From this we can see that the alien invasion and transformation of a civilization on a far-flung planet in a science fiction film is essentially no different to the colonization and transformation of the Wild West by the European settler in the Western.

So we have established, as proposed by Bakhtin, that genres are a means of understanding the world around us. But ultimately what we have identified is that we can use the vita activa and natality as the fundamental building blocks that underpin genre and according to Arendt define the infinite rebirth of the human condition.

WORKBOOK EXERCISE 3.1: USING GENRE & THE VITA ACTIVA TO DEVELOP A FILM IDEA

The following exercises offer insight into how to develop an idea for a film through cultural and contextual research and practical experimentation with the narrative interplay of character, layout design and soundtrack through the beat board animatic. These exercises build on the exercises in chapter two, which looked at how to break down the Writer's Journey, and apply the narrative formula of Hayao Miyazaki (his interpretation of Writer's Journey and also the animé genre) to the development of a story that has a deeper moral purpose.

Try making notes using the list below whilst watching *Star Wars: Episode IV—A New Hope*, *The Good, the Bad and the Ugly*, and also *Peter & the Wolf*:

- Define the semantic context of *Star Wars* using Arendt's vita activa and natality, i.e., define the natural environment, the work of the man-made environment and the arrival of a stranger or another civilization. Try and find parallels between Luke Skywalker's life on Tatooine in *Star Wars* and the rundown remote settlements in *The Good, the Bad and the Ugly*.

- Define the key paradigmatic theme in *Star Wars* by listing a set of motifs (defining objects of time/place), and find parallels to these in the spaghetti Westerns, e.g., X-Wing versus horse or light saber versus gun.

- Identify a range of key leitmotifs and iconic sound effects in the *Star Wars* soundtrack and contrast them with those from *The Good, the Bad and the Ugly*, e.g., sound effects of light sabers or gun shots.

- Compare the narrative journey of the hero Luke Skywalker the Jedi Padawan to 'The Man With No Name' the Western bounty hunter, using Vogler's simpler twelve-stage Writer's Journey (the model for which is outlined in chapter two). Try to identify the ordinary world, the call to adventure, tests, enemies and allies and so on.

- Identify the seven archetypal characters common to *Star Wars* and *The Good, the Bad and the Ugly*, such as the Hero, Villain, Donor and so on, as defined by Vladimir Propp.

- Define the binary relationship between the key protagonist and antagonist in *Star Wars*.

INTRODUCTION | SPACE COWBOYS: GENRE & CONTEXT | TO INFINITY & BEYOND: THE HUMAN CONDITION & GENRE | WORKBOOK EXERCISES 3.1 & 3.2 | CASE STUDY: FROM *MODERN TIMES* TO *WALL·E* | YOU KANT BE SERIOUS: COMEDY GENRE & THEORIES OF HUMOR | THE BIG DEBATE: GENRE OR STYLE? | CASE STUDY: *DOMESTICATED* | CHAPTER SUMMARY & FURTHER READING | KEY WORDS, NAMES & WORKS

WORKBOOK EXERCISE 3.2: APPLYING GENRE & SOUND TO A BEAT BOARD ANIMATIC

- Assemble a beat board animatic by drawing from a set of film stills from a scene in *Star Wars*.

- Set your beat board animatic against the sound effects, leitmotifs and soundtrack from a similar scene in *The Good, the Bad and the Ugly*.

- Make notes on how this changes your perceptions of what you are viewing.

Figures 3.8 and 3.9 are photos of an immersive audio-visual installation-performance that featured as part of *The Boiler Room* programme at Suspense Puppetry Festival, London 2015. The student-made production aimed to broaden the paradigm of animation by exploring different storytelling formats and types of exhibition space. The project was directed by Japanese audio-visual artist Noriko Okaku and involved projection mapping with VJ techniques resembling a vaudeville magic lantern show, developed in response to a fairy tale soundtrack written by Italian screen composer Enrica Sciandrone.

The venue was transformed with the panoramic scenes from the fairy tale *Rapunzel* appearing across two windows, giving audiences the sense that they have been transported into a fairy tale world. The three and a half minute piece was structured according to a twelve-stage narrative and the soundtrack. It was retold several times in different genres including fairy tale, Western and science fiction, reinterpreting motifs such as trees with cacti or castle towers with space rockets. The three genres were then intercut across the two windows, remixing genre-specific sound effects to reinforce the parallels between the hybridized genres.

3.8 & 3.9
Rapunzel (2015). Fairy tale-Western-sci-fi hybrid projection mapping performance, stills by Noriko Okaku and Tom Salo (Cass Film & Animation, London Metropolitan University, 2015). The hero features as a surreal prince in the fairy tale version, and as a Native American Indian climbing a totem pole instead of a tower in the Western version.

CASE STUDY:
FROM *MODERN TIMES* TO *WALL•E*

> **"The most radical change in the human condition we can imagine would be an emigration of men from the earth to some other planet. Such an event, no longer totally impossible, would imply that man would have to live under man-made conditions, radically different from those the earth offers him. Neither labour nor work nor action nor, indeed, thought as we know it would then make sense any longer. Yet even those hypothetical wanderers from the earth would still be human; but the only statement we could make regarding their 'nature' is that they still are conditioned beings, even though their condition is now self-made to a considerable extent."**
> Hannah Arendt (1958), *The Human Condition*, pp. 9–10

3.10
Modern Times (1936). Chaplin's tramp character gets stuck in the giant cogs of a factory machinery after he starts to have a nervous breakdown from the pressure of working there.

3.10

Thus far we have considered the hero's journey, genre and the human condition from the point of view of man's conquest over his own destiny or other civilizations in the natural world, such as a child venturing into the woods or the impact on the natural environment of Native American Indians by European settlers. However, what we have not looked at in detail is the hero's journey within the *human* world. We will now look at how individuals and entire civilizations can become even more trapped by the conditions of their own man-made worlds—conditions principally defined by the ancient Greeks as the public and private realm.

According to Arendt, the 'private realm' in ancient Greek civilization was defined by the activities that took place in the home, largely the labour of slaves. The tough conditions of labour essential for human survival were hidden from public view. The public realm (the 'polis' or city state), on the other hand, was where work, leisure and political action of the ruling classes (which was dependent on the labour of the slave) was promoted by the construction of objects, images, monuments and buildings. Arendt refers to this as the 'axiom' (unquestioned norm) upon which many civilizations have been built right up to the present day.

The Everyman's Journey

What we increasingly observe in *modern* genre is how the slave or 'everyman' becomes the *hero* of the human world. Chaplin's hapless (unfortunate) 'tramp' character personifies the struggles of the everyman to escape his entrapment from the slavery and exhaustion of mechanized labour in the private realm and/or accept the option of poverty and loneliness in the public realm.

In the man-made world, the slave or everyman's life is therefore one of suffering conditions imposed upon him by the state. Although he is initially unaware of how the human world imposes these conditions upon him, deep down inside the everyman there is a sense of loss or longing that starts to take hold in him—to be free, part of something bigger and to be loved.

The 'call to adventure' for the everyman is a moment of action when something prompts him to break free from his routine. This might be a moment of frustration or madness caused by the pressure of his routine; his discovery of something that is highly sought after by others; the distraction of a love interest that leads him away from his labour to an unfamiliar world; or recognition by authorities that he has skills that make him of additional value in the public realm.

3.11

But in his hurry and desire to free himself from labour, transform his status and join the public realm from which he has been hidden, a chaotic and uncontrollable chain of events follow his unconventional actions, as the everyman struggles to make sense of the modern civilization into which he enters. This unsettles and morally transforms the civilization he was born to serve. The everyman ultimately becomes the unwitting hero, by simply trying to set himself free.

Arendt argues however that in modern civilization automation has enabled the mass-production of food and objects, such that the activities of labour and work have essentially merged. This adds further confusion to our identity or sense of purpose, in so far as both labourers and workers have now become a *society* of consumers, and it is this consumption of products that now defines our existence—more so than our labour or work.

Arendt also points out how our overwhelming consumption of increasingly meaningless 'stuff' distracts us all from recognizing the regenerative cycle of the natural environment from which we have become increasingly detached. We therefore *all* become slaves to the man-made system and environment. The heroic act is no longer one of conquering the natural *or* human world, but one of escaping from the human world altogether and returning to the cycle of the natural one.

3.11
WALL·E (2008). WALL·E and Eve dance in space outside the *Axiom* spaceship.
© 2008 Disney·Pixar

CASE STUDY:
FROM *MODERN TIMES* TO *WALL•E (continued)*

Contextual Analysis of *WALL•E*

The following case study compares and contrasts two films in which the human condition and narrative journey of the everyman is defined by the mechanization or automation of human civilization: *Modern Times* (directed by Charlie Chaplin, United Artists, 1936) and *WALL•E* (directed by Andrew Stanton, Pixar, 2008).

Modern Times is a film set in America during the Great Depression of the 1930s. This was a period in the modern industrialized age where the efficiency of mechanized production left many people out of work. Ironically, this efficiency actually resulted in over-production of food and goods, which could not be afforded by the many people it had put on the poverty line.

Modern Times follows the trials and tribulations of Chaplin's 'Tramp' character looking for work in factories. It features sequences of Chaplin going mad from the repetition of his work, getting stuck in the huge cogs of one of the machines driving the production line and being hospitalized after a series of escapades.

There are clear parallels between *Modern Times* and *WALL•E*. We are now living through a similar world recession in an automated society where the computer and Internet have left many people out of work, but also made some so rich that they do not need to work. Now the over-production of commodities (including fast food) distracts us from the reality that, whether we can afford them or not, we are hugely influenced by the interests of large corporations, like the overweight characters on board the Axiom in *WALL•E*, whose lives are totally controlled by 'Buy n Large'.

Both Chaplin and WALL•E are hospitalized in their films, which clearly symbolizes the affect the pressure of labour and work has on the modern everyman. However, there is a scene in *Modern Times* where Chaplin and his love interest go roller skating in a department store. This is not dissimilar to the scene in *WALL•E*, where he dances with Eve in space using a fire extinguisher. These moments are important as they evoke nostalgia for childish play and romance, which are all too often squeezed in modern adult working lives, and remind us of how we can find pleasure in the simplest things amongst all the commodities of the modern world.

WALL•E is essentially a science fiction-fantasy. Part of the success of the animation is that the film relocates what is going on in the present day into an exciting, futuristic fantasy. The drab environment and actions of a person operating a refuse vehicle on a landfill site are infinitely more exciting and engaging when transferred to a robot compacting blocks of waste into great towers in a post-apocalyptic planet earth hundreds of years from now. The environmental message is the same, but perhaps clearer, and enables us to escape our own reality for a short while.

3.12

3.12
A bulldozer working on a landfill site has parallels with the fantastical futuristic occupation of WALL•E.

INTRODUCTION

SPACE
COWBOYS:
GENRE &
CONTEXT

TO INFINITY
& BEYOND:
THE HUMAN
CONDITION
& GENRE

WORKBOOK
EXERCISES
3.1 & 3.2

CASE STUDY:
FROM *MODERN
TIMES* TO
WALL•E

YOU KANT
BE SERIOUS:
COMEDY GENRE
& THEORIES OF
HUMOR

THE BIG DEBATE:
GENRE OR
STYLE?

CASE STUDY:
DOMESTICATED

CHAPTER
SUMMARY
& FURTHER
READING

KEY WORDS,
NAMES & WORKS

Cultural Analysis of *WALL•E*

There are many parallels between the story in *WALL•E* and the issues covered in *The Human Condition* by Hannah Arendt. 'Axiom' is a term Arendt uses on several occasions to explain how in human society we often take for granted how the human or man-made world has become the conditioned norm and how we are oblivious to the natural world outside this. The *Axiom* is the name given to the giant spaceship in *WALL•E*, and is a neat illustration of how divorced mankind has become from his natural environment.

Arendt talks about the *labour* of the slave in the private realm and about *political action* in the public realm. WALL•E's labour clearly involves clearing up the discarded overproduction of meaningless objects left on planet Earth. WALL•E's main political action involves escaping the solitude of servitude on planet Earth and leaving a trail of chaos behind him onboard the *Axiom*, as he tries to find his love interest Eve and ensure the safety of the small shrub that signifies the possibility of mankind returning to Earth.

The term *natality* is used by Arendt to talk about the birth or rebirth of a civilization. She talks in various ways about how consumerism and the human world have trapped modern society. The end of the film *WALL•E* illustrates this arc of mankind overcoming the human world, by returning to Earth, planting the shrub and reconnecting with the regenerative cycle of the natural world throughout the end credits.

Clowning Around: Comedy & Tragedy

The next section of this chapter will introduce the comedy genre and theories of humor, but it is important to look at humor while discussing *Modern Times* and *WALL•E*. Charlie Chaplin became famous for the 'physical shtick' of his Tramp character, which was the very personification of the everyman and class struggle in Europe, America and indeed around the world. Films such as *Modern Times* also show Chaplin's great ability to make comedy out of tragedy and hardship.

Like many immigrants who travelled to America from all over the world, Chaplin came from a tough working class background, emigrating from England to America in 1910 in search of a better life. He therefore he had a natural empathy (complete understanding) for the large audiences of non-English-speaking immigrant labourers and workers who flocked to his cheap silent films shown in the nickelodeon cinemas.

Thus, Chaplin's success lay in the fact that he knew how to make people laugh about their shared human condition, using the universal language of slapstick (physical humor) in silent cinema. The clumsiness of WALL•E is quite Chaplinesque, and although he makes very basic speech sounds, large portions of the film are also essentially without dialogue.

3.13

There is no doubt that the combination of humor and pathos (behaviour that evokes sadness) seen in both WALL•E and Chaplin is a powerful way of connecting with an audience, particularly when we can identify with the world of the protagonist. In the cases of *WALL•E* and *Modern Times*, there is a strong sense of being overwhelmed by technology, repetitive labour and the sense of loneliness these can create that resonate deeply within us all.

3.13
A nickelodeon cinema from the early 1900s, where audiences could pay just a nickel (five cents) to see a film such as those by Charlie Chaplin.

YOU KANT BE SERIOUS:
COMEDY GENRE &
THEORIES OF HUMOR

From our study of the human condition to genre, the morphology of the folk tale and synchronic images, the discussion of narrative in the book so far has perhaps all seemed a little serious. This is largely because we have been looking at how so much of storytelling is a way of recording, explaining and understanding human existence and survival. But by looking at *WALL•E* and *Modern Times*, we can see how the essence of a lot of humor is actually based around the same kinds of serious themes or subjects.

A conclusion we can draw from the study of *WALL•E* is that the dramatic tension and suspense created by series of serious or exciting actions and the anticipation of what is going to happen next in each scene is a key aspect to telling a good story. Anticipation or suspense is also one of the main ways in which humor is created. The key difference between humor and drama is the *outcome* of a series of narrative events.

The suspense and emotional tension built up in any number of scenes in *WALL•E* could turn it into a very serious film, but in most of the scenes the seriousness of a series of actions is relieved by a twist in events. For example, there is a scene in which WALL•E falls down a waste shoot on board the *Axiom* during a fight sequence on the captain's deck. But just when we think all is lost, WALL•E's head pops up in the mouth of the waste shoot—with the all-important shrub on his head. This unexpected and somewhat silly turn in events releases the emotional or nervous tension that has built up in the audience, and it is this process that creates laughter in humans.

The film *WALL•E* is primarily a science fiction-fantasy film, but features comedy as a key narrative component, so it might be more apt to describe it as a science fiction-fantasy-comedy hybrid or sub-genre. The idea of comedy as genre in itself follows narratives that place an emphasis on humor as the main overarching outcome of everyday events and gives the audience an emotional release (known as catharsis) from the experiences of the human condition. Once again, this is an idea that can be traced back again to ancient Greek philosopher Aristotle (384–322 BC), who defined this balance between humor and drama with the distinct literary and theatrical genres of comedy and tragedy.

> **"There is only one way of making comedy richer—and, paradoxically, funnier—and that is by making it more serious."**
> **Walter Kerr (1990),** *The Silent Clowns*, **p. 162**

3.14

3.14
An ancient Greek
theatrical mask.

INTRODUCTION

SPACE
COWBOYS:
GENRE &
CONTEXT

TO INFINITY
& BEYOND:
THE HUMAN
CONDITION
& GENRE

WORKBOOK
EXERCISES
3.1 & 3.2

CASE STUDY:
FROM MODERN
TIMES TO
WALL•E

YOU KANT
BE SERIOUS:
COMEDY GENRE
& THEORIES OF
HUMOR

THE BIG DEBATE:
GENRE OR
STYLE?

CASE STUDY:
DOMESTICATED

CHAPTER
SUMMARY
& FURTHER
READING

KEY WORDS,
NAMES & WORKS

Comedy Sub-Genres

There are a number of modern comedy sub-genres. Each explores a particular form of narrative relating to the human condition. The situational comedy or sitcom explores the everyday politics of a small group of people often focused around family and home or the workplace. Sitcoms are usually televised as a series of episodes, exploring a range of different social issues each week. *The Simpsons* was revolutionary for pioneering a new wave of *animated* sitcom.

Animated sitcom often involves other forms of more subversive humor, such as parody and satire, which will be investigated further in chapter five. Other sub-genres of comedy include the romantic comedy or romcom. These are usually feature films that explore the complexity of modern relationships. The black comedy explores the extremes between tragedy and comedy with often perverse or surreal and very intense scenes exploring the darkest aspects of the human condition such as mental illness, addiction and murder.

RECOMMENDED VIEWING

Here are examples of three comedy sub-genres:

Romcom: *Pretty Woman*, directed by Garry Marshall, Touchstone Pictures (1990)

Sitcom: *The Simpsons*, created by Matt Groening, Gracie Films (1989–)

Black Comedy: *Withnail & I*, directed by Bruce Robinson, HandMade Films (1987)

Theories of Humor

So far we have explored comedy in terms of genre, that is, identifying the different narrative contexts and types of subject matter. We have also looked at the narrative function of comedy—to find relief from the human condition through laughter. We will now explore some of the main theories of humor and other layers of comic practice that underpin how and why we find things funny.

Incongruity Theory

It could be argued that incongruity theory is the core form of humor used in structuring comedy narrative. This has essentially already been explored in our discussion of anticipation and suspense. Immanuel Kant (1724–1804) was a German philosopher and a key proponent of incongruity theory who studied the fundamental concepts that shape the human mind and human experience. He believed that our sense of humor was based on emotional reactions to sudden or unexpected and unrealistic changes to expected chains of events.

Within this theory there are different forms of incongruity, such as social incongruity, where a character is a social misfit and whose behaviour or actions are out of keeping with their environment. This essentially describes both WALL•E and Chaplin and underpins how their behaviour drives the unexpected events that unfold in their stories.

Relief Theory

Sigmund Freud (1856–1939) was the founder of psychoanalysis. He advocated that relief is the process by which laughter enables nervous release from more deeply rooted, pent-up or repressed (often sexual) feelings. Comedy often gives us a safe place to let go of our inhibitions, and explore things that we feel we cannot freely discuss in society. It allows us to laugh about things we do not fully understand, such as our weirdest desires and fantasies. This form of humor is more commonly expressed in black comedies, and independent animations.

Superiority Theory

The concept of superiority theory has evolved under a number of philosophers, from Plato in ancient Greece to French philosopher Henri Bergson (1859–1941). On the surface, superiority theory is defined by laughing at the misfortune of others, who we either perceive as being inferior to us in some way or who we view as being set in their ways and incapable of changing their circumstances. At its core, superiority theory enables us to laugh at and correct our own innate prejudices.

Further Comic Practices

In his book *Scriptwriting (Basics Animation)*, Paul Wells summarizes a range of comic practices that might feature within the various theories of humor above. These include accidental/physical and object-response. Accidental/physical can be used to describe the slapstick comic clumsiness we see in *WALL•E*, such as losing control while playing with an unwieldy fire extinguisher.

Object-response describes how objects can seemingly take on a life of their own, breaking down and disrupting human activity—this can be seen in *Modern Times* when Chaplin is used as a subject to test an automated feeding machine that goes wrong, or in the malfunctioning robots that have been taken to a secure unit for mending or recycling in *WALL•E*.

End Note on Comedy Genres and Theories of Humor

We can see how comedy can be defined as specific genre, but is also a useful way of sustaining an engaging narrative across a range of genres. The different comedy sub-genres, theories of humor and comic practices also help us break down narrative into a series of components for developing a narrative structure. We have also discussed how humor is another important narrative device that helps us empathize with the protagonist, explore difficult subject matter and find emotional release from the human condition of our daily lives.

3.15

3.15
'Object response' is a term used in comic practice to describe the humor that results from objects seemingly taking on a life of their own, often depicted as malfunctioning, like many of the robots on board the *Axiom*.

RECOMMENDED VIEWING

Here are three classic examples of film noir:

Double Indemnity, directed by Billy Wilder, Paramount Pictures (1944)

The Big Heat, directed by Fritz Lang, Columbia Pictures Corporation (1953)

The Big Sleep, directed by Howard Hawks, Warner Bros. (1946)

THE BIG DEBATE: GENRE OR STYLE?

One of the important things to remember when studying genre is to understand the difference between genre and style. So far, we have seen that genre is essentially the study of narrative structure, contexts, themes and representation of the human condition. We will now explore whether there can be other aesthetic considerations when determining genre in film and animation, through the contentious subject of film noir.

Film noir has parallels with the crime fiction genre and detective sub-genre, but whether it can be defined as a genre itself is a matter of debate amongst theorists, in part due to the fact that it does not follow the same narrative structure or clear underlying moral themes shared by the fairy tale, Western or science fiction genres. Rather, film noir is a term used later on by French film critics such as André Bazin to describe certain highly stylized filmmaking trends, influenced by a range of filmmaking conventions and production values that emerged in America after the Second World War, from the mid 1940s and into the 1950s.

But film noir *is* useful for exploring some of the more stylistic aspects of film genre through its distinctive use of filmic composition known as mise-en-scène, as well as the narrative concepts of the fabula and syuzhet, defined by Russian formalist theorist and writer Viktor Shklovsky (1893–1984), and the application of these terms to film narrative as prescribed by Russian formalist screenwriter Juri Tynianov (1894–1943).

The Russian formalist term *fabula* loosely translates as the 'story' and is defined by the character relationships and chronological plot order we recognize in Propp's Morphology. The Russian formalist term *syuzhet* is the *stylization* of the plot and looks at how the linear story can be challenged by the reordering of events, parallel plots and the use of a range of different accounts of the same narrative. Juri Tynianov argued that the syuzhet or stylization of the plot order is a key factor in determining film genres.

Such narrative stylization can clearly be seen in noir films where the protagonist's journey often no longer follows a chronological metanarrative. Instead, the plot is pieced together by the viewer through flashbacks and the interweaving parallel narratives of a range of protagonists. Further, contrary to dominant genres, there are no clear binary opposites or universal moral themes in film noir. The distinction between the protagonist and the antagonist or law and crime becomes blurred, and there is also a shift in the historical power balance between genders.

In noir films the 'hero's journey' often becomes a descent into unresolved moral confusion. The main character, an upstanding male citizen or troubled detective, is drawn into a criminal underworld by an archetypal seductress known as the femme fatale, where his morals are challenged by a web of corrupt cops in cahoots with criminal gangs. Deeper underlying themes include suspicion, paranoia, disillusionment and betrayal.

3.16

3.16
Domesticated by Vaida Kereisyte (University of Bedfordshire, 2013). Animation still from the film noir and science fiction-inspired narrative.

105

Mise-en-Scène & Sound

As well as the stylization of plot, film noir is distinctive for its mise-en-scène. Literally translated from French, mise-en-scène means 'to put in scene'. In simplest terms, mise-en-scène is the stylized composition and lighting of shots in film. It was another term devised by French film critics such as André Bazin to describe another aspect of filmmaking that defined the distinctive techniques of the auteur introduced in chapter two.

Mise-en-scène is essentially also the filmic equivalent of the narrative composition in painting, such as the genre paintings by Vermeer discussed in chapter one. That is to say, mise-en-scène is an important way of creating further narrative meaning through the symbolic composition of objects in a shot—the use of syntagmatic, paradigmatic and semantic analysis of the narrative composition of objects, the importance of lighting and so forth—that tell us about the different activities or private and public realms of the people within the image.

What makes mise-en-scène in film noir so distinctive are the highly stylized settings, types of objects, lighting and camera angles that are used to reinforce deeper psychological themes such as suspicion and paranoia. This stylization was heavily influenced by the work of German Expressionist filmmakers such as Fritz Lang, who migrated to America in the build-up to World War Two. We will look at German Expressionism in discussing modernism (chapter four).

3.17

Film noir scenes are largely set in modern cities at nighttime or in dark indoor locations. These include offices, bars and back alleys where lighting could make maximum use of shadows and silhouettes created by a range of elements including venetian blinds, fans and steam. Cage-like shadows and silhouettes reinforce feelings of entrapment and confusion central to the overarching narrative theme. Three-point chiaroscuro lighting also adds intensity to the psychological state of the characters—whereby three light sources create artificially heightened lighting on the actors, set against intense shadows in low-lit spaces.

3.17
Still from film noir-themed 3D animation by Nick Smith, BA (Hons) Animation, Cass Faculty, London Metropolitan University, 2014. The animation is a useful example of film noir lighting, which used three light sources to create additional drama through techniques such as silhouette, shadow and chiaroscuro (image features *Morpheus Rig* by Josh Burton).

> **"Filmic syntagms...include the spatial syntagms found also in still photography (in *mise-en-scène*: the composition of individual frames)."**
> Daniel Chandler (2007), *Semiotics: The Basics*, p. 86

INTRODUCTION

SPACE
COWBOYS:
GENRE &
CONTEXT

TO INFINITY
& BEYOND:
THE HUMAN
CONDITION
& GENRE

WORKBOOK
EXERCISES
3.1 & 3.2

CASE STUDY:
FROM *MODERN
TIMES* TO
WALL·E

YOU KANT
BE SERIOUS:
COMEDY GENRE
& THEORIES OF
HUMOR

THE BIG DEBATE:
GENRE OR
STYLE?

CASE STUDY:
DOMESTICATED

CHAPTER
SUMMARY
& FURTHER
READING

KEY WORDS,
NAMES & WORKS

End Note on Film Noir

Unlike narrative composition in painting, mise-en-scène in film has an added narrative dimension—the use of sound. Whereas indexical signifiers such as footprints can indicate the presence of people not in shot in either painting or film, film can also use the *sound* of footsteps to indicate the presence of someone not in shot. This is known as diegetic sound—sound that comes directly from the world within the film (whether on screen or off screen).

Music can also be considered as an aspect of mise-en-scène. However, if the music is there to embellish the mood but does not come directly from the world within the film, then it is known as non-diegetic sound. This would apply to the soundtrack and leitmotif. In the case of later film noir movies, the iconic leitmotif of the jazz saxophone was often used to signify the on or off-screen presence or imminent arrival of the femme fatale.

The leitmotifs and soundtracks of film noir are also very different to those of the Western, for example. 'Crime jazz' typifies later film noir, through a 'seedy' association with back street nightlife, whereas modernist orchestral music with dissonant chords (clashing rather than harmonic notes), often played by the trumpet, is typical of earlier film noir. As with the exaggerated lighting and non-linear plot order, the atonal musical composition (not written in any key) further unsettles the viewing experience, which could not be more different to the nostalgic and often triumphant music of the earlier Westerns.

Narration is another defining characteristic of many noir films. The monotone flat voice of the main character, a kind of monologue of internalized thoughts, gives a commentary of the plot at key moments throughout the film. This form of narration is known as homodiegetic narration (a form of diegetic sound), classified by French literary theorist Gerard Genette (b. 1930), whose work is closely connected with structuralism. This can be key to help the audience make sense of the unfolding plot, but also give a sense of experiencing the film in the first person.

Film noir became a collective definition for films that turn many of the clear-cut formalist and structuralist conventions underpinning narrative genre theory upside down. Film noir did this using non-linear narratives, highly stylized mise-en-scène, modern music and often a homodiegetic narration.

Though aspects of film noir have in fact been used as stylistic components in a range of genres, including the Western and science fiction, I would argue that film noir could be seen as its own distinctive emerging genre—particularly in the light of a wave of more recent films consolidating film noir into an *intentional* and recognizable narrative convention.

RECOMMENDED VIEWING

Here are four examples of modern film noir:

Blade Runner, directed by Ridley Scott, The Ladd Company (1982)

L.A. Confidential, directed by Curtis Hanson, Regency Enterprises (1997)

Mulholland Drive, directed by David Lynch, Les Films Alain Sarde (2001)

Sin City, directed by Frank Miller & Robert Rodriguez, Dimension Films (2005)

CASE STUDY:
DOMESTICATED

3.18
Domesticated by Vaida Kereisyte (University
of Bedfordshire, 2013). Sequence of animation
stills from the film noir and science fiction-
inspired narrative.

INTRODUCTION

SPACE
COWBOYS:
GENRE &
CONTEXT

TO INFINITY
& BEYOND:
THE HUMAN
CONDITION
& GENRE

WORKBOOK
EXERCISES
3.1 & 3.2

CASE STUDY:
FROM MODERN
TIMES TO
WALL·E

YOU KANT
BE SERIOUS:
COMEDY GENRE
& THEORIES OF
HUMOR

THE BIG DEBATE:
GENRE OR
STYLE?

CASE STUDY:
DOMESTICATED

CHAPTER
SUMMARY
& FURTHER
READING

KEY WORDS,
NAMES & WORKS

Domesticated by Vaida Kereisyte (University of Bedfordshire, 2013) is an example of how research into genre and the human condition informed the development of her BA (Hons) Animation major project.

Excerpts from her online workbook that summarize how she responded to these influences are included below, illustrated with a series of stills from her 2D animated short.

Synopsis: *Domesticated* is a 2D animated film about a man that gets abducted by an alien spaceship and is made into a pet.

Analysis: By looking at the synopsis it is clear that this film falls into the science fiction genre. The film features extraterrestrial life forms, spaceships and interstellar travel. Interstellar travel does not exist yet, nor is there any official proof of alien life. According to Welch Everman these are some of the main elements that define science fiction.

To make the workload easier for myself I did the storyboard very quickly in black and white. By also minimizing the use of colour in the development of the actual film, using dynamic shadows from only a few light sources and sometimes putting characters into silhouette, I realized that film noir would be a useful reference for developing the look of my film.

I referred to 1950s science fiction movies, including *The Day the Earth Stood Still* (1951) and *War of the Worlds* (1953), and based much of my design on this period because it would coincide with the film noir visual style more naturally. I also used a jazz soundtrack at the beginning of the film to fit with the film noir genre.

I also used *Blade Runner* directed by Ridley Scott (1982) as an influence for my film, as it combines science fiction with film noir as well. *Blade Runner* also has an interesting theme about what it means to be a real human being, and who we really are, by implying that the main protagonist Roy Deckard, who investigates replicants, may be one himself. Roy Deckard represents the audience, and by doing so the audience is made to question its own humanity.

My film has parallels with *Blade Runner* in its narrative. In the first shot we see a fish swimming in a fish bowl. At the end of the film we see the owner of the fish being dropped into a bowl by an alien, recreating the environment from which he was abducted. In the same way that *Blade Runner* makes us question our humanity, I tried to question the idea of freedom in my own film—are we truly free, or are we controlled by someone else. If so what difference does it make to our daily lives if we are unaware of this.

CHAPTER SUMMARY & FURTHER READING

From the myth and fairy tale to the Western and science fiction, discussion of genre and the human condition has illustrated how different civilizations have reflected on mankind's place in the world, using stories to understand what defines their society and the humans within it. We have identified some of the dominant genres and learned how to interpret or even invent other less familiar genres.

We have seen how comedy can be defined as specific genre, explored its different sub-genres, as well as theories of humor and comic practices, to help us break down narrative in other entertaining and cathartic ways. We have also identified how the vita activa and natality can be used as the fundamental building blocks of any genre, and according to Hannah Arendt define the infinite rebirth of the human condition.

In doing so we have understood how the hero's journey, genre and the human condition define man's conquest over his own destiny. We have seen increasingly how in the modern narrative, the slave or everyman becomes the *hero* of the human world. We have highlighted the importance of contextual research in developing knowledge of historical events and current affairs, in order to have a fuller understanding of films and the parallels between their narratives—from *The Good, the Bad and the Ugly* to *Star Wars* and *Modern Times* to *WALL•E*.

Overall, we have understood how these aspects of genre define the quest of human civilization to make sense of its place in the universe. But ultimately we have learned how we have *all* become slaves to the man-made environment. From *Laputa* (in chapter two) to *WALL•E*, we can understand that now the heroic act is one of escaping not from planet Earth, but from the limitations of our own man-made environment, and returning to the natural world from which we originally came.

From changes in the use of words in different languages to identifying new genres, throughout the book so far we have seen how technology has come to define us more than anything else and how it has changed our understanding of our world and who we are. We now live in an age where narrative genres evolve and hybridize as quickly as the human world and consume our imagination with concerns about our present and also our future.

In practical terms, we have consolidated our knowledge of the main conventions used in developing universal narrative structures, as well as our understanding of the ways in which narration, music, sound and mise-en-scène enhance narrative meaning in film and animation. This offers us valuable insight into the narrative interplay between character, layout design and soundtrack through the beat board animatic when developing an idea for a film.

Through the study of film noir we have also started to challenge some of the clear-cut formalist and structuralist conventions underpinning narrative genre theory, such as the use of non-linear narratives, highly stylized mise-en-scène and modern music. In the next chapter of the book, you will be introduced to modernism. This was a period in which many writers, artists and filmmakers broke away from the universal rules of genre altogether.

Chapter four will therefore reconsider representation of the human condition by looking at a modernist visual language of more individual and abstract forms of artistic expression—expressing the confusion experienced by the everyman in the modern world. It will also explore how animation is able to uniquely express some of these more abstract and personal feelings. The first three chapters, however, will have hopefully opened your eyes to how we can reflect real world issues within more literal, yet fictional animation narratives.

FURTHER READING

Film Theory & Genre

Chandler, D. (2007) *Semiotics: The Basics*, Routledge: Abingdon

Duff, D. (2000) *Modern Genre Theory*, Pearson Education Ltd: Harlow

Grant, B. (2011) *Film Genre: From Iconography to Ideology*, Wallflower Press: Brighton

Stam, R. (2000) *Film Theory, An Introduction*, Blackwell Publishers Ltd: Oxford

Stam, R., Burgoyne, R. & Flitterman-Lewis, S. (2006) *New Vocabularies in Film Semiotics*, Routledge

Wells, P. (2002) *Animation Genre and Authorship*, Wallflower Press: London

The Human Condition & Cultural Materialism

Arendt, H. (1998) *The Human Condition*, The University of Chicago Press Ltd: London

Baudrillard, J. (Glaser, S. translator, 1994) *Simulacra and Simulation*, University of Michigan Press: Ann Arbor

Comedy Genre & Theories of Humor

Hoover, S. (2013) *What's So Funny? Theories of Comedy*, Stephen Hoover: USA

Kerr, W. (1990) *The Silent Clowns*, Da Capo Press: Cambridge, MA

Wells, P. (2007) *Scriptwriting*, AVA Publishing SA: London

Mise-en-Scène & Film Noir

Copjec, J. (1993) *Shades of Noir*, Verso: London

Gibbs, J. (2007) *Mise-en-Scène, Film Style and Interpretation*, Wallflower Press: London

3.19

3.19
An image of planet Earth by day and night as it orbits the sun reveals how humans have attempted to overcome the natural world with a man-made world—evident by the city lights at night.

KEY WORDS

Axiom
The unquestioned norms of a society or civilization

Black Comedy
Explores the extremes between tragedy and comedy with often perverse or surreal and very intense scenes

Catharsis
The psychological healing process of release from repressed emotions or memories, often as the result of creating or experiencing art, film or music

Chiaroscuro
The use of three light sources to create artificially heightened lighting on actors, set against intense shadows in low-lit spaces

Crime Fiction Genre
A genre that includes a broad range of sub-genres, but differs from other mainstream genre as it is largely built around a crime rather than a 'Hero's Journey' as such

Diegetic Sound
Sound that comes directly from the world within the film (whether on screen or off screen)

Dystopian
Decaying and dictatorial worlds

Fabula
Story defined by the character relationships and chronological plot order

Fairy Tale Genre
The written form of the folk tale

Fantasy Genre
Set in more mythical worlds based around adventures with magic and supernatural forces

Film Noir
A stylised form of filmmaking that has parallels with the crime fiction genre, but challenges conventions of genre in general by playing with the order of events and components of the standard narrative structure

Greek Tragedies and Comedies
Some of the earliest forms of literary and theatrical genre from ancient Greece

Homodiegetic Narration
A kind of monologue of internalized thoughts, giving a commentary of the plot at key moments throughout the film

Human World
A natural world conquered and controlled by the activities of mankind

Hybrid Genre
A newer and less established genre, more specific in terms of its historical context (time and place in which it is set)

Mise-en-Scène
Filmic composition, which also takes into consideration meaning of objects, lighting, as well as things outside the shot, including sound

Monologue
A speech by a single actor

Narrative Genre
A means of classifying narratives across a range of historical contexts that all essentially follow the same structure and 'Hero's Journey'

Natality
How a civilization is defined and held together by its own unique combination of human activity and the arrival of the activities of new civilizations

Natural World
The natural world, unexposed to the activities of mankind

Nickelodeon
Cinemas in the early 1900s, where audiences could pay just a nickel (five cents) to see a film

Non-Diegetic Sound
Music used to embellish the mood but that does not come directly from the world within the film

Object-Response
How objects can seemingly take on a life of their own

Pathos
Behaviour that evokes sadness

Private Realm
The tough conditions of labour essential for human survival hidden from public view—largely the labour of slaves

INTRODUCTION

SPACE
COWBOYS:
GENRE &
CONTEXT

TO INFINITY
& BEYOND:
THE HUMAN
CONDITION
& GENRE

WORKBOOK
EXERCISES
3.1 & 3.2

CASE STUDY:
FROM *MODERN
TIMES* TO
WALL·E

YOU KANT
BE SERIOUS:
COMEDY GENRE
& THEORIES OF
HUMOR

THE BIG DEBATE:
GENRE OR
STYLE?

CASE STUDY:
DOMESTICATED

CHAPTER
SUMMARY
& FURTHER
READING

**KEY WORDS,
NAMES & WORKS**

Psychoanalysis
A form of psychological therapy focused on releasing repressed memories and emotions

Public Realm
Where work, leisure and political action of the ruling classes (dependent on the labour of the slave) is promoted by the construction of objects, images, monuments and buildings

Romcom
Films that explore the complexity of modern relationships

Royal Genre
A dominant or universal narrative such as the fairy tale, which is seen to impose certain conventions on other subsequent genres

Science Fiction Genre
Set in the context of either alternative and theoretically possible worlds or technologically advanced societies

Sitcom
A sub-genre of comedy exploring the everyday politics of a small group of people, often focused around the family and home or workplace

Slapstick
Comic clumsiness (and comic violence)

Social Incongruity
A theory of humour that depends on a character who is a social misfit and whose behaviour or actions are out of keeping with their environment

Spaghetti Western
More action and gun fights than the traditional Western

Sub-Genre
A body of films or books that follow the same narrative format as the texts of a dominant parent genre, but shift the emphasis to the development of a particular aspect of the narrative theme

Syuzhet
The *stylization* of the plot order, parallel plots and use of a range of different accounts of the same narrative

Utopian
Perfect and idealistic worlds

Vita Activa
A system used to explain the relationship between three key forms of human activity that define the human condition

Western Genre
Set in the context of European settlers in the American 'Wild West'

KEY NAMES

Aristotle
Hannah Arendt
Roland Barthes
Mikhail Bakhtin
Henri Bergson
Charlie Chaplin
Sigmund Freud
Gerard Genette
Immanuel Kant
Fritz Lang
Sergio Leone
Claude Lévi-Strauss
Ennio Morricone
Ireneusz Opacki
Plato
Ridley Scott
Viktor Shklovsky
Andrew Stanton
Juri Tynianov

KEY WORKS

Big Heat, The
Blade Runner
Good, the Bad and the Ugly, The
Lord of the Rings, The
Matrix, The
Modern Times
Sin City
Star Wars
Toy Story
WALL·E

CHAPTER FOUR
MODERNISM: THE END OF GENRE & THE METANARRATIVE

CHAPTER OVERVIEW: RETHINKING NARRATIVE FORM

In this chapter, you will learn:

- **How modernist art movements challenged mainstream forms of visual narrative and artistic expression in the first half of the twentieth century.**

- **How these art movements represented a shift away from universal genres and narrative structures to a more subjective, pluralistic and abstract visual language.**

- **How artists of this period reflected on the human condition and how the historical events that influenced them have direct relevance today.**

- **How narrative themes covered in the previous chapters can be reinterpreted using examples of modernist animations and films.**

4.1
Anatomy of a Murder (title sequence) animated by Saul Bass, Otto Preminger Films (1959). The animated title sequence reflects many of the principles of modernist design.

INTRODUCTION

This chapter begins by outlining the historical developments that led to radical changes in literature, art, design and film. These changes included a dramatic shift away from the universal genres and narrative structures discussed so far to a modern visual language of more subjective (personal interpretations), pluralistic (of multiple individuals), abstract forms of artistic expression that collectively became known as modernism. This chapter looks at how this cultural shift ultimately challenged the dominance of realism in animation.

It is important to note before going any further that modernism does not necessarily come historically after the theories we have explored so far. Rather, a broad range of modernist art movements (distinctive approaches to art used by groups of artists) challenged more *mainstream* or *dominant* forms of visual narrative and artistic expression in the first half of the twentieth century (around 1900–1960).

These movements included cubism, expressionism and German Expressionism, which are used as the focus for the investigation of modernism in this chapter. Such movements spanned across literature, music, theatre, film, animation, painting, sculpture, design and architecture. They challenged preconceptions not just of what art should portray and express about the world, but also *how* it could express it.

We will see how modernism also places strong emphasis on the theme of the human condition and how many of the historical events that influenced the artists discussed in this chapter still have direct relevance to the events going on in the world today. Narrative themes covered in previous chapters are also reinterpreted using examples of modernist animations and films dealing with some of the darkest subject matter in this book. There is also discussion of how more humorous animation finds a place in modernism too.

The second case study in this chapter, *When the Day Breaks* directed by Wendy Tilby and Amanda Forbis (1999), illustrates some core aspects of modernism useful in developing more experimental solutions to animation narrative. The first case study and workbook exercises in this chapter will look mainly at the use of montage, rotoscoping and anthropomorphism (giving animals or things human attributes) in film and animation. These methods will help us understand how to represent deep and challenging narrative themes in more abstract ways, building on the semiotic and narrative set design exercises in chapter one.

"Even when there is not mention of 'rules' or 'conventions' (its usual corollary), the term [genre] seems almost by definition to deny the autonomy of the author, deny the uniqueness of the text, deny spontaneity, originality and self-expression."
David Duff (2000), *Modern Genre Theory*, p. 1

INTRODUCTION

COFFEE,
STEAM & TANKS:
PUTTING
MODERNISM
IN CONTEXT

SPACE, TIME
& REALITY:
DEFINING
MODERNISM

WORKBOOK
EXERCISE 4.1

WORKBOOK
EXERCISE 4.2

FROM THE
MUNDANE TO
MURDER: OTHER
ASPECTS OF
MODERNISM

CASE STUDY:
ZOI

CASE STUDY:
WHEN THE DAY
BREAKS

WORKBOOK
EXERCISE 4.3

CHAPTER
SUMMARY
& FURTHER
READING

RECOMMENDED VIEWING

Anatomy of a Murder (title sequence), animated by Saul Bass, Otto Preminger Films (1959)

Coloured Rhythm, made by Léopold Survage (1912–1914), filmed by Bruce Checefsky (2005)

'M', directed by Fritz Lang, Nero-Film AG (1931)

Pleasures of War, directed by Ruth Lingford, Fine Take Productions (1998)

Psycho, directed by Alfred Hitchcock, Shamley Productions (1960)

The Battleship Potemkin, directed by Sergei Eisenstein, Goskino (1925)

The Cabinet of Dr. Caligari, directed by Robert Wiene, Decla-Bioscop AG (1919)

The Typewriter, directed by Richard Haynes & Mikolaj Watt, Arts University Bournemouth (2003)

Triangle, directed by Erica Russell, Gingco (1994)

When The Day Breaks, directed by Wendy Tilby & Amanda Forbis, National Film Board of Canada (1999)

Zoi, directed by Amanda Curl, University of Bedfordshire (2013)

ADDITIONAL RECOMMENDED VIEWING

A Christmas Carol, directed by Robert Zemeckis, Walt Disney Pictures (2009)

Death and the Mother, directed by Ruth Lingford, Channel Four Films (1988)

Metropolis, directed by Fritz Lang, Universum Film (1927)

Mr. Magoo, directed by Pete Burness, United Productions of America (1949–)

Mrs. Dalloway, directed by Marleen Gorris, First Look International (1997)

Sleeping Beauty, directed by Clyde Geronimi, Walt Disney Productions (1959)

The Hours, directed by Stephen Daldry, Paramount Pictures (2002)

Tim Burton's The Nightmare Before Christmas, directed by Henry Selick, Touchstone Pictures (1993)

2001: A Space Odyssey, directed by Stanley Kubrick, Metro-Goldwyn-Mayer (1968)

COFFEE, STEAM & TANKS: PUTTING MODERNISM IN CONTEXT

The Enlightenment

Although modernism is a term used to describe a period of radical developments in the arts in the first half of the twentieth century, to understand modernism more fully, it is helpful to first explore the dramatic shifts in society following previous periods and events in history, including the Enlightenment, the Industrial Revolution and the First World War.

The Enlightenment began in the late seventeenth century (1600s) and was a period of intellectual reform (a change in the way we think about things) in the western world that continued up until the end of the eighteenth century (1700s). During this time science began to replace superstition and also dominate over religion as means of understanding the world. Leading philosophers of the period included René Descartes (1596–1650), Baruch Spinoza (1632–1677) and John Locke (1632–1704). They belonged to different schools of thought known as Rationalism and Empiricism.

Rationalists such as Spinoza and Descartes believed that the world could be understood through logical reasoning of the mind, whereas Empiricists such as Locke believed that the world was mainly understood through firsthand, human, sensory experience. Following the invention of the printing press in Europe by German blacksmith Johannes Gutenberg in the mid to late 1430s, the Enlightenment was also a period in which knowledge was being distributed ever more quickly and widely, outside the traditional channels of the church, state and universities.

With the introduction of coffee in Europe, coffee houses became a popular alternative meeting place to alehouses, or the gin houses in London, where the proliferation of cheap gin had given rise to extensive alcoholism and social problems. However coffee houses provided a 'sober' place to distribute printed pamphlets and newspapers, where people from all walks of life could meet publicly to discuss new ideas. We can see parallels today with the provision of 'Wi-Fi' in coffee houses, which are often used as meeting places by professionals to discuss work projects.

4.2

4.2
The Gutenberg printing press
(mid to late 1430s).

The Industrial Revolution & Capitalism

The industrial revolution took place from the mid-eighteenth to mid-nineteenth century (1700s–1800s). This was a period of rapid mechanization and urban expansion, which started in Britain and quickly spread throughout Europe and America. It was a period in which the production of objects went from being made by hand to mass production using steam-powered machinery.

Great numbers of people moved from the countryside into the cities to work the machinery in the factories, producing textiles and iron goods. There was a huge rise in affluence amongst the ruling classes with the global export of commodities (objects made more for profit than for practical use). But there was also severe poverty as well as terrible working and living conditions amongst the working classes. A similar rate of rapid industrialization can be seen in China today.

Karl Marx (1818–1883) was a German philosopher and socialist revolutionary who wrote some of the most influential theories on modern society, economics and politics, which later became known as Marxism. In 1867 Marx published the first of three volumes called *Das Kapital*. These volumes explored political ideas to empower the working classes—ideas that later became known as socialism—in an attempt to educate people about their exploitation by what later became known as industrial capitalism.

The Human Condition, written by Hannah Arendt (discussed in chapter three), was partly informed by her interpretation of Marx. But, whereas Arendt's discussion extended to the political action of whole civilizations and the relationship between the human and natural world, Marx looked more specifically at the processes and mechanics of modern capitalism and the potential collective action of the working classes against the ruling classes.

A Christmas Carol, written by Charles Dickens (1843), captures the essence of conditions during the industrial revolution, by contrasting the merriment of Christmas with the harsh realities of the working class life in the industrial cities, where many of the workers were also children. *A Christmas Carol* has been made into several films and animations, including Disney's computer animated version starring the voice of Jim Carrey (2009). The film *Modern Times* and animation *WALL•E* discussed in the last chapter also echo many of the ideas of Marx, highlighting the exploitation of the working classes and the mass production of commodities.

The First World War

The First World War (1914–1918) in many ways marks a point in history that defines the modern age. This was a period of international conflict and mechanized destruction on a scale never seen before, between the main world economic powers as they sought to expand their territories and resources needed in their continuing mechanization and modernization.

These economic powers included Germany, Austria-Hungary and the Ottoman Empire, fighting against countries including America, Britain, France and Russia. The new machines of the modern age, such as tanks and airplanes, were used to tear apart countries, killing millions of people and changing the physical, political and economic landscape of the world forever.

❝Marx demonstrates that capitalism is based on the *exploitation* of working women, men and children. All the basic facts of modern society are analysed, from prices and profits to wages and the working day. Why labour products are 'commodities', why money is so all-powerful, where capital originates and why economic crises happen.❞
David Smith & Phil Evans (1982), *Marx's Capital for Beginners*, p. 21

SPACE, TIME & REALITY:
DEFINING MODERNISM

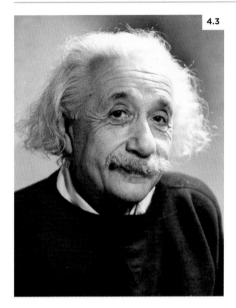

4.3

Modernism was not a conscious school of thought. Rather, it was a term applied later on to the broad range of forms of artistic expression that emerged in the first half of the twentieth century, in response to the radical human transformations of the world outlined so far in this chapter, from scientific thought, to industrial capitalism and global warfare.

By the twentieth century science had become increasingly abstract compared to the period of the Enlightenment. The introduction of theories such as Albert Einstein's Theory of Relativity (1905) and Max Planck's Quantum Theory (1901) challenged our perceptions of space, time, matter and observable reality.

Philosophers such as Friedrich Nietzsche (1844–1900) challenged the existence of God and the nature of religion, as did Sigmund Freud (1856–1939) the founder of psychoanalysis. Freud's work on the analysis of dreams and the nature of our subconscious mind had a big influence on the modernist art movements and also on advertising in the twentieth century (see chapter five).

The First World War also shook the human psyche and people's confidence in traditional belief systems and ideals, bringing into question the authority of government. People were also adapting to fit in with new social ideas of how to live and function, as they tried to make sense of the changes rapidly taking place in an accelerating, industrialized, capitalist age.

4.3
Portrait of theoretical physicist Albert Einstein. Einstein's Theory of Relativity (1905) challenged our perceptions of space and time. Artists responded with abstract paintings that also challenged our views on art.

❝Art was capable of diagnosing, and pointing beyond, alienating social and economic conditions. For Marx the best art served the cognitive function of piercing through the ideological clouds which enshroud social realities. Moreover, by graphically embodying this relative freedom from the mere reflection of external circumstances, aesthetic creations could develop the desire for greater freedom from a dehumanized alienating society. All art has the capacity to create a *need* for aesthetic enjoyment and education which capitalist society cannot satisfy.❞
Eugene Lunn (1984), *Marxism and Modernism*, p. 16

Aesthetic Self-Consciousness or Self-Reflexiveness

In his book *Marxism and Modernism*, the American academic Eugene Lunn (1941–1990) outlined Karl Marx's cultural theories on the purpose and relationship of art with capitalism. Under capitalism, the production of art had become as much a product of human labour for sale and profit as any other commodity.

But for Marx, subsequent neo-Marxists and modernist artists, a key function of *great* art was how it could be used as an aesthetic process (artistic experience) to educate people. Art could expose or challenge the reality behind many of the belief systems used by society, that condition people to accept the repressive and dehumanizing effects of capitalism as the 'normal' way of life. Equally it could provide an emotional escape from highly rationalized and industrialized society.

Lunn loosely defined the nature and range of modernist art movements using four key sets of characteristics that reflect many of the changes to society outlined so far. We will now look at key examples of modernist art movements, artists and theories that illustrate each of these characteristics. These are particularly relevant to understanding more modern animation techniques, subject matter, narrative structures and meaning, some of which are introduced in this chapter.

From the Enlightenment up until the modernist period, western art was largely preoccupied with producing a *rational*, measured, known representation of the world around us, generally referred to as realism. Realism in art followed the same principle as mimesis established by the ancient Greek philosopher Aristotle: to accurately represent aspects of our external reality. Artists focused on techniques such as perspective in painting to create a sense of depth on a flat canvas.

Realism was also the name of a specific art movement in the nineteenth century that strived to represent reality as closely as possible. As well as using techniques such perspective painting, subject matter was based wholly on 'real' life, excluding aspects such as more mythical narratives found in earlier perspective painting.

The paintings of English artist Joseph Wright of Derby (1734–1797) capture the essence of the Enlightenment era. His paintings, such as *An Experiment on a Bird in the Air Pump* (1768), are almost photographic in their attention to light and perspective, but also depict advances in science during the Enlightenment period.

4.4

4.4
An Experiment on a Bird in the Air Pump, by Joseph Wright of Derby (1768).

Expressionism

In the twentieth century, as scientific explanations of reality became increasingly abstract, artists began to focus on personal abstract *sensory experiences*, *internal spiritual feelings* or *states of mind* instead. Some artists expressed this through associations with vivid colours, geometric shapes and visual representations of sound—in some ways returning to more primitive mythical traditions in art. Artists also began to purposefully expose the flat plain of a painting, as well as the *techniques* they used to create works of art, rather than trying to represent a perfectly painted, photographic, external reality.

Thus, the relative realism achieved through use of perspective and narrative meaning conveyed in paintings such as those of Vermeer, for example, or animations such as *Snow White and the Seven Dwarfs* (discussed in chapter one), was challenged by images that exposed the flat plane of the canvass, the paint marks and subconscious mind or internal world of the artist.

This approach to painting defined a movement central to modernist art known as expressionism, established in 1911. Founding artists included Russian painter Wassily Kandinsky (1866–1944), who published his first book *On the Spiritual in Art* (1912), which outlined his own colour theories and ideas on abstract art.

Interestingly, Kandinsky's early paintings focused on subject matter from Russian folklore and fairy tales, but the majority of his later work explored the instability or rhythmic movement of different shapes, lines, colours and representations of sound or states of mind. He is best known for paintings such as *Composition VIII* (1923), produced whilst he taught at the famous modernist art school called the Bauhaus in Germany.

Music itself had also become more abstract. The highly influential Austrian composer Arnold Schoenberg (1874–1951), a friend and contemporary of Kandinsky, developed a compositional method of atonal sounds (music not written in any particular key) and dissonant chords (of clashing as opposed to harmonic notes) known as the Twelve-Tone Method.

This approach to sound also created a sensation of conflicting feelings (common to modernist movements), as well as widening the scope for more individual and expressive approaches to music and its use in film and animation. We have discussed in chapter three how the dissonant sounds of modernist orchestras or crime jazz helped to create an unsettled atmosphere in Noir films.

During the same period, another Russian artist named Léopold Survage (1879–1968) developed the earliest known theories and designs of abstract animation. He produced a series of watercolour images called *Coloured Rhythm* (1912–1914), which though not filmed until 2005 by Bruce Checefsky, set out an animated sequence of abstract, rhythmic, coloured shapes.

Survage essentially established the same abstract principles as Kandinsky in the medium of animation, but he stated specifically that the rhythmic colour and movement of shapes in his images was designed not to illustrate or represent sounds, rather to arouse feelings, in the same way that the mind understands or responds to music. However, many animators have subsequently placed equal emphasis on the abstract qualities and relationship between image and sound.

More recently, animators such as Erica Russell (born in New Zealand in 1951) have explored complex abstract feelings experienced in sexual relationships. Her Oscar-nominated short *Triangle* (1994) begins with highly choreographed dance sequences of a realistically drawn nude male and two nude female figures. As the film progresses and the relationship between the three figures become more complex, the anatomies dissolve into sequences of abstract rhythmic shapes and patterns. The sound track also evolves from a melodic tune to placing more emphasis on evocative leitmotifs, building up a range of emotions in the audience.

Other early experimental animators such as the German-American Oskar Fischinger (1900–1967) followed Survage, with stop motion animations including *Composition in Blue* (1934), using abstract coloured shapes and blocks—the influence of which can clearly be seen in the music video *With Every Heart Beat* by Swedish singer Robyn (2007).

4.5

Composition VIII by Wassily Kandinsky (1923).

"One very significant area is the huge shift in sensibility caused by developments in science and philosophy; these fundamentally affected our sense of reality, our understanding of the so-called real world and how we see it. They consisted essentially in a move from a static to a dynamic view of the world based on movement and change, to a view that shifted from the visible to the invisible, from a perceptual to a conceptual comprehension of the world and our place in it."

Mary Acton (2004), *Learning to Look at Modern Art*, p. 15

Simultaneity, Juxtaposition or 'Montage'

4.6

4.6
Student exercise illustrating examples of rhythmic montage in a rotoscoped version of the Odessa Steps sequence from *The Battleship Potemkin* (1925); Alice Barlow, BA (Hons) Animation, Cass Faculty, London Metropolitan University (2014).

Whereas some modernist artists or art movements rejected the constraints of narrative in favour of totally subjective forms of artistic expression, others experimented with narrative structure in their exploration of the human condition. As scientific theories challenged our sense of space and time, writers and filmmakers also found artistic expression through alternative approaches to the highly structured narrative genres and metanarratives such as those established by the Russian formalist Vladimir Propp.

Simultaneity & Juxtaposition
Writers and filmmakers experimented with nonlinear narratives, where events were no longer put into a clear order of beginning, middle and end, but were instead sometimes presented simultaneously (at the same time), creating juxtapositions (meaningful contrasts) through the viewpoints of different characters or parallel events from different moments in time. Later these techniques also found popularity in more mainstream film noir using the Russian formalist concept of the syuzhet—the *stylization* of plot using flashbacks and so forth—as discussed in chapter three.

❝Modernism is the moment at which art stops making sense.❞
Jeff Wallace (2011), *Beginning Modernism*, p. 12

Prominent English modernist writer Virginia Woolf (1882–1941) used these methods in her novel *Mrs. Dalloway* (1925). The novel focuses on the lives of two people who are connected by another character, and whose memories of the past (including thoughts of previous relationships and the traumas of the first world war), are presented to the reader as flashbacks through interior monologues (the spoken or written stream of thoughts of a character or person). These interior monologues are interwoven with the author's narration of present events during a single day. The novel enables the reader to experience the thoughts, memories and feelings of the characters.

The novel *The Hours*, written by Michael Cunningham (1998), uses similar narrative methods to those used by Woolf in *Mrs. Dalloway*. Both books have been made into films. The film adaption of *The Hours* (2002) is also set during just one day, but cleverly constructs a narrative around the troubled lives of three women in different decades of the twentieth century, whose stories are connected by their reading of the novel *Mrs. Dalloway*. One of the characters is a portrayal of Virginia Woolf herself writing the book and her personal struggle with depression.

Montage

Modernist filmmakers also explored the juxtapositions of moments in time to evoke abstract visceral feelings (deep, raw internal emotions) using an editing technique known as montage. Montage theory was established through the experiments conducted by Soviet filmmaker Lev Kuleshov (1899–1970), using an already common principle called the shot-countershot.

The shot-countershot is the standard process of cutting from a shot of an actor to the view that they see. However, Kuleshov experimented by juxtaposing the same shot and close-up passive facial expression of an actor with close-ups of different counter shots. These included a bowl of soup, a dead woman and a child playing.

The combination of the same expression of the actor with a different countershot evoked a very different interpretation of the emotion of the actor and resulting *feeling* in the audience, such as deep contemplation, sadness and joy. This juxtaposition technique of close-up shot-countershot became known as the 'Kuleshov Effect'. The use of close-ups was particularly important as it intensified the sense of experiencing the situation firsthand for the audience.

"The fourth dimension?! Einstein? Or mysticism? Or a joke? It's time to stop being frightened of this new knowledge of a fourth dimension."
Sergei Eisenstein (1949), *Eisenstein, Film Form*, p. 69

WORKBOOK EXERCISE 4.1:
THE KULESHOV EFFECT—YOU TRY

1. Take a 'selfie' in which you are smiling.

2. Take a series of photos or cut outs from magazines of random unrelated close-up images.

3. Pair these images with the same selfie, place them in an editing timeline and play the sequence.

4. Ask a number of people what emotion they feel or what narrative situation springs to mind for each pair of images and note these down alongside the image pairs in your workbook.

Another pioneer of Soviet montage theory was filmmaker Sergei Eisenstein (1898–1948), not to be confused with the scientist Albert Einstein (both however were fascinated with the concept of the fourth dimension, time). Filmmaker Eisenstein not only experimented with pairing and order but also duration of shots, the rhythms and direction of action within the shot and tonal composition of shots, which he broke down into five different methods of montage: metric, rhythmic, tonal, overtonal and intellectual montage.

One of Eisenstein's most famous films was *The Battleship Potemkin* (1925), a dramatized account of a Soviet naval mutiny in 1905. A sequence in the film titled 'The Odessa Steps' is a master class in Eisenstein's different montage methods. Although the mutiny and civil unrest were interpretations of real events, the Odessa sequence shows the *fictional* massacre of innocent civilians by Soviet government forces on the steps leading down to the harbor. Eisenstein's use of montage is so powerful, it almost becomes a believable portrayal of a real historical event.

Eisenstein described a defining feature of montage as "emotive structures applied to non-emotional material" (Eisenstein, 1949, p. 69). What Eisenstein essentially illustrates is how the subject of each shot in a film may carry little or no narrative meaning on its own, but carries meaning, and most importantly emotion, once edited into a larger sequence or narrative structure.

Therefore, what makes modernist montage theory fundamentally different to more classical formalist or structuralist approaches to narrative are the abstract associations between shots that evoke an emotional response in the audience, as opposed to a highly structured, more rational narrative. The audience therefore actively takes part in an experience, rather than passively witnessing a narrative. Furthermore, montage is able to condense information and the passage of time through editing, where more traditional narratives may take more time to reveal a plot.

INTRODUCTION

COFFEE,
STEAM & TANKS:
PUTTING
MODERNISM
IN CONTEXT

SPACE, TIME
& REALITY:
DEFINING
MODERNISM

**WORKBOOK
EXERCISE 4.1**

WORKBOOK
EXERCISE 4.2

FROM THE
MUNDANE TO
MURDER: OTHER
ASPECTS OF
MODERNISM

CASE STUDY:
ZOI

CASE STUDY:
*WHEN THE DAY
BREAKS*

WORKBOOK
EXERCISE 4.3

CHAPTER
SUMMARY
& FURTHER
READING

KEY CONCEPTS: SERGEI EISENSTEIN'S FIVE METHODS OF MONTAGE

- Metric montage uses the repetition of the same duration of time for each shot, creating dramatic tension though the acceleration and equal shortening of each shot by smaller and smaller mathematical fractions.

- Rhythmic montage works on similar principle as metric montage, but creates further emotional tension when the rhythm of the action within each shot is out of step with, or perhaps even more intense than the accelerating rhythm of the edit. For example, a close-up of the pace of someone's footsteps in a shot may be faster than the perceived pace of the edit. It can also include intercutting of things moving in opposite directions to add to a sense of tension or conflict.

- Tonal montage contrasts more dominant thematic aspects in the composition of one shot with less dominant elements of composition in another to create an overarching mood. This could quite literally be tonal in terms the amount of light in a shot, contrasting the panorama of a sunset with the close up of a candle burning itself out. It can also include *graphic* tonality in terms of the contrasting scale and angles of dominant shapes forms, such as a long shot of the parallel lines of some steps at one angle with the close-up of the parallel lines of some steps at another angle.

- Overtonal montage essentially uses different combinations and aspects of all the above methods to create a range of different tensions, moods and emotions.

- Intellectual montage is the final form of montage. It uses a visual metaphor in one shot to imply or reinforce meaning of a more literal image in another shot. For example, a person walking in a slow heavy-footed and unhappy manner down stairs in one shot could signify and reinforce a downturn in their fortune, such as losing their job, by then cutting to a shot of them in a queue at a job centre.

WORKBOOK EXERCISE 4.2:
RESEARCHING & APPLYING MONTAGE TO A STORYBOARD

This exercise is designed to help you develop your cultural and contextual analysis skills and apply them to the development of a storyboard. It uses the rhythmic montage in the Odessa Steps Scene of *The Battleship Potemkin* as the focus of your research and resulting storyboard.

1. Find out more about *The Battleship Potemkin*, making further cultural and contextual notes on montage and what the film is about (see further reading list at end of chapter).

2. Key words: Kuleshov, Eisenstein, Potemkin, montage, rhythmic

3. Watch the Odessa Steps sequence.

4. Try to describe examples of rhythmic montage, including the marching troops, the runaway pram and switching of camera angles.

5. Try drawing out two or three shots set out as a storyboard to illustrate your examples.

Montage & Suspense

The English film director Alfred Hitchcock (1899–1980) also firmly believed that montage and emotion defined filmmaking. Hitchcock was known as the 'Master of Suspense'. He worked on the principle that if an audience knows or has a sense that something is going to happen, but has to wait for a period of time before the event occurs, it builds up an emotional tension known as suspense (a concept explored in chapter three in relation to comedy and incongruity theory).

Therefore, the director has to reveal enough of an overarching theme or plot developments to set up the expectation of a murder, for example. The suspense is then heightened by using progressive montage sequences of close-ups and visual cues, which finally reveal the critical moment at which the sinister outcome takes place. The precise point of the critical moment may be stipulated early on, or may in some cases be a surprise. *Psycho* (1960) is one of Hitchcock's most famous films; it uses montage to build dramatic tension in a sequence depicting the stabbing and murder of a woman from behind a shower curtain.

4.7

Hitchcock also outlined three key forms of suspense. *Vicarious* suspense takes place when the audience is aware of the outcome of the unfolding events but the character is not. The audience therefore experiences feelings on the character's behalf. *Shared* suspense is more intense, when the audience and character are both aware of developments, and the audience experiences the growing intensity of the emotions with the character in the build up to a critical moment. *Direct* suspense enables the audience to experience the tensions of a situation in the first person (as if the camera view is their viewpoint), without being concerned for any specific characters.

4.7
A film still from the famous shower scene in *Psycho*, directed by Alfred Hitchcock (1960). The scene is a classic example of montage and suspense.

129

Paradox, Ambiguity & Uncertainty

4.8

4.8
The Bottle of Banyuls, cubist still
life by Juan Gris (1914).

Cubism is generally regarded as the art movement most central to the development of modernism and defined largely by the work of the Spanish artist Pablo Picasso (1881–1973) and French artist Georges Braque (1882–1963). Most radically, cubists explored the idea of representing a person or object from several different angles in one image, to reflect changes in how we perceive the world through new technology and forms of transport. Developments in supersized architecture, air travel and photography meant that people could travel faster than ever before and see the world from the multiple viewpoints of tall buildings and airplanes.

From as early as 1907, Picasso developed painting techniques using hard-edged abstract shapes, black outlines, flat patterns and flat colours (but often in more muted tones than the Expressionists). In a second phase, Picasso and Braque used a combination not seen before in painting, of flat colours and collage—pasting together pieces of paper and materials of different textures onto the canvas. The further combination of these flat colours and textured materials with multiple viewpoints of their subject matter gave their images a more sculptural quality.

INTRODUCTION

COFFEE,
STEAM & TANKS:
PUTTING
MODERNISM
IN CONTEXT

SPACE, TIME
& REALITY:
DEFINING
MODERNISM

WORKBOOK
EXERCISE 4.1

WORKBOOK
EXERCISE 4.2

FROM THE
MUNDANE TO
MURDER: OTHER
ASPECTS OF
MODERNISM

CASE STUDY:
ZOI

CASE STUDY:
WHEN THE DAY
BREAKS

WORKBOOK
EXERCISE 4.3

CHAPTER
SUMMARY
& FURTHER
READING

Paradoxically (in contradiction), these sculptural images had as much sense of depth as traditional perspective paintings, but were representing more ambiguous (open to interpretation) notions of reality. Picasso was also inspired by African tribal artifacts such as masks in his simplification of the human form. This added to the sculptural quality of his work and also exaggerated the visceral feelings closely associated with so many modernist movements.

The influence of cubism can be clearly seen in the stylized development of animation in the 1950s. Some animators grew frustrated with the pursuit of realism in mainstream animation. A number of new studios, including UPA, sprang up in America producing short animations and commercials that sought cheaper and therefore less realistic techniques.

Character designers such as Sterling Sturtevant (1922–1962) and animation background painters such as Bob McIntosh (1916–2010) worked on the *Mister Magoo* cartoons of the 1950s, which reflected the methods of Picasso and other cubists, including Fernand Léger (1881–1955).

Backgrounds in animations became more abstract with areas of angular flat colour used to emphasize mood. Printed textures were purposefully misregistered with outlines to reveal the expressive techniques of the artist. Characters too became more abstract in their design and movement, sometimes flattened to the extent that character and background became visually fused.

A term known as limited animation was also developed—an equally expressive approach to traditional animation— but using more exaggerated key frame poses and sometimes radical, seemingly illogical in-betweens. This was useful in expressing increasingly anarchic (intentionally disruptive and often violent) and absurd (nonsensical) actions common in modern animations, which like many forms of art challenged authority and ideas of what was acceptable behaviour, but for humorous effect.

Pairing such action with the atonal sounds and dissonant chords of modern jazz and orchestral music also added to the sense of anarchy. This helped to further exaggerate the humor in the Looney Tunes cartoon series produced by Warner Brothers from the 1930s to the 1960s, which included classics such as *Bugs Bunny*, *Daffy Duck* and *Wile E. Coyote and the Road Runner*.

Large studios such as Disney also experimented with a bold new approach of flattened colour in the feature-length animation *Sleeping Beauty* (1959) under the art direction of Eyvind Earle (1916–2000). While the sophisticated styling marked a significant shift in production values, the fairy tale format was still used in contrast to modernist approaches to narrative.

Modern or a Product of Its Time?

Although modern by comparison to the classical realism established in animation by Disney and other studios, the more radical approaches to design in 1950s animation cannot necessarily all be described as *modernist*. It is important to remember that although visual style and technique is a very conscious component of modernism, modernism is also defined by the expression of deeper ideas and emotions.

The majority of 1950s animation borrowed modernist techniques mainly to stylize and simplify animation for commercial purposes such as advertising, rather than explore a deeper psychology seen in the of experimental work of artists and animators such as Survage or Russell. Modern animation from the 1950s was therefore more a product of its time, rather than being truly modernist.

Exceptions to this can be seen in the iconic work of graphic designers such as Saul Bass (1920–1996), who developed semi-abstract, thematic animated title sequences for feature films. Semiotic associations of certain colours, flat fragmented shapes or broken lines would for example give a sense of the psychological human states of mind central to certain film narratives.

Notable examples of Bass' work include the title sequence for *Anatomy of a Murder* (Otto Preminger, 1959), as well as Hitchcock's films *Vertigo* (1958) and *Psycho* (1960). The legacy and influence of Saul Bass can still be seen in the twenty-first century, including the opening title sequence for *Catch Me If You Can* (Steven Spielberg, 2002), which appropriates Bass' techniques and compresses the essence of the whole film narrative into two and half minutes.

However, we still also see the important impact and stylistic legacy of 1950s animation today, even in three-dimensional computer animations such as *Madagascar* (DreamWorks, 2005). Here, subtly angular exaggerations of objects and buildings, and the decorative features of characters from nostrils to lion manes, echo the same fundamental design principles. The pre-production artwork for *The Incredibles* (Pixar, 2004) also infuses the final film with similar 1950s design sensibilities.

4.9

4.9
The Typewriter, directed by Richard Haynes & Mikolaj Watt, Arts University Bournemouth (2003). Animated short in which the protagonist escapes the routine of his job by playing with the typewriters in the office he is meant to be tidying. The animation is rendered in a typical 1950s style, with flat colours, semi-abstraction and limited animation synchronized to a musical score.

INTRODUCTION

COFFEE,
STEAM & TANKS:
PUTTING
MODERNISM
IN CONTEXT

SPACE, TIME
& REALITY:
DEFINING
MODERNISM

WORKBOOK
EXERCISE 4.1

**WORKBOOK
EXERCISE 4.2**

FROM THE
MUNDANE TO
MURDER: OTHER
ASPECTS OF
MODERNISM

CASE STUDY:
ZOI

CASE STUDY:
*WHEN THE DAY
BREAKS*

WORKBOOK
EXERCISE 4.3

CHAPTER
SUMMARY
& FURTHER
READING

Dehumanization

RECOMMENDED VIEWING

Here are some examples of modern animation (1950s):

Anatomy of a Murder, directed by Otto Preminger, Otto Preminger Films (1959)

Catch Me If You Can, directed by Steven Spielberg, DreamWorks SKG (2002)

Madagascar, directed by Eric Darnell & Tom McGrath, DreamWorks (2005)

Mr. Magoo, directed by John Hubley, United Productions of America (1949—)

Sleeping Beauty, directed by Clyde Geronimi, Walt Disney Productions (1959)

The Incredibles, directed by Brad Bird, Pixar (2004)

Vertigo, directed by Alfred Hitchcock, Paramount Pictures (1958)

Wile E. Coyote and the Road Runner, directed by Chuck Jones, Warner Bros. (1949—)

Modernism brought attention to the dehumanizing effect of industrialism and the horrors of war. As we have already discussed, Chaplin captured the impact of industrialism on the everyman in his film *Modern Times*, as had other filmmakers. Picasso's approach to painting also reflected a new level of awareness around the fragmentation, loss of identity and destruction of the individual.

In 1937 Picasso painted one of his most famous works of art, Guernica. The large panoramic image expressed the violence of the Spanish Civil War, which coincided with the Second World War. He used his trademark angular contortion, fragmentation of the human form and intense tonal contrasts to express the horrors of the massacre of innocent civilians in Guernica, the capital of the Basque region of Spain.

German Expressionism

The German artist Käthe Kollwitz (1867–1945) also produced some of the most striking and enduring images of the human condition in the twentieth century. Using highly expressive tonal drawing and later using striking black and white woodcut prints, Kollwitz produced figurative images which intensified the portrayal of the dehumanizing suffering, poverty and starvation experienced by women and children before, during and after the First World War.

Though very different to the abstract, colourful and rhythmic work of artists such as Kandinsky, the later work of Kollwitz can also be described as a form of Expressionist art. Whereas the work of Kandinsky created abstract states of mind through abstract coloured shapes, Kollwitz's highly visceral images evoked intense emotions including confusion, fear, isolation and grief.

4.10

4.10
Death and the Mother, directed by Ruth Lingford (1988), resembles the work of Käthe Kollwitz in both style and subject matter.

133

A famous example of her work included a poster image known as *The Survivors* (1923). The poster was designed to commemorate the outbreak of the First World War and shows children huddled with a mother figure that almost resembles the Grim Reaper (death). All the figures in the painting look quite lifeless, with dark eye sockets, which in some cases are bandaged over.

The animation director Ruth Lingford used similar techniques to Kollwitz in her film *Death and the Mother* (1988), based on a Hans Christian Andersen fairy tale, depicting a mother struggling to save her child from death. This was an early example of digital drawn animation, which like the woodcut prints of Kollwitz used high contrast black and white marks to add to the intense visceral feelings of the story.

Lingford's later film *Pleasures of War* (1998) combined the same woodcut print style with a digital collage and montage of real war footage. The film shows how a female victim of war becomes so dehumanized that she becomes equally violent, using her sexuality to seduce and take vengeance on her oppressors. The film suggests how women, men and children can become equally conditioned and militarized by the horrors of war.

German Expressionism also encompassed a modernist film movement that emphasized intense psychological feelings of anger, fear, anxiety, despair, paranoia and madness that emerged out of the same impoverished inter-war period and environment as the work of artists such as Käthe Kollwitz. Moreover German Expressionist film reflected "the institutionalized madness of German life" (Stam, 2000, p. 78).

From around 1919–1933 filmmakers such as Fritz Lang and Robert Wiene looked at how the modern industrialized and militarized world was repressing feelings of mounting frustration and anger, which could emerge from anyone in perverse and sinister ways. We only need to think of the erotic images from Ruth Lingford's *Pleasures of War*. Under the irrational ideology of Nazism, the sanity of many of those in power was brought more into question than those repressed under it.

The Cabinet of Dr. Caligari directed by Robert Wiene (1919) is one of the most famous examples of German Expressionist film. It is a story about a 'freakshow' exhibit called the Cabinet of Dr. Caligari. The exhibit is a man in death-like sleep whose murderous activities cause havoc in a small town.

Due to the limited funds for production, the director could not afford realistic film sets. Instead, highly stylized, theatrical sets were created containing exaggerated angular buildings with intense shadows painted onto them partly for dramatic effect. (The influence of *The Cabinet of Dr. Caligari* is evident in the films of Tim Burton, such as *The Nightmare Before Christmas*, 1993.)

There are parallels here with cubism, not only in the level of abstraction, but also in drawing attention to the stylized methods of the director rather than concealing them. If anything, these methods enhanced the madness and drama of the narrative, creating in many ways a sense of the state of mind of the murderous and crazed-looking character called Cesare. Amongst the many visual and narrative devices, the film is also told through the use of flashbacks.

❝Lang's films consistently depict an entrapping, deterministic world in which the characters are controlled by larger forces and internal desires beyond their understanding. In this cruelly indifferent world, people struggle vainly against fate and their own repressed inclinations towards violence. As in Hitchcock's films, Lang's often deal with the violent potential lurking within the respectable citizen and suggest that social order requires controlling the beast within.❞
Barry Keith Grant (2007), *Film Genre: From Iconography to Ideology*, p. 71

FROM THE MUNDANE TO MURDER: OTHER ASPECTS OF MODERNISM

Whilst Lunn's four categories have opened up an extensive discussion about what may define modernism, as illustrated by a number of theories and movements, techniques and subject matter, these categories by no means cover all aspects of modernism—nor can this one chapter come anywhere near to fully explaining such a complex range of concepts.

However, one of the main things to have been reinforced about modernism so far is how the artists of different movements looked beyond the conventional narrative themes and structures of genre to focus on the self-expression of individual experiences. However, what is also important to note is how the subject matter of many forms of modernist expression also focused on the minutia (small details) and humdrum (routine activities) of everyday life.

In her book *The Human Condition*, Hannah Arendt had described how the labour of the 'slave' in the *private realm* of the home was concealed from society. For centuries, however, artists such as Vermeer and great novelists such Mary Ann Evans (1819–1880), known famously for her novel *Middlemarch* (1874) written under her pen name George Eliot, had explored the activity and politics in the everyday lives of laborers and women using the principles of realism: to depict things as they were without heavily romanticizing them.

Vermeer used the semantic association of objects, while Mary Ann Evans used similar principles of interweaving plots to those used later by Virginia Woolf to create deeper layers of meaning. However, modernist novelists, artists and filmmakers were able to explore the deeper *psychological* significance of mundane objects, as well as a greater level of abstraction in the activities and feelings of those people traditionally 'hidden' in the private realm of the home.

> **"Modernism is, however, by its very nature multifaceted, and characterized by the invention, dissolution and recombination of genres and their boundaries."**
> Jeff Wallace (2011), *Beginning Modernism*, p. 1

MODERNISM: THE END OF GENRE

'M' is for Murder

4.11
'M' directed by Fritz Lang (1931). A scene introducing the audience and a young victim to a child murderer. The use of shadows was one of the defining devices for creating narrative meaning in German Expressionist films.

The German Expressionist filmmaker Fritz Lang was one of the most influential filmmakers of the twentieth century. One of his most powerful films, *'M'* (1931), illustrates how he could masterfully create deeply psychological scenes filled with suspense out of the mundane (uninteresting) details of everyday life. Lang's films, and the films of other German Expressionist directors, also explored many of the same fears and morals as fairy tales, while adding a whole new repertoire of stylistic and psychological storytelling techniques.

Allegedly based on real events, *'M'* is the story of a city living in fear of a child murderer known in the film as Hans Beckert. In the first ten minutes of the film he introduces himself to a young female character called Elsie, without his identity being revealed to the audience, through the clever casting of his shadow over a street poster that warns the public about him, then followed by long shots of him in his hat with the young girl who is bouncing a ball along the sidewalk.

Lang builds up a *shared suspense* of the inevitable disappearance of Elsie using a long slow montage of her mother nervously awaiting her return from school and shots of the stranger buying Elsie a balloon. The staging of the mother and daughter's home is reminiscent of Vermeer's typical compositions of domestic labor.

The mother is depicted in her routine preparation of dinner for her daughter and doing the laundry by the window of the room. The mother's mounting concern that Elsie is running late is indicated through the intercutting of her looking out of the window, checking outside the front door of their flat as other residents come and go and laying the table, as well as several references to a shot of a clock on the wall.

As the mother's panic mounts, we hear her voice calling out several times for 'Elsie', with increasing intensity set against an otherwise silent montage of empty spaces, looking down the stairwell of the block of flats, across the attic spaces where laundry is dried and to a table set with an empty plate and a seat for Elsie. Then, finally, the sequence cuts to a shot of the Elsie's ball rolling out from under a bush and the balloon she was bought by the child murderer caught in some telephone lines—leaving the audience with the powerful suggestion of the girl's murder.

Lang uses various forms of tonal and intellectual montage in this sequence. He also employs the use of dynamic high and low camera angles known as the 'German angle', as well as high contrast lighting and shadows and obsession with clocks and time typical of German Expressionist film. All these aspects add to psychological intensity of the montage and unfolding plot, which is even more unnerving due to the everyday familiarity of the shots that make up the horrifying sequence.

Many of the deeply psychological narrative techniques and approaches of mise-en-scène used by German Expressionist filmmakers influenced the period of filmmaking now known as film noir in the United States (as discussed in chapter three). Fritz Lang immigrated to America along with many other filmmakers fleeing the Nazi regime and war in Europe, where he made several noir films.

CASE STUDY:
ZOI

Zoi (2013) directed by Amanda Curl, BA (Hons) Animation, University of Bedfordshire

Production team: Duncan Patterson, Charlene Spence, Joel Coomber

Music & sound: Peter Fabri (running time: three minutes)

The abridged notes below are from the workbooks compiled by students who made the 3D animated short *Zoi*. These explain how and why they incorporated various modernist influences amongst others in the production. They focused on German Expressionist film in particular, which lends itself well to the medium of computer animation, as the filmmaker has so much control over camera and lighting. *Zoi* can be viewed on Vimeo: http://vimeo.com/69160811

4.12
Zoi, directed by Amanda Curl, BA (Hons) Animation, University of Bedfordshire, 2013.

INTRODUCTION

COFFEE, STEAM & TANKS: PUTTING MODERNISM IN CONTEXT

SPACE, TIME & REALITY: DEFINING MODERNISM

WORKBOOK EXERCISE 4.1

WORKBOOK EXERCISE 4.2

FROM THE MUNDANE TO MURDER: OTHER ASPECTS OF MODERNISM

CASE STUDY: ZOI

CASE STUDY: WHEN THE DAY BREAKS

WORKBOOK EXERCISE 4.3

CHAPTER SUMMARY & FURTHER READING

Workbook Notes by Amanda Curl

Synopsis: *Zoi* is an allegory about an oppressed factory worker struggling against the system and with his own conscience, realizing that he must become part of the system in order to beat it. This anthropomorphic short draws influence from German Expressionist film, Charlie Chaplin, Stanley Kubric and real life experience.

Identity & Character Design: For my major project I am collaborating with three other animation students to direct a 3D animated film that attempts to explore the subject of identity that is lost and then found again, through the story of a creature breaking free from a mundane task he is forced to undertake in an evil factory. The film is based on my own personal experience of discovering a much more creative way of life than that of working for a large corporation. I feel that such a life-changing event is something other people will be able to relate to.

The book *Jane Eyre* (1847) by Charlotte Brontë has always been a favourite of mine, because the female character Jane is very independent and self-reliant, which is unusual for the time it was written. It has been seen as an influential feminist text because of this. My first intention was to have a female worker, either based in an office or a factory,

struggling with her mundane day-to-day situation before discovering an object that would lead her to leave this existence. My aim was to show a contrast between the mechanical actions she was performing and the passionate thoughts in her head.

However, I am finding that it is less important to make it explicit whether the character is female or not, as I think this could lead to explorations of feminism and women's rights, which are subjects that interest me, but would take away the focus of the film being about the ability of the individual to find the power to make change. I am also worried about my technical abilities—to be able to create a very realistic human character that is capable of conveying deep emotions—in my chosen medium of 3D animation.

So I have taken the decision to design a creature using anthropomorphism. This decision is the most important one I have made, as it I believe it will influence all other aspects of the film. I have designed a frog-like character, based on research into nocturnal animals, as I want the film to be set in a dark building, and so need a creature that will look as if it would inhabit this type of place. I feel the character design is the part of the film design that I am most pleased with so far.

Narrative Influences: I was initially heavily influenced by the German Expressionist film *Metropolis* directed by Fritz Lang (1927). The film is set in a futuristic city where society is divided in to two classes: the workers and the planners. The workers' environment is a vast underground factory full of machines, while the planners' environment is a more utopian and palatial world.

In *Metropolis* the workers are shown as having no independent thought or life of their own, by the way they mechanically go to work with their heads bowed and marching as if they were one unit. This is the kind of acting that I will try to get across in my characters. In *Metropolis* a female worker predicts a prophet will come to unite the divided classes. She and a planner fall in love and have to stop a robot created by an insane scientist from preventing these predictions.

CASE STUDY:
ZOI (continued)

4.13

Set Design Influences: Another source of inspiration was the film *The Cabinet of Dr. Caligari*, directed by Robert Wiene (1920). The exaggerated sets almost give the houses personalities, with doors becoming like the gaping jaws of creatures. A mouth-like entrance is also used in the film *Metropolis*, through which chained workers are dragged.

We have been inspired to do something similar (see fig. 4.13), because I think it is something an audience could empathize with—the feeling of being swallowed up by the place you work. We have decided that the factory and the machines inside will also be used in this way so that the factory itself, or the factory whistle, potentially becomes the main antagonist of the film. The sets in our film will also be used to convey atmosphere and meaning and to give an insight into the psyche of the characters.

The factory in the film Zoi is intended to look very metallic and angular so that it is the opposite of the rounded organic character of Zoi. We have chosen orange rusty tones for the textures, to create a good colour contrast to the blue-grey of the character. It has been a struggle to make the factory interior as dark and as shadowy as we wanted, in keeping with the German Expressionist style, but still make it bright enough to show all of the action.

Plot Devices: The clock in our film is also influenced by the use of clocks in the film *Metropolis*. The clock in the factory was designed on a large scale not only to reinforce the passage of time but also bring attention to the mortality of the creatures (see fig. 4.14). The creatures' work will involve removing faces from photographs on a conveyor belt to represent the loss of identity of others trapped 'in the system', using the everyday object of an office stamp, while the monotonous job they are doing also has the effect of removing their *own* identity (see fig. 4.15).

The crucial moment in our film will be when the character finally snaps and can no longer stand doing the work in the factory. Montage will be used to compress time and show how the main character is beginning to feel the pressure of his work, by switching between images of the clock ticking, the whistle watching his every move, and finally the horror of realizing what his job has led him to—with the intention of creating the same intense feelings in the audience.

4.14

4.15

4.13–4.15
Zoi, directed by Amanda Curl,
BA (Hons) Animation, University
of Bedfordshire, 2013.

CASE STUDY:
ZOI (continued)

2001: A Space Odyssey, directed by Stanley Kubrick (1968), has formed part of my research as it also contains a machine that is a villain, trying to destroy the hero. The film's theme is of the human condition and evolution. Primitive ape becomes man, and man becomes a future being. The spaceship's computer HAL evolves a personality and a sense of self-preservation, something that man and ape both share.

HAL is the ultimate symbol of a system that goes wrong. Although HAL is a computer, of which we see only a red eye and a voice, he is very much a main character, just as the whistle character with red eyes that supervises the frogs in my film has become more of a central character (see fig. 4.16 & 4.17). In fact, HAL seems more human than the astronauts of the film, with his neurotic behaviour. It is the humans that act in a mechanical method, in their everyday tasks, rather like the workers in *Metropolis*.

4.16–4.18
Zoi, directed by Amanda Curl, BA (Hons) Animation, University of Bedfordshire, 2013.

Workbook Notes by Duncan Patterson

Narrative Influences: Our film narrative has many parallels to Chaplin's *Modern Times.* We have referred to Chaplin's tramp character working on a production line conveyor belt, struggling to keep up with its increasingly fast pace after the factory president orders the speed of the belt to be increased.

Although these two films can be directly compared in terms of narrative, they couldn't be further apart when we look at the genres/ movements of the films. Chaplin turns a stressful situation into something of a comedy, as his tramp character loses control on the assembly line and runs riot in the factory tightening anything resembling the shape of bolts with his hand tools. However, in our film we will see both a physical breakdown of the factory clock as well as a psychological breakdown of the character, using a more expressionist combination of influences.

Initially the factory setting alone was designed to show Zoi's entrapment, but as more research goes into the developing the narrative of the film, looking particularly at films such as *I, Robot* and *WALL•E*, we have been realizing that all of our influences featured a character which was not human but a technological or mechanical system. A system which knew only of what it had been programmed to do, but in some cases a system which learns to ignore it's programming, turning against its 'master' or 'programmer'.

Music & Sound: In Amanda's original storyboard animatic there is a small steam whistle on top of the factory summoning the creatures to work. This was a really interesting idea as the piercing sound alone of the steam whistle can help create an intense atmosphere that is ideally suited to German Expressionism. We are working closely with a musician/ sound designer to develop an intense soundtrack of atonal music to add to the dramatic tension.

4.18

143

CASE STUDY:
WHEN THE DAY BREAKS

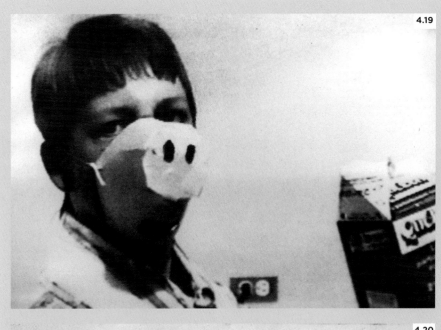

4.19

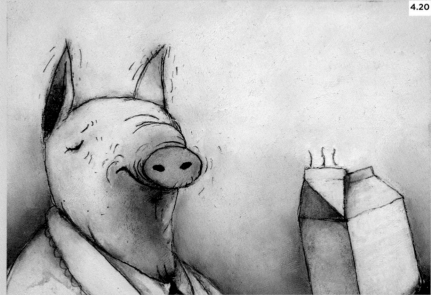

4.20

We will now look at a professional case study of an animated short that demonstrates a masterful combination of painterly expressionist techniques, elements of cubism and montage, with the concepts of the private realm, city life, dehumanization, anthropomorphisis, interweaving narratives and a simple but fascinating comment on the human condition.

When the Day Breaks was directed and animated by Wendy Tilby and Amanda Forbis (National Film Board of Canada, 1999). The animated short tells the story of two strangers living in a city, a female pig and male chicken, whose brief encounter with one another changes both lives forever.

4.19 & 4.20
When the Day Breaks, directed and animated by Wendy Tilby and Amanda Forbis, National Film Board of Canada (1999). The images illustrate the process of rotoscoping in the animation.

INTRODUCTION

COFFEE, STEAM & TANKS: PUTTING MODERNISM IN CONTEXT

SPACE, TIME & REALITY: DEFINING MODERNISM

WORKBOOK EXERCISE 4.1

WORKBOOK EXERCISE 4.2

FROM THE MUNDANE TO MURDER: OTHER ASPECTS OF MODERNISM

CASE STUDY: ZOI

CASE STUDY: WHEN THE DAY BREAKS

WORKBOOK EXERCISE 4.3

CHAPTER SUMMARY & FURTHER READING

Both characters set out to buy some groceries. The pig is in a hurry and accidentally bumps into the more reserved chicken as they cross paths entering and leaving a grocery store. This distracts the chicken as he goes to cross the road, and he is killed by an oncoming car. The audience then experiences a montage of images and sounds that indicate what has happened, which then lead into a montage of memories from the chicken's life.

After witnessing what has happened, the pig returns home in a hurry, where she contemplates how her innocent actions affect others. The audience experiences her thoughts by viewing a semi-abstract and rhythmic montage of electric wires, telephone cables and drains leading from one home to another, where other anonymous characters go about their daily activities. The film essentially illustrates how everyone's lives and actions are interconnected.

The film is distinctive for its simple yet multi-layered narrative and also for the diverse range of animation techniques that it uses. Combined with a 1930s-style sound track, the piece is highly atmospheric. The narrative is open to a level of interpretation, but leaves the audience with a distinct feeling rather than a specified moral message.

All of the characters and most of the sequences in the film are created and animated by painting over printed out video footage of real actors, whose heads and main features are replaced by those of different animals— essentially a form of rotoscoping (drawing or painting over live action footage; see figs. 4.19 & 4.20).

The montage sequence of memories and some of the backgrounds are formed of individual painted-over photographs, medical and scientific diagrams and elements of collage. The semi-abstract sequence of the pig's internal thoughts is also somewhat diagrammatic, resembling blueprints from technical manuals.

The soundtrack includes a range of pastiche (imitation), upbeat, gentle jazz and big band songs popular in the 1930s. These songs were a form of escapism from an era defined by the poverty of the American Great Depression and act as a useful counterbalance to the drama in the animation.

The soundtrack also pays close attention to a range of sound motifs, such the noise of the subway and police sirens that reinforce the impersonal nature of the city environment, while the noises of domestic appliances, electricity and dripping taps reinforce the humdrum nature of our everyday lives. The lack of dialogue also helps the audience to focus on the atmosphere of the piece.

CASE STUDY:
WHEN THE DAY BREAKS (continued)

**Interview with Wendy Tilby & Amanda
Forbis on *When the Day Breaks***

As previously discussed, one of the defining aspects of modernist literature, art and film was to focus on the minutia of everyday life. In the film *'M'* director Fritz Lang juxtaposes the mundane domestic objects and everyday chores of the mother in the home with the events leading up to the murder of her daughter. The montage of the empty spaces in the block of flats, the daughter's abandoned toy ball rolling out from under bush and her balloon caught in telephone cables symbolize her murder.

We can see parallels in *When the Day Breaks*, when the imminent death of the chicken is represented by one of the lemons he has bought and dropped falling down the drain, leading into a montage of his possessions scattered over the road and the memories of his life. But what are the mundane domestic objects used to represent, particularly in the sequence depicting the pig's internal thoughts after she has returned from the public realm to the privacy of her flat?

Just as one can glean much about a person by studying the items in their shopping basket, Ruby the pig learns about the chicken by seeing his groceries strewn on the road. Those commonplace artifacts are the pathway to the more symbolic imagery of his physical being, his thoughts and his past. We wanted

4.21

to suggest an entire life laid on the road—bones, experience and personality intermingled with eyeglasses, lemons and cans of soup.

When Ruby returns to her flat following the accident, she feels alone and traumatized. The sight of the bowl of potato peels and the chair lying on its back are reminders of her innocence before the accident. She locks the door and draws the shade in an effort to close off the world which, at that moment, feels dangerous and hostile.

Drawn by the sound of her electric kettle, her mind escapes through the walls and wires she shares with her neighbours. She imagines their mundane domestic activities and the intertwining tangle of pipes and circuitry that connects her, ultimately, to the chicken's empty flat and the remnants of his breakfast. Along with running water and electricity, she senses and is reassured by the common current of human experience that courses through the city.

Mundane objects and mundane activities tie the larger points in the narrative together. We very much wanted to suggest a parallel between the organism that was the chicken and the organism that is the city. Though made up of flesh and bones and vessels, the spirit of the chicken is in his groceries, his thoughts, or his grandfather—just as the city is 'animated' by its inhabitants shaving, ironing or watching a hockey game.

INTRODUCTION

COFFEE, STEAM & TANKS: PUTTING MODERNISM IN CONTEXT

SPACE, TIME & REALITY: DEFINING MODERNISM

WORKBOOK EXERCISE 4.1

WORKBOOK EXERCISE 4.2

FROM THE MUNDANE TO MURDER: OTHER ASPECTS OF MODERNISM

CASE STUDY: ZOI

CASE STUDY: *WHEN THE DAY BREAKS*

WORKBOOK EXERCISE 4.3

CHAPTER SUMMARY & FURTHER READING

4.22

4.22
Shot from montage sequence illustrating the death of the chicken character in *When The Day Breaks*.

CASE STUDY:
WHEN THE DAY BREAKS (continued)

You self-consciously reveal your filmmaking methods to the audience in a similar way to the cubists Picasso and Braque. What is the reason for doing this, what do all the different techniques from collage to painting over video print outs add to the narrative? Is it to play with our senses, and our sense of reality?

The use of video in *When the Day Breaks* very much shaped the film. We had experimented with various styles and techniques before discovering the video printer. We were immediately attracted to the photographic images that were neatly contained in film-like strips. As we had both previously been 'under camera' animators, drawing and painting directly onto these images (without tracing) appealed to our need for spontaneity yet gave us more control. It also allowed us to respond to the photographs, which was both constraining (in a good way) and fun.

Most importantly, the technique inspired us to change the characters into animals. Beaks, snouts and large pointed ears were much more interesting to draw than subtle human features. In our minds, the transformation to animals rationalized the rotoscopy. Also, the photo-realism retained in some of the backgrounds lent substance to the characters and the city and gave the film a gritty documentary tone that we felt suited the story.

As detailed backgrounds were technically challenging, we made a point of avoiding wide shots. To counter the claustrophobic effect of close ups, we created 'postcard' paintings of wide cityscapes which we shifted directly under the camera. The same method was used to depict the chicken's ancestors.

Video was also not an option for the more surreal sequences so we looked for interesting ways to realize our ideas that would be in keeping with the character scenes. Images of bones, cells and blood vessels were derived from medical illustrations while the pipes and wires were line drawings that we squashed or stretched using the photocopier then inverted digitally to create a dark, blueprint look. With the exception of the pipes and wires, we unified the look by rendering in paint.

Although in many ways timeless, there is a general sense from the soundtrack, clothing and vehicles that the film could be set sometime between the 1930s and 1950s. Was this purely for personal nostalgia, or was there an aspect of this period such as modernist literature, film or art that particularly inspires you, or was this just an intuitive mix of techniques and ideas?

We didn't deliberately set the story between the 1930s and '50s but would agree that it seems of that era. This is partly due to the limited palette but also because we couldn't resist a good fedora hat. The music is deliberately nostalgic. When we were growing up in the '60s, musicals were still a big part of the cultural landscape and we are both very fond of the genre. The power of the musical is that it can encapsulate an emotion and translate it into lush, full-throated song. Wouldn't we all love to express ourselves by belting out a tune and dancing down the street?

INTRODUCTION

COFFEE, STEAM & TANKS: PUTTING MODERNISM IN CONTEXT

SPACE, TIME & REALITY: DEFINING MODERNISM

WORKBOOK EXERCISE 4.1

WORKBOOK EXERCISE 4.2

FROM THE MUNDANE TO MURDER: OTHER ASPECTS OF MODERNISM

CASE STUDY: ZOI

CASE STUDY: WHEN THE DAY BREAKS

WORKBOOK EXERCISE 4.3

CHAPTER SUMMARY & FURTHER READING

We were also greatly inspired by Dennis Potter's series *The Singing Detective*. Potter understood the beauty and strangeness of contrasting the sweet optimism of a 1930s pop song with harsh reality. We were trying for something similar in *When the Day Breaks* and asked our composer, Judith Gruber-Stitzer, to compose three songs—one for each act of the film.

The first, *When the Day Breaks*, expresses Ruby's easy cheer. The second piece is an instrumental that falls outside the 1930s pop style. It has a haunted, wistful tone that underscores the chilling aftermath of the accident and Ruby's vision of the chicken's life. The third number, *Prairie Blue*, is the most nostalgic of all, evoking a lost bucolic paradise as we move through the guts of the city.

Anthropomorphic animals are commonly used in animation. Animation directors such as Hayao Miyazaki use anthropomorphic animals to explore the tensions between mankind and the natural world. Animation directors such as Suzie Templeton have used animals to symbolize different human qualities. What is the main purpose of the anthropomorphic characters in *When the Day Breaks*—was it in any way a means of illustrating the dehumanizing aspects of modern life?

The original story featured humans, but we found ourselves struggling to create a simple, appealing female character who was not primarily defined by her age and attractiveness. Turning Ruby into a pig solved the problem immediately. As we both love animals, the animation process was instantly

much more fun and the animal characters brought lightness and comic potential into the dark story. Also, we liked the notion of turning the convention of animals in cartoons on its ear in that, unlike Wile E. Coyote, the chicken does not bounce back after being hit by the car.

It was not our intention to suggest that these characters had been dehumanized. To our minds, 'animalizing' them had the opposite effect. As animals, they were warmer, funnier and more sympathetic. That said, we were also interested in the notion of farm animals in the city, far away from their rural roots. Just after the chicken dies, we see a bucolic scene of blue skies and pastures. For us, this is a glimpse of the chicken's afterlife but it also hints at the pig's nostalgia for a (supposedly) safer, simpler time.

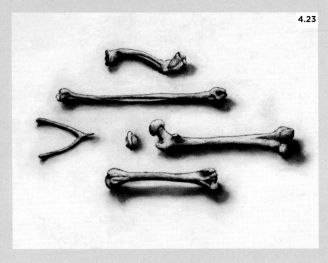

4.23

4.23
Shot from montage sequence illustrating the death of the chicken character in *When The Day Breaks*.

WORKBOOK EXERCISE 4.3:
EXPERIMENTING WITH ROTOSCOPING,
ANTHROPOMORPHISIS, MONTAGE & SOUND

This exercise explores a combination of techniques from *When the Day Breaks* with a German Expressionist film. It also looks at how these techniques affect the audience. Furthermore, it builds on the semiotic and narrative set design exercises from chapter one by thinking about how a montage of objects within a space creates narrative meaning.

- Take a series of screen shots from the Odessa Steps montage sequence in *The Battleship Potemkin* or the opening montage sequence from '*M*'.

- Print out the screen shots and paint into them taking influence from *When the Day Breaks*. Replace the heads of the main characters with hand painted or collage animal heads, thinking carefully about the mythical associations of different creatures, e.g., a wolf to represent evil characters, a rabbit to represent both fear and (ironically) good fortune.

- Change the objects in the close-ups, for example replace the empty plate of the child in '*M*' with an uneaten carrot.

- Drop the montage images into an editing time line (also try a random reordering of shots).

- Add a jazz soundtrack such as *Mack the Knife*, composed by Kurt Weill, lyrics by Bertolt Brecht (1929); pay close attention to the lyrics.

- Add sound motifs such as gunshots or kitchen sounds, depending on the choice of film.

- Write down audience reactions to how your edit of the sequence changes the perception of the relationship between the Soviet troops and civilians in *Potemkin*, or between the girl, murderer and mother in '*M*'.

- Write down audience reactions to how the music and sound motifs change the mood or intensity of the sequence.

- Write down audience reactions to how the painting onto shots and anthropomorphic animal heads affect the impact of the piece. Does it make it easier or harder to watch?

Further Reading

Wells, P. (2009) *The Animated Bestiary*, Rutgers University Press: London

INTRODUCTION

COFFEE,
STEAM & TANKS:
PUTTING
MODERNISM
IN CONTEXT

SPACE, TIME
& REALITY:
DEFINING
MODERNISM

WORKBOOK
EXERCISE 4.1

WORKBOOK
EXERCISE 4.2

FROM THE
MUNDANE TO
MURDER: OTHER
ASPECTS OF
MODERNISM

CASE STUDY:
ZOI

CASE STUDY:
WHEN THE DAY
BREAKS

WORKBOOK
EXERCISE 4.3

CHAPTER
SUMMARY
& FURTHER
READING

4.24

4.24
Student exercise illustrating example of exploring
a combination of techniques from *When the
Day Breaks* with film footage from *'M'*, directed
by Fritz Lang (1931); Michael Evans, BA (Hons)
Animation, Cass Faculty, London Metropolitan
University (2014).

CHAPTER SUMMARY & FURTHER READING

Whilst there is a stylistic element to the look of many modernist art forms, the important thing to remember is that the techniques are used to express deep feelings, abstract ideas and narrative meaning. Form follows function. Picasso's cubist paintings looked the way they did because he was trying to express how the world could be understood from many perspective viewpoints, but also to reflect that the sense of human self was being fragmented and destroyed by war.

Animation was born out of experimentation with forms such as shadow puppetry, optical toys such as the zoetrope and stop motion visual effects in early film, but mainstream animation very quickly became an industrialized process, synonymous with the popular comedy and fairy tale genres of the large commercial studios. Dominant animation techniques included principles of classical realism such as perspective, anatomy and fluid movement in hand drawn form.

Historically however, as we have seen, many independent animators have preferred to work with a range of techniques that reflect more modernist approaches in film, art and design. Survage and Russell's work experiments with expressionist colours, shapes, rhythms and sensations. Animation artists including Sturtevant, McIntosh and Bass explored cubist-like approaches to design. Directors such as Ruth Lingford and Tim Burton incorporated the intense influences of expressionism in their filmmaking.

In each case we can see how animation can uniquely combine principles of realism and modernism, by blending film methods with principles of painting and sound. Animators perhaps more than any other kind of artist are able to play with space, time and emotion—by squashing and stretching human form, editing sequences in any order they please and using sound to evoke abstract feelings.

This complete flexibility in many ways defines animation as a modernist art form, through its unique combination of technology, self-expression and storytelling. Animation was once perceived as being limited to including only a few genres, such as fairy tale and comedy, or even simply as being a genre in itself. But in fact, we can now see that within animation there is the potential to identify as many genres, sub-genres and art movements as in any other area of the arts.

The final chapter will include discussion of a particularly distinctive and increasingly popular genre, animated documentary, which juxtaposes aspects of realism and modernism to produce something both factual and expressive. But before discussing animated documentary, in the next chapter we will first explore how governments learned to control people using the emotive tools of propaganda and realism in order to continue driving the agenda of capitalism.

❝Animators, drawing upon a fine art background, not merely explore approaches and stylings, but also self-consciously explore theoretical principles and ideas generated within fine art, and play them out afresh using the animated form. This has already been noted in the ways that animators use expressionist, impressionist, cubist and surrealist approaches and so on.❞
Paul Wells (2002), *Animation Genre and Authorship*, pp. 36–37

FURTHER READING

Marxism

Lunn, E. (1984) *Marxism and Modernism*, University of California Press: Berkeley

Smith, D. & Evans, P. (1982) *Marx's Capital for Beginners*, Writers and Readers: London

Modernism, Cubism & Expressionism

Acton, M. (2004) *Learning to Look at Modern Art*, Routledge: Abingdon

Behr, S., Fanning, D. & Jarman, D. (1993) *Expressionism Reassessed*, Manchester University Press: Manchester

Wallace, J. (2011) *Beginning Modernism*, Manchester University Press: Manchester

Montage & Suspense

Adams Sitney, P. (1990) *Modernist Montage*, Columbia University Press: New York

Eisenstein, S. (1949) *Eisenstein, Film Form*, A Harvest/HBJ Book: New York

Smith, S. (2000) *Hitchcock, Suspense, Humour and Tone*, British Film Institute: London

German Expressionism

Eisner, L. (2008) *The Haunted Screen*, University of California Press: Berkeley

McGilligan, P. (1998) *Fritz Lang: The Nature of the Beast*, Faber and Faber Ltd.: London

Film Theory & Genre

Duff, D. (2000) *Modern Genre Theory*, Pearson Education Ltd: Harlow

Grant, B. (2011) *Film Genre: From Iconography to Ideology*, Wallflower Press: Brighton

Stam, R. (2000) *Film Theory: An Introduction*, Blackwell Publishers Ltd: Oxford

Wells, P. (2002) *Animation Genre and Authorship*, Wallflower Press: London

Wells, P. (2007) *Understanding Animation*, Routledge: London

Modern, Modernist & Experimental Animation

Amidi, A. (2006) *Cartoon Modern*, Chronicle Books: San Francisco

Bass, J. & Kirkham, P. (2011) *Saul Bass: A Life in Film & Design*, Laurence King: London

Pilling, J. (2012) *Animating the Unconscious*, Wallflower Press: London

Russel, R. & Starr, C. (1998) *Experimental Animation: Origins of a New Art*, Da Capo: London

Wells, P. (2009) *The Animated Bestiary*, Rutgers University Press: London

Miscellaneous

Chion, M. (2001) *Kubrick's Cinema Odyssey*, British Film Institute: London

4.25

4.25
Wayang Kulit, Shadow Puppet Show, Malaysia. Shadow puppetry has existed for centuries all around the world. A precursor to animation, cut out puppetry continues to find popularity in modern digital and craft-based animation.

KEY WORDS

Aesthetic
Artistic experience of viewing an image or listening to music

Anthropomorphic
Giving animals human physical attributes or using particular animals to symbolize certain human qualities

Collage
Pasting together pieces of paper and materials of different textures onto the canvas

Commodities
Objects made for profit rather than practical use

Cubism
The exploration of representing a person or object from several different angles in one image, to reflect changes in how we perceive the world through new technology and forms of transport, using new techniques such as collage

Empiricism
A school of thought based on first-hand sensory experience

The Enlightenment
A period of intellectual reform (a change in the way we think about things) from late 16th to late 18th century

Expressionism
A modernist art movement, in which images exposed the flat plane of the canvas, the paint marks and subconscious mind or *internal* world of the artist

German Angle
Dynamic high and low camera angles often used by German Expressionist filmmakers

German Expressionism
Modernist film and art movements that emphasized intense psychological feelings of anger, fear, anxiety, despair, paranoia and madness experienced in inter-war Germany

Juxtaposition
Meaningful contrasts of images, and/or words, sounds etc.

Limited Animation
An animation technique using more exaggerated key frame poses and sometimes radical, seemingly illogical in-betweens

Marxism
A body of influential theories by philosopher Karl Marx on modern society, economics and politics

Mimesis
The accurate representation of our *external* reality

Modernism
A modern visual language of more subjective, diverse and abstract forms of artistic expression, in reaction to the huge, global, political, scientific and technological changes in the first half of the 20th century

Montage
An editing technique similar to the shot-coundershot, which juxtaposes different images to evoke abstract, raw internal emotions

Quantum Theory
Planck's theories that challenged perceptions of matter and observable reality

Rationalism
A school of thought based on logical reasoning of the mind

Realism
A specific art movement in the 19th century that strived to represent reality as closely as possible

Rotoscoping
Drawing or painting over live action footage

Shot-Counteroshot
The standard process of editing from a shot of an actor to the view that they see

Socialism
Political ideas for empowering the working classes, partly informed by Marxism

Suspense
The buildup of emotional tension, often through the use of montage in film

Theory of Relativity
Einstein's theories that challenged perceptions of space-time

Twelve Tone Method
A modernist approach to musical composition, not written in any particular key, and with chords made of clashing as opposed to harmonic notes

KEY NAMES

Saul Bass
Tim Burton
René Descartes
Charles Dickens
Eyvind Earle
Albert Einstein
Sergei Eisenstein
George Eliot
Oskar Fischinger
Amanda Forbis
Sigmund Freud
Alfred Hitchcock
Wassily Kandinsky
Käthe Kollwitz
Fritz Lang
Fernand Léger
Ruth Lingford
John Locke
Eugene Lunn
Karl Marx
Bob McIntosh
Otto Preminger
Pablo Picasso
Max Planck
Erica Russell
Arnold Schoenberg
Baruch Spinoza
Sterling Sturtevant
Léopold Survage
Wendy Tilby
Robert Wiene
Virginia Woolf
Joseph Wright of Derby

KEY WORKS

Christmas Carol, A
Anatomy of a Murder
Battleship Potemkin, The
Cabinet of Dr. Caligari, The
Coloured Rhythm
Composition in Blue
Composition VIII
Death and the Mother
Experiment on a Bird in the Air Pump, An
Guernica
'M'
Metropolis
Middlemarch
Mr. Magoo
Mrs. Dalloway
Pleasures of War
Psycho
Sleeping Beauty
Survivors, The
Tim Burton's The Nightmare Before Christmas
Triangle
Typewriter, The
When the Day Breaks
Zoi

CHAPTER FIVE
REPRESENTATION: FACT VERSUS FICTION

CHAPTER OVERVIEW: INTERROGATING NARRATIVE FUNCTION

In this chapter, you will learn:

- How knowledge and information is communicated to us through the media and how this shapes our identity and beliefs.

- How propaganda is used to exaggerate and distort facts and truths in both the still and moving image.

- How advertising has used the same principles as propaganda to shape our opinions and identities and to condition us as consumers.

- How advertising, entertainment and gaming have perpetuated harmful stereotypes and how animators are able to challenge these stereotypes.

5.1
World War I lithograph poster (1917) encouraging people to use less cooking fat in order to aid supplies to troops. The poster reflects methods in which image and text have been used in both propaganda and advertising to similar effect.

INTRODUCTION

In the last chapter we looked at how the technology of the industrial revolution, First World War and modern science had changed society irrevocably. We explored how artists had reacted against these developments and the established traditions of genre and realism in the arts, with new forms of self-expression in modernist literature, music, painting, film and animation.

Looking at a range of case studies we examined how principles such as cubism and montage had been used to communicate the horrors of war, from the massacre of innocent civilians to the more personal tragedies of individuals. In all instances we have understood how conventional narrative structures and belief systems were challenged by artistic practices that evoked emotional rather than rational responses from their audiences.

Identity formation and 'otherness' are the underpinning themes of this chapter. We will discuss how knowledge and information is communicated to us through the media and how this shapes our identity and beliefs. In turn, we will look at how societies will often alienate those whose cultures, lifestyles and values deviate from those held as the established norm.

In breaking down the different ways in which our public identity or persona and values are formed, we will consider the notion of the home, or private realm, and how the political actions of the public realm (introduced in chapter three) have now invaded every aspect of our personal lives through the pervasive nature of modern media. We start by thinking about home in the broadest sense as the region we grow up in and the communities we are part of, then move to our private identities and interactions in the home itself.

We will begin by looking at the function of propaganda and how it is used to exaggerate and distort facts and truths in both the still and moving image, by referring to First World War propaganda posters and the animation *The Sinking of the Lusitania* by Winsor McKay. We will see how the art of Socialist Realism has also been used by communist states to condition people to believe in a prevailing government ideology. We will contrast this with the animation *Tale of Tales* by Yuri Norstein, which opposed the censorship endured by artists who did not work within the restrictions of Socialist Realism.

We will then look at how advertising has used essentially the same principles as propaganda to evoke an emotional response from the spectator, shape our opinions and identities and condition us as consumers. In doing so, we will consider how the media often misrepresents people and how advertising, entertainment and gaming have perpetuated certain harmful stereotypes and aspirational myths about the society we live in.

Once again, we will discuss the idea of authorship, with a particular focus on issues of representation, and will consider how animators have not only perpetuated stereotypes of ethnicity and gender, but also how they have been able to challenge them. We will consolidate discussion around the purpose and nature of animated sitcom, with examples including *The Boondocks*, *Family Guy*, and the cartoon series *The Powerpuff Girls*.

The chapter also includes a student case study that provides an example of how issues of representation and propaganda have informed an original and off-the-wall campaign by a social organization to promote the production of community-owned enterprises in West Africa to a global market. The case study illustrates how viral advertising can be used in a positive and ethical way that challenges preconceptions of identity and benefits producers and consumers without the hard sell of a brand.

The first workbook exercise in this chapter explores how we can use the natural qualities of stop motion in advertising to create myths about the lifestyle associated with certain types of products. The second exercise is designed to encourage critical analysis and discussion between you and your peers about issues of representation in animated sitcom.

INTRODUCTION

HAMMERING
IT HOME:
PROPAGANDA
& SOCIALIST
REALISM

THE IDEAL
HOME:
ADVERTISING

WORKBOOK
EXERCISE 5.1

HOME SWEET
HOME: TV
SITCOM &
GAMING

WORKBOOK
EXERCISE 5.2

CASE STUDY:
MAKE BAOBAB
FAMOUS

CHAPTER
SUMMARY
& FURTHER
READING

KEY WORDS,
NAMES & WORKS

RECOMMENDED VIEWING

Betty Boop, created by Max Fleischer, Fleischer Studios (1930–1939)

Dot, produced by Sumo Science, Aardman (2010)

Family Guy (*Husband, Father, Brother*, Season 3 Episode 14), created by Seth MacFarlane & David Zuckerman, 20th Century Fox Television (1999–)

Good Times, created by Mike Evans, Norman Lear & Eric Monte, Bud Yorkin Productions (1974–1979)

Gulp, produced by Sumo Science, Aardman (2011)

Lara Croft Tomb Raider: The Cradle of Life, directed by Jan de Bont, Paramount Pictures (2003)

Scrub Me Mamma with a Boogie Beat, directed by Walter Lanz, Universal Pictures (1948)

Tale of Tales, directed by Yuri Norstein, Soyuzmultfilm (1979)

The Boondocks (*Good Times*, Season 4 Episode 2), created by Aaron McGruder, Adelaide Productions (2005–)

The Cosby Show, created by Bill Cosby, Bill Cosby (1984–1992)

The Fresh Prince of Bel Air, created by Andy Borowitz & Susan Stevenson, NBC Productions (1990–1996)

The Incredibles, directed by Brad Bird, Pixar (2004)

The Powerpuff Girls, created by Craig McCracken, Hanna-Barbera Productions (1998–2005)

The Sinking of the Lusitania, directed by Winsor McKay, Universal Film Manufacturing Company (1918)

HAMMERING IT HOME:
PROPAGANDA & SOCIALIST REALISM

Propaganda

5.2

5.2
Uncle Sam, 'I Want You' US
Army recruiting poster (1917)
by James Montgomery Flagg,
one of America's most famous
propaganda poster artists.

The term 'propaganda' is usually used
to describe the spread of exaggerated
or false information that is presented
as true fact through the media, by
governments or organizations trying
to persuade the public to support
political ideology and political actions.
The meaning of the term 'propaganda',
however, has changed in its emphasis
and usage.

Today it generally has a negative
association with war, but it was
originally a term used by the Catholic
Church in the seventeenth century
to *propagate* or spread the Catholic
faith around the world in reaction to
the rise of Protestantism. The idea of
propagation or spreading of knowledge
can also be extended to other actions,
such as raising awareness of the work
of charitable organizations or educating
the public about how to prevent the
spread of diseases.

It was not until the First World War that
the concept of propaganda and its term
became commonly used to describe the
strategic, systematic and relentless
use of every form of media possible by
governments to build up a picture of
a threat to peace at home by a foreign
enemy, and to persuade pacifist peoples
into supporting military action against
other nations.

Posters would often depict alleged or fictional atrocities and dramatized military scenarios rendered as semi-realistic images to rouse a general sense of public fear, or use allegorical images such as a German troop crushed under the weight of a British coin, to encourage the public to invest in government bonds to help finance Britain's role in the First World War. Other nations, including America and France, ran similar poster campaigns.

Edward Bernays (1891–1995) was the Austrian-American nephew of Sigmund Freud. Bernays was one of the most influential minds on propaganda. His knowledge on manipulating public opinion—which incorporated the psychoanalytical theories of his famous uncle, who examined the repressed emotions, fears and desires of the subconscious mind—was used extensively in propaganda by the American government during the First World War.

Posters with provocative images and simple bold text were used to arouse deep prejudices, incite racial hatred and perpetuate a state of fear and anxiety about the activities of other nations. In his book *Propaganda*, Bernays explains that the repetition of information all around us reinforces a set of ideas as the norm. Further, using emotive images to create a state of fear makes it easier for people to believe in false information. These methods were also used extensively by Nazi and Allied propaganda in the buildup to and during the Second World War.

Propaganda can also be used to boost morale and build a collective sense national pride based on a *consensus* of romanticized ideals around national identity. A prime example is the iconic image of 'Uncle Sam' dressed in the motifs of the American flag, used by the United States government to encourage men to enlist in the armed forces during the First World War. The poster singles out the individual spectator with a pointed finger to reinforce a sense of patriotism with the jingoistic caption "I Want You" (see fig. 5.2).

" The manipulators of patriotic opinion made use of the mental clichés and the emotional habits of the public to produce mass reactions against the alleged atrocities, the terror, and the tyranny of the enemy. It was only natural, after the war ended, that intelligent persons should ask themselves whether it was possible to apply a similar technique to the problems of peace. "
Edward Bernays (2005), *Propaganda*, p. 55

PROPAGANDA IN ANIMATION: *THE SINKING OF THE LUSITANIA*

The Sinking of the Lusitania, made in 1918 by pioneering American animator Winsor McCay (1867–1934), is one of the prime examples of early propaganda in animation. The animation essentially served as news footage of the sinking of a British civilian ocean liner by a German submarine in 1915 during the First World War. The *Lusitania* was carrying a large number of American passengers, several of who were prominent figures in sport, the arts and philosophy.

"Germany, which had already benumbed the world with its wholesale killing, then sent its instrument of crime to perform a more treacherous and cowardly offense."—Caption card from *The Sinking of the Lusitania*

McCay's prolonged semi-realistic animated sequence, rousing classical music soundtrack and embellished caption cards can be seen as a clear attempt to later recreate but also dramatize actual events for which there was no real film footage. The animation was generally promoted and accepted as the 'first record' of actual events.

Although the real event did not directly provoke American involvement in the First World War, the animation can be viewed as a clear example of propaganda, used to rouse patriotism in American and British Allies and stir anti-German sentiment. The level of realism employed in the creation of the animated images of people falling from the stern of the sinking ship may have had a similar impact on the viewer as did the horrific real footage of people jumping from the Twin Towers during the 9/11 terrorist attack in New York. We will revisit this animation in chapter six when discussing animated documentary.

5.3

5.3
The Sinking of the Lusitania, animation directed by Winsor McCay (1918). The animation was generally promoted and accepted as the 'first record' of actual events.

Socialist Realism

Socialist Realism is a form of painting and visual communication (as well as music and literature) that was used in the production of propagandist hyperrealism—realistic yet often stylized images that enforced a very clear state ideology on citizens—an ideology of a strong youth and hard work generating a better future and the national supremacy of a country over other nations.

Such ideology was particularly important to governments in countries such as Russia and Germany after the collapse of their monarchies and economies following the end of the First World War. Socialist Realism was used to reinforce a new national ideology based on the need to rebuild the countries' infrastructures and national pride.

Images typically depicted bright, youthful, peasant men and women harvesting crops, alongside workers involved in construction and dynamic looking military troops. These images often appeared as giant paintings or posters in state buildings and around cities. The hammer and sickle became recurring motifs in these images, symbolizing national unity between peasants and workers, and was featured on the flags of Soviet states from around 1923 until the fall of their union in 1991.

5.4

Socialist Realism had emerged in various forms throughout Europe, but became part of state policy in the Soviet Union during the 1930s in the buildup to the Second World War under the Soviet leader Joseph Stalin. As in Germany and Austria under the authority of Adolf Hitler and the Nazi Party, under Stalinist rule many modernist works of art and ambiguous forms of individual artistic expression were heavily censored, banned or destroyed.

Socialist Realism spread to many communist states as the dominant form of art. It also influenced other forms of cultural expression, such as civic architecture and monuments, which reflected a sense of simplicity, solidity and permanence. The legacy and practice of Socialist Realism can still be seen today in communist countries such as North Korea (see fig.5.4).

5.4
Propaganda posters using the conventional style, ideology and subject matter of socialist realism, Pyongyang, North Korea (photo by Shelda Cohen, 2010).

Tale of Tales:
Socialist Realism & Censorship

Although post-war changes in Russian government gave rise to a more liberal period of artistic expression in the 1950s, the legacy of such censorship of art, film and literature in Russia continued during other political eras well in to the 1970s and 1980s. Yuri Norstein (b. 1941) is one of the most famous Russian animation directors to have been faced with such censorship.

Norstein began his professional career as an animator for the Russian animation studio Soyuzmultfilm in 1961. Animation did not generally face the same level of state censorship of its scripts as film or literature, as it was largely viewed by the authorities as children's entertainment rather than a political art form. However, Norstein's work did cause controversy.

He was born in Russia during the Second World War. His family was Jewish. Although they were not deported to concentration camps like many Jews throughout Europe, he grew up in an era still dogged by anti-Semitic prejudice after the war. Norstein was sheltered from much of this prejudice by his parents as a child, but his later films reflected his deeper awareness of the impact of these traumatic conditions on his life, the life of his father and others around him.

Norstein started to gain recognition in the 1970s for directing a series of animations that experimented by combining cut out stop motion puppets with expressively drawn and painted textures on layers of animation cel (transparent plastic sheets traditionally used to create the ink traced and painted version of the rough animation). The simple folkloric stories such as *The Hedgehog in the Fog* (1975) had a dream-like quality to both their visual style and narrative techniques.

Norstein really established his reputation as a director with his animation *Tale of Tales* (1979), which received widespread critical acclaim at many international festivals. Russian author Lyudmila Petrushevskaya wrote the initial film treatment for Norstein. Her script focused carefully on the positive feelings and memories of childhood, a theme that was accepted by the state censors and sponsors. Norstein's wife Yarbusova was responsible for the visual style of the film, developing the dream-like qualities similar to Norstein's earlier films.

During production, however, Norstein experimented with a more abstract narrative structure informed by his love of poetry, particularly Japanese poetry. The film is made up of an eclectic mix of scenes that represent a web of memories, tracing the impact of the Second World War on the community in the Maryina Roshcha district of Moscow, where Norstein grew up.

An open-air summer party is the subject of possibly one of the most nostalgic and haunting sequences of the film. Tables are laid out with tablecloths and bottles of wine, as couples dance under streetlamps to the gentle somewhat melancholy sounds of a male singer, an accordion and clarinet playing the wartime tango *Weary Sun*.

The sequence then develops a more foreboding atmosphere. One by one the men are transformed into soldiers wearing military capes, floating away from their dancing partners as a draught somewhat symbolically unsettles the tablecloths. The sequence concludes with an abstract impression of the sound and lights from the trains that took troops away to war.

Whilst Norstein's film was not overtly political it had, somewhat intentionally, largely become an abstract criticism on postwar Russian society. Happy childhood memories, and many of the scenes in the film, came to represent the disappearance of communities and lost values, as areas of the city were demolished and redeveloped.

Such imagery was at odds with the optimistic and clear messages of the original treatment that satisfied the ideology of Socialist Realism. Thus, there was mounting concern by the state censors over the ambiguous and potentially subversive nature of the story. The film therefore faced various challenges before the Russian authorities officially allowed its release.

Image, Text, Otherness & Consent

Perhaps the main conclusion we can draw about the function of Socialist Realism and propaganda is that the prime aim is to create images of a hyper-real world with no room for any doubt or imagination. Doubt is total taboo! The medium controls the consumer!

Roland Barthes (whose work on the concept of 'myth and meaning' of images in modern society was covered in chapter two) argued that it is the accompanying text that forms the critical component of an image. The image of 'Uncle Sam' or animation footage in *The Sinking of the Lusitania* on their own could have any number of connotations (be interpreted in any number of ways). But it is the text with which they are paired that ultimately denotes (indicates) meaning.

The popular loyalty-building image of Uncle Sam could, for example, have easily been produced as part of a German propaganda campaign, with the caption 'I want to kill you'. Or the same footage from *The Sinking of the Lusitania* could have been made with German captions heralding the heroic bravery of the submariners and the triumph of killing key figures from the enemy nations.

The moral supremacy of one nation is often depicted as an image of a heroic act that commands respect or by an atrocity committed by the other nation that provokes condemnation. In each case a caption denotes how the viewer should respond or what they should consent to believe in order to help validate retaliation or attack and defeat of the enemy.

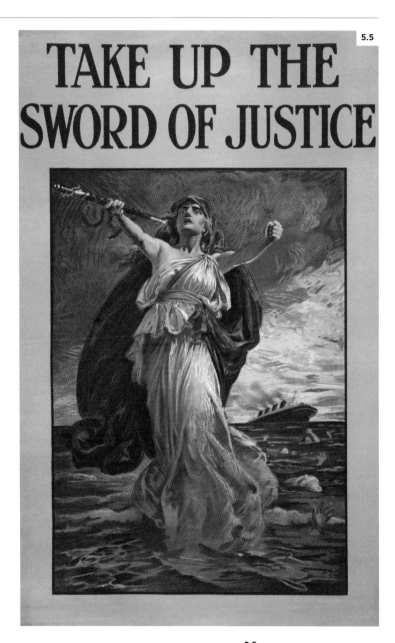

5.5

5.5
British World War I poster illustrating the sinking of the *Lusitania* (1915). The melodramatic image and text are a clear example of propaganda.

One of the key principles of political propaganda, therefore, is to project the idea of 'otherness'. As we have seen in previous chapters on folklore and fairy tale, this is how we collectively project our fears of the unknown onto strangers, who according to the structuralists operate on the principle of binary opposites (see chapter two).

The French philosopher Jacques Derrida (1930–2004) argued that there is always a dominant binary, indicating the normality or moral supremacy of the first binary over the second. Therefore, propaganda is used to build up an 'us and them' scenario, whereby it is always 'them' that are the aggressor and threat to the peaceful and humanitarian values held by 'us'.

In many cases this is known as 'moral relativism' (Chomsky 2002, p. 78), whereby terrorist acts of violence by a more powerful government are self-justified as a defense against the supposed terrorist actions or even unsubstantiated threats of another less powerful government or organization.

The American writer and political commentator Walter Lippman (1889–1974) was a key critic of the American government's propaganda machine. He defined the use of news media by governments and large organizations to filter facts and influence public opinion as the 'manufacture of consent'. The American philosopher and political commentator Noam Chomsky later popularized and explained this term and concept in a book of a similar title.

People who do not share commonly inculcated values (ideas repeatedly reinforced by society) and speak out against them often have their views ridiculed or censored and become socially isolated by governments, large organizations and society itself. In modern society these practices still play out in politics and war, but for a long time they have also established particularly powerful ways for governments and large organizations to manipulate public behaviour by not only controlling the news media, but also advertising and entertainment.

❝❝A propaganda model focuses on this inequality of wealth and power and its multilevel effects on mass-media interests and choices. It traces the routes by which money and power are able to filter out the news fit to print, marginalize dissent, and allow the government and dominant private interests to get their messages across to the public.❞❞
Edward Herman & Noam Chomsky (1994), *Manufacturing Consent*, p. 2

CHARLIE HEBDO: SATIRIZING ONE, AND FILTERING OUT THE 'OTHER'

In many societies minority groups often become the scapegoats for irrational tensions and fears. The Jewish populations in countries throughout Europe became the scapegoat for many of the economic and cultural tensions during the period between the two world wars, leading to the Holocaust—the mass slaughter of Jews in concentration camps by the Nazis.

Today the media in western society often stigmatizes Muslims, who fall victim to the conflict between Islamists (Islamic fundamentalist groups) and western governments. Satirical cartoons may ridicule deeply held beliefs, but can be damaging by generating ill-informed stereotyping, and therefore can be dangerous by perpetuating harmful prejudices such as Islamophobia.

On January 7, 2015, two gunmen of Algerian origin stormed the Paris offices of the satirical weekly French newspaper *Charlie Hebdo* and shot dead eleven of the staff working there. The abhorrent attack was a reaction to the newspaper's ongoing satirical commentary on Islam and offensive cartoon portrayals of the Prophet Muhammad, whose depiction is forbidden by the Islamic faith.

The public responded immediately with mass vigils and peaceful protests throughout European cities, which also remembered a further six murders by the gunmen in the same week. Members of the public carried distinctive black banners with white and grey text declaring 'Je suis Charlie', to show solidarity for the victims of the attacks. The banners became a symbolic stand against attack on the freedom of speech.

The events that week raised a number of important questions about the popular press. Firstly, there was discussion about the responsibility that comes with freedom of speech and the fine line drawn between this and propaganda. The attacks highlighted the extraordinary degree of influence and responsibility held by a very small group of people in one small circulation publication. But, equally, it illustrated how the global reach of the Internet has become a propaganda machine of 'the people', as innumerable cartoons satirizing the shootings paired with the caption 'Je suis Charlie' were posted online by the public.

The massacre underlined the power of cartoon image and text as a propaganda tool, prompting the question of whether the satirical images of Muhammad could themselves be deemed as an act of aggression, by 'othering' a minority faith group in Western Europe. The attacks were also followed by the global distribution of a poster on the cover of a newspaper memorial edition, depicting the Prophet Muhammad rather than an image of the gunmen with the phrase 'All Is Forgiven', further confusing Islam with religious extremism and terrorism.

Events also exposed a disturbing deeper aspect of propaganda covered extensively by Chomsky, which is how selective the media can be on reporting one atrocity while neglecting another. In the very same week of the Paris attacks, the massacre of two thousand innocent civilians in the town of Baga in Nigeria by the Islamist group Boko Haram went virtually unreported by the western press. Paris was much closer to home. But above all this was a week that exposed the extraordinary power of the cartoon image in shaping and expressing public feelings.

5.6

5.6
Iconic text 'Je Suis Charlie' used as banners in solidarity for victims of the *Charlie Hebdo* attacks in Paris. The text also accompanied many cartoon images drawn and uploaded to the Internet by the public in support for the right to freedom of speech.

THE IDEAL HOME: ADVERTISING

Advertising: Mass Psychology, Expert Advice & Celebrity Endorsement

Bernays' analysis of propaganda also underpinned many forms of advertising that developed between the First and Second World Wars. His legacy is so significant that he became known as the 'Father of public relations'. Public relations is a term that came to be used in advertising and politics in place of the word propaganda, to avoid negative associations with warfare.

In his book *Propaganda*, Edward Bernays outlined methods used by psychologists to identify how information could be used systematically to affect human behaviour and the habits of the consumer. The following section of this chapter considers and interprets some aspects of Bernays' insights as to how advertising has used many principles of propaganda to condition us as consumers of products, using powerful emotional tactics such as mass psychology.

Advertising often relies on habitual consumer choices born out of the security of purchasing something that is endorsed by a 'trusted' source of information or respected celebrity role model. Dentists are often used to recommend the benefits of toothpaste brands, for example, whereas beauty products, razor blades, dietary supplements or footwear are frequently promoted by famous celebrities or sports personalities, who claim that a certain brand helps improve their concentration, confidence and performance on stage or on the sports field.

Bernays highlighted how the choices we make are also often not the conscious or rational decisions that we might believe them to be. Rather they are driven by impulsive emotions, governed by mass psychology—that is, the way we are collectively conditioned to absorb 'artificial' values that are *repeatedly* presented to us as the norm and in such a way that the need to think for ourselves is removed or swayed by following the *subconscious* perception of what 'everyone else' is doing.

So, more often than not, we subconsciously develop brand loyalty to products not on the rational basis of their price, quality or usefulness, but because we believe in a complex web of ideas that we have repeatedly absorbed through the bombardment of our senses by an ever-growing network of media tools, from digital advertising hoardings to Internet viral videos. This is essentially the same way that posters were repetitively used by 'trusted' governments during the First and Second World Wars to build up a climate of national pride or nationalism.

Increasingly, advertising enhances not only the appeal of a product to the consumer, but also acts as a powerful public relations tool that reinforces the profile of the celebrity endorsing it to an almost mythical status. What is problematic for the consumer is how this creates an artificial and increasingly unobtainable aspirational social stereotype, which comes to represent the perceived norm. We keep buying things in order to try and 'keep up' our appearance with society and avoid becoming the spectacle of otherness ourselves.

5.7

5.7
Times Square, New York, United States. The public space popular with tourists is saturated with digital advertising promoting global brands and Broadway theatrical shows.

INTRODUCTION

HAMMERING
IT HOME:
PROPAGANDA
& SOCIALIST
REALISM

THE IDEAL
HOME:
ADVERTISING

WORKBOOK
EXERCISE 5.1

HOME SWEET
HOME: TV
SITCOM &
GAMING

WORKBOOK
EXERCISE 5.2

CASE STUDY:
MAKE BAOBAB
FAMOUS

CHAPTER
SUMMARY
& FURTHER
READING

KEY WORDS,
NAMES & WORKS

Lifestyle & Morality: Happiness, Anxiety & Public Goods

We can begin to see that many of our decisions made about the material goods we buy are driven by the desire to associate ourselves with aspirational activities or personalities, which reinforce our own social status and identity. Another trend we have witnessed in advertising today is an emphasis on how digital technology has blurred the boundaries between work and leisure, and how this depicts or imposes upon us a new set of values and aspirations about how we live.

We are probably all too familiar with the relentless touch screen technology brand advertisements that project the ideology that mobile technology enables us to achieve a healthy, carefree life-work balance. For example, imagine a youthful adult depicted completing her work day walking home along the seafront taking a digital photograph of a playful and cool urban activity such as parkour.

She then sends the photo to her editorial team at the fashionable design agency she works for as the front cover of the next edition of a magazine. Finally, she makes videophone call to her partner—who is smiling, waving and blowing bubbles with their child on a hammock—to let them know that she is on way home. The self-conscious hazy lighting and lens flare in all the shots gives a sense of warm summer memories captured on an old-fashioned home movie camera.

5.8

5.9

5.8 & 5.9
A fictional advertisement illustrating how the mechanisms of propaganda are used in modern advertising of consumer goods, such as mobile technology, to sell us a lifestyle over the product itself.

169

This is a fictional advertisement, but it exposes a series of common desirable clichés often used to create a myth about buying into a lifestyle. Bernays identified that it is the *lifestyle* associated with a brand, rather than the product itself, that is used to persuade us to purchase consumer goods. This lifestyle is of course very appealing, but is also very socially desirable.

Identity and social status allied to leisure time is nothing new. It was something that brought great anxiety to many people in Victorian Britain (1837–1901), for whom promenading at seaside resorts or discussing the latest opera that they had been to demonstrated their wealth in terms of their ability to afford leisure time and aspirational leisure activities.

In the twenty-first century social media and advertising has perpetuated similar anxiety. It is the 'fear of missing out' on socially desirable experiences that becomes a part of the driving strategy in much advertising, with slogans such as 'while limited stocks last' and 'sell-out performance' further prompting an anxious rush to purchase. Therefore, we live once again in an era where our identity has become defined as much by the demonstration of leisure time activities as the impossible pursuit of a permanent state of happiness through the purchase of material goods.

In his book *Endless Propaganda*, Paul Rutherford illustrates how our social conscience, freedom of speech and thoughts have also become commoditized and controlled by the media. He uses the term 'public goods' to refer to a growing trend by which charitable organizations are using the media in the same way as advertising to promote awareness of their causes. This now extends to the demonstration and essentially even the purchase of our moral beliefs and humanitarian concerns through social media.

The 'Ice Bucket Challenge' social media campaign (2014) for the ALS Association (Amyotrophic Lateral Sclerosis) involved public demonstration of support for raising awareness of the condition by pouring an ice-cold bucket of water over the heads of celebrities, who then donated to the charity. The campaign went viral due to the socially desirable nature of public demonstration of social conscience, pursuit of fun and association with celebrity. Critics were soon asking why it was necessary for individuals to feel the need to publicly demonstrate that they gave to charity. Patrons of charities such as Water Aid also highlighted the moral complexity of using water in such a way, when the shortage of clean water in so many parts of the world is something that also is deserving of greater public awareness.

The campaign highlighted the positive effect propaganda can have on provoking public action. However, it also demonstrated how powerful the influence of large organizations and social media continues to be on the manufacture of consent over people's moral beliefs, as well as both public actions and private actions in the home.

❝All publicity works upon anxiety.❞
John Berger (1972), *Ways of Seeing*, p. 137

Nostalgia: Motifs & Leitmotifs

Let us imagine another fictional technology commercial using a number of trends in advertising. Cardboard cutouts emerge from a pop-up book using a stop motion aesthetic. As the screen fills with a carnival of craft, we hear a soundtrack of carefully layered leitmotifs. There is an upbeat rhythm of hands clapping as a banjo strikes up a loop of gentle rhythmic chords and a xylophone harmonizes with someone whistling a light-hearted melody. The pop-up book then closes and is transformed into a shiny digital tablet surrounded by a range of craft tools and materials.

We are left with a nostalgic feeling of an innocent and simpler childhood era, when there was 'more time' for craft activities and learning musical instruments. In a 'time poor' generation, we begin to form the impression through such advertising that the tactile interactive nature of the tablet will enable us to rediscover our own childhoods.

As with the expressive and emotive use of experimental animation discussed in the last chapter, we see once again how the tactile and playful nature of stop motion in particular is a powerfully emotive way of appealing to a broader audience in a modern culture obsessed with digital technology. Thus, the irony is that in order to sell technology or a modern lifestyle, it is that human connection and association with real tactile materials, human sounds and traditional ways of life that has an ever more potent nostalgic appeal to the consumer in an accelerating technology saturated age.

5.10

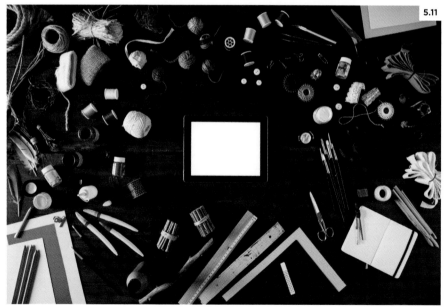

5.11

5.10 & 5.11
A fictional commercial illustrating how the use of stop motion has become increasingly popular in advertising to create nostalgic associations with simpler and more human lifestyles in a rapidly accelerating world saturated with digital technology.

WORKBOOK EXERCISE 5.1:
DECONSTRUCTING ADVERTISEMENTS & VIRALS

The trend of combining the tactile qualities of a stop motion or 2D pop-up book aesthetic with the sounds of simple musical instruments has extended beyond commercials for digital technology to the promotion of brands and services from a broad range of companies, including food products and eco-friendly organizations, for whom the need to appear down to earth, friendly and wholesome has become ever more important. Many use the format of lighthearted 'infomercials', incorporating playful motion graphics comprised of stylized charts and diagrams.

1. Try making a list of advertisements and virals that are made using stop motion or 2D pop-up animation, as well as nostalgic leitmotifs such as whistling, clapping, xylophone etc.

2. For each one note down what the advertisement or viral is promoting, e.g., touchscreen technology, food products or eco-friendly organizations.

3. Note down the time duration of the animation as well as the number of shots and their duration (or stages for a continuous sequence).

4. List out the key facts or brand values (e.g., lifestyle benefits) presented against a beat board of screenshots for each of the shots or stages from the animation.

5. Comment on how effective you think the commercial is in communicating a clear message and whether you think the sound and visuals used are appropriate to the brand or are simply copying stylistic trends.

6. Now try to identify other trends in advertising that use a different combination of animation techniques and musical structures for particular kinds of product, services or organizations.

"Just as during the war, propaganda would at once exalt the nation and advance the civilizing process, teaching immigrants and other folks of modest means how to transform themselves, through smart consumption, into happy and presentable Americans."
Mark Crispin Miller (2005), *Propaganda* (Introduction), p. 13

INTRODUCTION

HAMMERING
IT HOME:
PROPAGANDA
& SOCIALIST
REALISM

THE IDEAL
HOME:
ADVERTISING

WORKBOOK
EXERCISE 5.1

HOME SWEET
HOME: TV
SITCOM &
GAMING

WORKBOOK
EXERCISE 5.2

CASE STUDY:
MAKE BAOBAB
FAMOUS

CHAPTER
SUMMARY
& FURTHER
READING

KEY WORDS,
NAMES & WORKS

The American Dream
& Issues of Representation

The US government and large corporations used public relations and advertising extensively to encourage consumerism (the buying of commodities) in order to reinvigorate the American economy during the Great Depression of the 1930s and also after the Second World War. Promoting a materialistic lifestyle was achieved under the guise of 'educating' the population on how to improve their living standards and live in pursuit of happiness.

This was a concept that built on what was known as the 'American Dream', and was one that became embedded in the national psyche—a belief in social mobility, amongst other things—that anyone could afford a better life and happiness through hard work. However, consumerism shifted the emphasis from achieving social mobility and happiness through hard work, to also achieving the same goals through the purchase of material goods. This was a stark contrast to the propaganda of Socialist Realism used by communist governments, which promoted the belief that a better future could be achieved for *everyone* on the basis of *collective* hard work.

Just as today, much of western manufacturing and advertising of products from the 1930s to the 1950s focused on technology for the home. Advertisements encouraging the purchase of domestic goods would often depict how these items could improve lifestyle in the home, making household chores such as cooking and cleaning easier—and freeing up more time for leisure activities.

Advertising agencies also consciously perpetuated stereotypical gender roles. Invariably, the products would be endorsed by the trope (overused cliché) of a carefree, well-dressed, happy housewife seeing to the needs of her husband, who might be depicted relaxing in an armchair with a newspaper after a busy day at the office. The consumer was not only buying into a lifestyle, but the media was also shaping their sense of gender, gender roles and overall identity.

5.12

5.12
Advertising in the 1950s used images of the 'ideal home' and family to encourage the purchase of commodities by the public. Advertising of commodities in the 1950s often featured the trope of the 'happy housewife'. Advertising therefore not only influenced lifestyle aspirations, but also gender roles.

THE INCREDIBLES & THE AMERICAN DREAM

The Incredibles (Pixar, 2004) is in part a parody (tongue-in-cheek caricature) of how the consumer culture of interwar and postwar America is still relevant today, but also how many of the gender stereotype roles associated with it are now being challenged. The film is based on the comic book superheroes of the 1950s and has many references to the 1950s and 1960s design era. The narrative highlights how a family of superhero 'outsiders' tries to blend in with 'normal' consumer society.

The father in particular struggles with living in a house and lifestyle cluttered by consumer objects, activities and values—not least assuming the stereotypical role of office commuter dad, while the mother contends with the stereotypical housewife role heavily perpetuated by advertising in the 1950s. Symbolically, in the end we see the mother come to the rescue of the father's escapade, which essentially represents the western male midlife crisis and emerging modern female empowerment.

Commodity Racism

THE ORDER OF THE BATH

"Use PEARS' SOAP for the Skin & Complexion"

5.13

The mechanisms and binary tropes of American cultural imperialism (imposition of values from one dominant culture on others, often through the export of commodities that include forms of entertainment such as film and television) can be traced back to the cultural imperialism of other nations, in particular the British Empire.

The Zimbabwean born, white, feminist scholar and academic Anne McClintock has written extensively on issues of gender, race, class and imperialism. In her famous book *Imperial Leather: Race, Gender and Sexuality in the Colonial Contest*, McClintock points to the propagandist use of images and text to promote the commodities exported by large trading companies.

The propagandist use of advertising by large British trading companies was largely done with the intention to build national pride and to promote the 'superiority' of the British Empire over other nations. In particular, it was aimed at the indigenous peoples of the colonies from where many of the raw materials for the products were sourced.

5.13
Bath Time circa 1890, an advertisement for Pears' Soap. The caption 'The order of the bath' is a reference to an honor awarded by a British monarch to high-ranking military officers or senior civil servants for their service to the British Empire. The association of such text with products was commonly used by nations to reinforce a sense of national pride and cultural imperialism.

INTRODUCTION

HAMMERING
IT HOME:
PROPAGANDA
& SOCIALIST
REALISM

THE IDEAL
HOME:
ADVERTISING

WORKBOOK
EXERCISE 5.1

HOME SWEET
HOME: TV
SITCOM &
GAMING

WORKBOOK
EXERCISE 5.2

CASE STUDY:
MAKE BAOBAB
FAMOUS

CHAPTER
SUMMARY
& FURTHER
READING

KEY WORDS,
NAMES & WORKS

At the height the British Empire, consumer goods such as tea, coffee and soap flooded the market. The packaging and advertisements for many of these goods, which were primarily targeted at domestic users, perpetuated gender stereotypes in similar ways to the American products of the 1950s. However, they also created mythical associations with the exoticism of all the new products being imported from around the world that cluttered the homes of the Victorians.

McClintock used the term 'commodity racism' to describe how in the late 1800s brands such as Pears' Soap created harmful tropes of race in the promotion of their product. One of Pears' most famous advertisements depicted how the soap would cleanse black skin, thereby intimating the 'civilizing' impact of the supposed intellectually superior British Empire over the racist depiction of 'savage' and intellectually inferior populations of its colonies.

Such images permeated western popular culture and public perception of black cultural identity by white populations, with many animated cartoons perpetuating racist tropes of African-Americans well into the twentieth century. In 1948 the American cartoon producer Walter Lantz came under extensive criticism from a range of public pressure groups for releasing the cartoon *Scrub Me Mamma with a Boogie Beat*.

The cartoon depicts an African-American community called 'Lazy Town' with racist tropes of sleepy or lazy black men, women and children. The whole community is enlivened when a sexualized black female jazz singer steps off a paddle steamer. A musical sequence follows with a series of racist visual gags, including tropes of black children being washed in tubs reminiscent of the Pears' Soap advertisements.

The enduring legacy of commodity racism can still be seen through the promotion of products in western society today. Perversely, this is manifested through 'celebrating' rather than condemning otherness. Advertising and packaging may often unintentionally patronize the nations from which the products or raw materials are sourced, by the use of romanticized folksy motifs, sounds and tropes of developing nations. Whether used consciously or not, advertising can still be susceptible to reinforcing a deeply rooted sense of western intellectual superiority and romantic preconceptions of other 'less developed' cultures.

HOME SWEET HOME:
TV SITCOM & GAMING

Issues of Representation
in Domestic Sitcom

5.14

People had migrated to America for several centuries in the hope of a better life built on the promise of civil liberty (the rights to freedom of speech, fair trial, ownership of property etc.) and social mobility. But the reality of the modern economy was that capitalism had created extremes of wealth and poverty, particularly a racial divide in affluence, also attributable to the legacy of slavery. American documentary photographer and first female war correspondent Margaret Bourke-White (1904–1971) captured such division in her iconic photograph known as *Kentucky Flood* (1937).

The photograph is dominated by an American advertising billboard propagating the relatively true slogan "World's Highest Standard of Living", under which an image of an affluent well-dressed, well-fed, rosy-cheeked, Caucasian-American (white) family can be seen driving through the countryside in a shiny car. The image also includes the slogan "There's no way like the American Way".

5.14
The 1970s American television sitcom *Good Times*
used humor in the representation and examination
of the lives of black Americans in the Chicago
housing projects.

INTRODUCTION

HAMMERING
IT HOME:
PROPAGANDA
& SOCIALIST
REALISM

THE IDEAL
HOME:
ADVERTISING

WORKBOOK
EXERCISE 5.1

HOME SWEET
HOME: TV
SITCOM &
GAMING

WORKBOOK
EXERCISE 5.2

CASE STUDY:
MAKE BAOBAB
FAMOUS

CHAPTER
SUMMARY
& FURTHER
READING

KEY WORDS,
NAMES & WORKS

But what the photograph of this advert ironically and symbolically highlighted below the image of a wealthy, middle-class, Caucasian-American family, was a real line of destitute African-American men, women and children queuing for food and clothing following flooding in the state of Kentucky.

The poster itself is not a direct example of commodity racism in 1930s America. But the photograph illustrates how the media often misrepresents real life for many, or alienates whole sections of modern, increasingly multicultural societies by depicting what is an unobtainable level of financial security and way of life for many as the aspirational norm.

The complexity of the relationship between the American Dream and social mobility largely defines the subject matter of many television sitcom series. We will now consider how sitcom, including animation sitcom, often uses the domestic setting to document, analyse and challenge ideas around social mobility, with further analysis of how identity is affected by consumerism.

As discussed in chapter three, sitcom uses humor to explore and document real life situations or scenarios. *Domestic sitcoms* emerged on US and UK television from the 1930s onwards. Since the 1980s there has been a continuing growth in the number of prime time domestic sitcoms, such as *The Cosby Show* (USA) and *Only Fools & Horses* (UK); *Roseanne* and *Fresh Prince of Bel Air* (USA) in the 1990s and 2000s; and animated sitcoms such as *The Simpsons*, *Family Guy* and *The Boondocks* (USA).

English academic Andy Medhurst describes comedy as a 'social thermometer'. That is to say, many forms of comedy record changes in attitude towards different aspects of cultural identity—primarily those of class, ethnicity and gender. So, whilst sitcoms are essentially fictional, they provide an important way for society to examine itself, and to ridicule ourselves for our own commonly held and often repressed prejudices.

In countries largely defined by social mobility, American and British sitcoms often focus upon class conflict to drive the overarching narrative of a series, usually reinforcing white middle-upper class status and undermining working class values. Humor is achieved by contrasting the stereotypes of different classes, often by plunging an everyman protagonist from one class environment into another.

Class conflict then arises when the protagonist behaves in ways uncharacteristic of their new environment, creating a paradox whereby the stereotypical behaviour of each class is both confirmed and also challenged. Sitcom (and comedy in general) therefore has great power to either reinforce the status quo or, conversely, influence change in the commonly held values of society.

The Cosby Show (1984–1992), set around a professional middle-class African-American family called the Huxtables, was one of the most popular American television sitcom series of the 1980s. It was significant for the universal appeal of an all-black cast making prime time viewing on national and international television networks. It also marked an important shift from previous television sitcom series such as *Good Times* (1974–1979), which built narratives around the challenges faced by African-Americans living in the notorious Chicago housing projects.

However, critics have often accused *The Cosby Show* of creating "a misleadingly cozy picture, a sugar candy world unfettered by racism, crime, and economic deprivation" (Jhally, S. & Lewis, J. 1992, p. 2). The main criticism of the show has often been that it essentially reinforced and transferred white middle class concerns onto a professional black family, with little reference to the reality of the difficulties faced by many working class and/or African-Americans in achieving social mobility and the 'American Dream' in that era.

Later successful African-American domestic sitcoms such as *The Fresh Prince of Bel Air* or *The Boondocks*, have followed the challenging journey of the everyman from one social class structure to another. This creates a dynamic tension between preconceptions and prejudices around class and race, which are all too often synonymous in real life, but also in the representation of modern American and British society.

❝By presenting the Huxtables as hard-working, successful people who maintain their middle class existence comfortably and not pointing out the difficulties in becoming wealthy if you're black, the suggestion is that failure to be so successful is purely a personal matter. That is, by embodying the American Dream, the Huxtables imply that failure is nothing more than an individual trait.❞
Brett Mills (2005), *Television Sitcom*, p. 131

INTRODUCTION

HAMMERING
IT HOME:
PROPAGANDA
& SOCIALIST
REALISM

THE IDEAL
HOME:
ADVERTISING

WORKBOOK
EXERCISE 5.1

HOME SWEET
HOME: TV
SITCOM &
GAMING

WORKBOOK
EXERCISE 5.2

CASE STUDY:
MAKE BAOBAB
FAMOUS

CHAPTER
SUMMARY
& FURTHER
READING

KEY WORDS,
NAMES & WORKS

The Boondocks

The popular animated sitcom *The Boondocks*, created and written by Aaron McGruder, explores the influence of 'The American Dream' on modern black families by following two young brothers who move from the city and try to adapt to life in an affluent, predominantly white suburb with their grandfather. The characters are used to explore a number of controversial and complex issues in contemporary American society, often through the opposing views of the two boys.

The older brother Huey and his precocious left-wing politics often conflict with the values of his younger brother, Riley, that perpetuate the nouveau riche and hedonistic stereotypes more closely associated with gangsta rap. The contrast in attitudes between Granddad, also known as Robert Freeman, and a black character called Uncle Ruckus (who works for the Wunclers, the white property owners of the suburban estate) is also used to debate a number of issues around African-American identity.

Robert Freeman is portrayed as being generally submissive to white authority and exploited by capitalist culture— his attempted involvement as a soft young man in civil rights protests and surname being a clear reminder of the legacy of segregation and slavery on African-American identity. As an ironic contrast, Uncle Ruckus often creates commotion (as his name suggests) by violently rejecting black culture. This is continually reinforced by his humorous but tragic claim that he has 'revitiligo'—a fictional reversal of the skin condition vitiligo, the loss of pigment from the areas of the skin—inferring that he is actually a white man.

In the episode *Good Times* (season four), Granddad reveals to the children that he has run up serious debts, whilst at the same time trying to conceal the possibility of home repossession from them. The episode focuses on prejudices surrounding home ownership and the challenges of living in a predominantly white capitalist society.

The title of the episode and soundtrack are a direct reference to the 1970s sitcom series *Good Times.* This immediately gives a broader context to the plot and the events that unfold. The white landlord sublets rooms in the Freeman's home without their consent, relocating them to sleep in the garage in an attempt to resolve the Granddad's unpaid debts. This creates a tension in the episode that essentially ghettoizes the Freeman family within the affluent white suburb to which they belong.

This episode in particular is contentious. Some reviewers have criticized it on social media forums for a bizarre plot that involves the Freeman family ultimately signing themselves into slavery to pay off debts owed to the white landlord. The episode might be intended as a political comment on the fact that the legacy of slavery still runs deep in modern American society, with many people also bound to large organizations by crippling debts.

It also highlights an issue with authorship, as the first Boondocks season not to involve the original creator and writer. *Good Times* is a stark contrast to episodes in previous seasons. Rather than pursue socially progressive agenda, the episode perpetuates negative tropes of both black and white identity. In the previous season involving Aaron McGruder, the ironic hypocrisy of society as a whole is interrogated ruthlessly, but in such a way that it gives the audience more time to understand, if not agree with, the motives of the individual lead characters.

Whilst animated sitcoms such as *The Boondocks* and films such as *The Incredibles* present fictional accounts of modern American life, they highlight many of the issues faced by modern Americans regarding racial and gender stereotypes and the effect of capitalism on the modern family. Even so, there is the danger that parodying 'The American Dream' in sitcoms, and indeed academic debate itself, can perpetuate harmful unrepresentative norms and stereotypes or outdated criticism, depending on who the authors of the material are.

WORKBOOK EXERCISE 5.2:
DISCUSSING AUTHORSHIP & AUDIENCES

5.15

5.15
The animated television sitcom *Family Guy*
employs a cast of different character tropes to
parody and expose frequently conflicting values
or issues in modern American society.

INTRODUCTION

HAMMERING
IT HOME:
PROPAGANDA
& SOCIALIST
REALISM

THE IDEAL
HOME:
ADVERTISING

WORKBOOK
EXERCISE 5.1

HOME SWEET
HOME: TV
SITCOM &
GAMING

WORKBOOK
EXERCISE 5.2

CASE STUDY:
MAKE BAOBAB
FAMOUS

CHAPTER
SUMMARY
& FURTHER
READING

KEY WORDS,
NAMES & WORKS

Animation sitcom series such as *Family Guy*, created by Seth MacFarlane, often develop controversial plots that satirize and interrogate American values. The episode *Husband, Father, Brother* (season three) satirizes white prejudices around black identity, when the main character Peter Griffin grows concerned about his son developing the speech mannerisms of his black basketball teammates.

Peter Griffin decides to educate his son about his supposed Irish-American ancestry in a prejudiced attempt to counter his assimilation of black culture. But upon researching his family history, Peter Griffin discovers he has African-American ancestry. The episode focuses on a white male exploring his own identity through his naïve preconceptions of Irish and African-American culture and through a series of excruciating attempts to integrate with black society.

Family Guy and *The Boondocks* raise a number of interesting questions about the ethics and function of animated sitcom that are important for us to think about in devising characters, themes and narrative plots. The following questions and answers are extracts from a discussion between a mixed group of UK animation students. Try writing your own answers to these questions.

Audiences are generally fairly receptive to the use of stereotypes in animated sitcom. Do you think this is because they help us laugh at our own commonly held prejudices, rather than mock particular tropes? Do you find this treatment of such subject matter funny or sometimes offensive, and why?

Elora Aboua: People usually laugh at their own stereotypes and prejudices openly, but behind closed doors also laugh at the tropes of other groups. Personally I don't find it offensive at all—if I can relate to the prejudices. This is something that I see as a form of healing. It is good to laugh at things, time moves on, and unless it is clearly hateful then there is no problem.

Bartosz Kastner: For me it can be offensive, because serious issues can become so commonplace that people become desensitized to them. For instance the racially offensive use of the 'N word' has become trivialized as it is often used in the media, music, everyday life as an informal 'friendly' greeting.

***The Boondocks* is preoccupied with the human condition of a black male in a white capitalist society. *Family Guy* is preoccupied with a white male's naïve understanding of all identities that differ from his own. Do you think we still need to explore such issues or are we past this kind of debate?**

Elora Aboua: These are subjects that should be explored in sitcom, as it provides a safe environment for different viewpoints on otherwise difficult subject matter to be talked about. It teaches, informs and opens minds to different points of view.

Marsha Williams: Yes, we do still need to explore these issues, to educate all generations to share and understand different viewpoints. Especially when old-fashioned perceptions of 'all black people looking the same' are still perpetuated. For example in the *Family Guy* episode *Husband, Father, Brother* you get a few quick glimpses in various shots of over fifteen black characters who all had the same complexion, just different hairstyles. But when the whole Griffin family is shown together, we see a skin colour palette of several different shades of pale yellow, pink and orange.

WORKBOOK EXERCISE 5.2:
DISCUSSING AUTHORSHIP & AUDIENCES *(continued)*

Both series often divide public opinion on their audience appeal. Why might this be? Is the subject matter and humour more hard-hitting or confrontational in one or the other? Is the humour and subject matter directed towards a more specific audience?

Elora Aboua: Yes. *Family Guy* has a lighter feel to its humour, making it more comfortable for people to laugh at subjects when in a mixed audience. Humour in *The Boondocks* is heavier and seems to be aimed at one particular point of view. *The Boondocks* looks at issues in ways that are typical of 'black/African American' humour, for example the open use of particular language and tropes such as 'hood/ghetto' brother versus 'philosophical African-American' brother.

However this can be an awkward way to present these topics to more general audiences. This is because they might be unsure if they are 'allowed' to find this funny, or they may not fully understand the trope-related jokes—which may therefore be seen as offensive and more awkward for a mixed audience to watch.

Emeka Uzoh: *The Boondocks* and *Family Guy* confront the same issues but in different ways. For example, *The Boondocks* confronts slavery in a serious context with the main black characters having to work for the white characters in order to pay off their debts, whereas *Family Guy* deals with slavery in a funny context in terms of having the white main male character find out that one of his ancestors was black.

Do you think the fact that a black male created *The Boondocks*, and that a white male created *Family Guy* is important to the way in which issues are presented to the audience? In the case of *Family Guy* for example, we have a black character created by a white writer and voiced by a white actor. Does this affect the credibility and appeal of the show to wider audiences?

Emeka Uzoh: I think that it is important because it gives the audience an insight into the different issues that black and white people face from different perspectives.

Marsha Williams: Most people wouldn't notice. But from a black perspective, yes, because there have been many black actors and actresses that have had roles in movies involving the subjects of slavery and racist stereotypes. But why pay a black person when you just need a voice with some type of accent, that can add a few slang words in, I guess that's the power of voice-overs.

INTRODUCTION

HAMMERING
IT HOME:
PROPAGANDA
& SOCIALIST
REALISM

THE IDEAL
HOME:
ADVERTISING

WORKBOOK
EXERCISE 5.1

HOME SWEET
HOME: TV
SITCOM &
GAMING

WORKBOOK
EXERCISE 5.2

CASE STUDY:
MAKE BAOBAB
FAMOUS

CHAPTER
SUMMARY
& FURTHER
READING

KEY WORDS,
NAMES & WORKS

Does the semi-realistic animé influenced style of _The Boondocks_ or the level of fantasy seen in _Family Guy_ affect how we feel about the different series?

Emeka Uzoh: Yes, the type of animation style that an animated series adopts can affect how we feel about the animation. If the animation style is more cartoon-like we will usually think that the animation does not take itself seriously.

Bartosz Kastner: Animation is often still largely seen as being for kids, but in my opinion it is of as much value as live action. The problem is not the form of presentation, or the subjects explored by the authors, but the audience perception of what the medium can do. For instance the 2008 BAFTA winner for 'Best Animated Film' was _WALL•E_. The runners up were _Persepolis_ and _Waltz with Bashir_. All three films were covering topics that are equally important and current in the way they can change people's opinions about the issues presented. But in my opinion it was the sugar sweet story that won over the general audience, and this might the bigger problem of popular animation.

Sex Sells:
Representation of Gender

5.16

5.16
A promotional image for the feature
film *Lara Croft Tomb Raider: The
Cradle of Life* (2003) that illustrates
contradictions of male oriented
depictions of female empowerment.

INTRODUCTION

HAMMERING
IT HOME:
PROPAGANDA
& SOCIALIST
REALISM

THE IDEAL
HOME:
ADVERTISING

WORKBOOK
EXERCISE 5.1

HOME SWEET
HOME: TV
SITCOM &
GAMING

WORKBOOK
EXERCISE 5.2

CASE STUDY:
MAKE BAOBAB
FAMOUS

CHAPTER
SUMMARY
& FURTHER
READING

KEY WORDS,
NAMES & WORKS

The Australian academic and feminist activist Germaine Greer has written extensively on how society is structured around the male psyche. In her book *The Female Eunuch*, she examined how men and women have been conditioned to perceive the female identity largely around either the tropes of the housewife or sex object. Although the book was published in the 1970s, many of the sexist tropes of female identity challenged by Greer are still perpetuated in the media today, perversely often by those who are attempting to empower female identity.

In fact, there has been a noticeable upsurge in recent years of more extreme depictions of hyper-sexualized females and sexual violence towards women in advertising, as various types of brands from fashion retailers to fast food outlets seek ever more shocking tactics to compete for attention in an age saturated by a wide range of mobile media. Examples in fashion have included the overt suggestion of rape by Dolce & Gabbana (2007), whilst it is not uncommon to see the act of a female eating food in an erotic manner as a euphemism for oral sex, such as the 'Seven Incher' advertisement by Burger King (2009).

English artist and critic John Berger highlighted in his book *Ways of Seeing* how the act of looking at the female body as an idealized object has been ingrained in European painting for centuries, and how in western culture the way a woman appears will determine how she is treated. What is also assumed in western culture is that the ideal viewpoint of the female is that of the heterosexual male.

In the twentieth century the female prostitute openly became a common nude subject for artists such as Picasso and Toulouse Lautrec. Although the gaze of Picasso's female nudes in *Les Demoiselles d'Avignon* (1907) confronted the gaze of the male viewer by staring directly out from the canvas, and despite Lautrec's paintings often revealing a more sympathetic insight into his subjects as real people with the same everyday human concerns as the viewer, such paintings still do not resolve the female subject's status as essentially being reduced to that of an *object* to be looked at from a male perspective.

Historically, many animation companies have had cartoons edited, censored or banned for depicting overtly sexist stereotypes as objects of desire or racist stereotypes as subjects for mocking and amusement. *Betty Boop* (created by Max Fleischer, 1930) was the first highly sexualized female animated cartoon character, whose scantily clad appearance was later toned down due to the implementation of censorship laws in America during the 1930s.

As discussed in chapter two, mainstream feature length animation has begun to mature in its representation of women as 'makers of meaning' (Mulvey, 2009, p. 15), increasingly taking on the role of the protagonist rather than remaining a passive 'carrier of meaning', a helpless heroine or an object of desire. But contemporary feminists, such as Anita Sarkeesian, the Canadian-American media critic and creator of the web series *Feminist Frequency*, point out that there is still a lack of strong females depicted as lead roles in entertainment, such as among the many superhero franchises.

❝If marriage and family depend on the castration of women let them change or disappear. The alternative is not a brothel, for brothels depend upon marriage and family for their existence.❞
Germaine Greer (1970), _The Female Eunuch_, p. 111

Sarkeesian's criticism focuses on gaming in particular, which has perpetuated the use of the female as a passive sexual object. She highlights how women are frequently used in this way, with little narrative purpose other than infusing the gaming experience with an edgy and arousing atmosphere, which assumes and perpetuates gaming as a being a space primarily for heterosexual men. In the few instances where there is an empowered female avatar, such as Lara Croft in the *Tomb Raider* games and spin off films, once again we see the female physique become highly sexualized.

A Patriarchal Problem: The Otherness of Villainy

Despite the rise of 'Girl Power' in the 1990s and feminist attempts to address female empowerment in animation and other media, submissive fairy tale princesses have somewhat paradoxically been superseded by increasingly sexualized characters in animated television series such as *Bratz*. This continues to send out a dangerous message that further engenders an unhealthy misunderstanding of 'normal' body image and identity formation in girls, and in turn perception of the female individual by boys.

Part of the problem underlying stereotyping is that many video games played and animations watched in the home are still largely created by white males. In his analysis of the animated superhero series *The Powerpuff Girls*, Ewan Kirkland notes two key problems with white middle class male authorship of female empowerment. Firstly the "heroines express a recognizable Western femininity" (Kirkland, 2010, p. 13) highlighting that the girls all have diminutive physiques, and that they are all still subservient to a male character—their scientist father, with no mention of a mother.

Secondly, what is equally questionable is that the creators perhaps unwittingly project the notion of villainy onto stereotypes of those that deviate from a patriarchal norm (the influence of male authority as the established norm). That is to say, signifiers of race, class and sexuality that do not fall within the westernized, white, heterosexual, male norm are used to characterize the villains that the girls come into combat with. Such villains include mocking stereotypical caricatures of highly sexualized females, gender-queer males and Asian monkeys.

❝Sexualized female bodies often occupy a dual role as both sexual playthings and the perpetual victims of male violence.❞
Anita Sarkeesian (2014), *Feminist Frequency*, Women as Background Decoration (Part 2) August 25, 2014

❝An assessment of the limitations of this 'Girl Power' series reveals the marginalization and vilification of certain identity formations outside the white middle-class heterosexual girlhood represented by the show's protagonists.❞
Ewan Kirkland (2010), *Animation: An Interdisciplinary Journal Online*, The Politics of Powerpuff: Putting the 'Girl' into 'Girl Power', p. 9

INTRODUCTION

HAMMERING
IT HOME:
PROPAGANDA
& SOCIALIST
REALISM

THE IDEAL
HOME:
ADVERTISING

WORKBOOK
EXERCISE 5.1

HOME SWEET
HOME: TV
SITCOM &
GAMING

WORKBOOK
EXERCISE 5.2

CASE STUDY:
MAKE BAOBAB
FAMOUS

CHAPTER
SUMMARY
& FURTHER
READING

KEY WORDS,
NAMES & WORKS

> **"The program text may indeed have cross-gender (and generational) appeal, but, the commercial intertexts almost uniformly represent girls and young women as the ideal consumers of puff stuff."**
> **Joy Van Fuqua (2004), *Prime Time Animation*, p. 207**

Combining repetitive stereotyping with humor is a powerful tool used to reassert a point of view and authority of any dominant group over those whose identities and values fall outside the mainstream. The combination of humor with otherness was frequently used in wartime propaganda. *Tokio Jokio* (Warner Brothers, 1943) is an example of World War II propaganda that mocked the Japanese with unsympathetic caricature of body features, language and culture. Such cartoons have subsequently been banned or censored for their offensive nature.

Interestingly, the female academic Joy Van Fuqua is more positive about *The Powerpuff Girls*. She points out how the series promotes female protagonists that are not defined by highly sexualized physical characteristics, and how it included other female characters in roles more traditionally assumed by male characters, such as astronauts and explorers. She also notes how the show has had equal appeal with both female and male audiences.

However, Van Fuqua also points out that the matter of reinforcing gender stereotypes does emerge if we pay attention to merchandise from the series. The merchandise exclusively targets a young female consumer market with branded products ranging from handbags and make-up to fanzines that resemble female teenage fashion magazines.

While there are arguments that both support and criticize its intentions, and there are also dangers of overanalyzing the content of animated series such as *The Powerpuff Girls* or *The Boondocks*, two points seem clear. Firstly, we should be aware about the cumulative effect of stereotyping perpetuated by the media (without a sufficient variety of authorship), and secondly how the commodities of consumer culture such as toys can impose a sense of identity and values on us from a very early age—even in the safety of the home.

CASE STUDY:
MAKE BAOBAB FAMOUS

In this chapter, we have explored how many of the mechanisms of propaganda can be applied to advertising and how large organizations have used the media in the 'manufacture of consent' around consumer and public goods. That is to say, we have seen how the public can be led to believe in a network of carefully controlled myths about the products they buy, the lifestyles they lead and the values they hold.

The following case study is used to illustrate how the Africa-inspired, London-based health and beauty brand and social business Aduna developed an authentic public goods campaign called 'Make Baobab Famous'. The campaign was designed to raise awareness about the nutritional and economic benefits of the African baobab fruit to its consumers and producers, whilst consciously aiming to avoid the tropes of commodity racism. It includes an interview with the cofounder of the campaign, Andrew Hunt, and student animator Emeka Uzoh, who developed an animation viral for part of the campaign.

5.17

5.17
A promotional image from the 'Make Baobab Famous' campaign run by Aduna (2015) demonstrating how imagery can be used to positively and realistically portray contemporary Africa in the West.

INTRODUCTION

HAMMERING
IT HOME:
PROPAGANDA
& SOCIALIST
REALISM

THE IDEAL
HOME:
ADVERTISING

WORKBOOK
EXERCISE 5.1

HOME SWEET
HOME: TV
SITCOM &
GAMING

WORKBOOK
EXERCISE 5.2

CASE STUDY:
MAKE BAOBAB
FAMOUS

CHAPTER
SUMMARY
& FURTHER
READING

KEY WORDS,
NAMES & WORKS

Interview:
Andrew Hunt, Cofounder of Aduna

What is Aduna, and what is the mission of your brand?

Aduna is a social business whose mission is to create demand for under-utilized natural products from small-scale producers in Africa. Our mission is also to breathe the vibrancy of Africa into the daily lives of people all around the world, whilst creating a virtuous circle that feeds positive impacts back to the source.

What is the baobab fruit and why is it so special?

Our hero product is baobab, 'The Feel Good Fruit'—an exceptionally nutrient-dense 'superfruit' that is rich in vitamin C, fibre and antioxidants. Baobab has the potential to bring health and vitality to our customers around the world while providing sustainable income flows to the estimated 10 million rural households in Africa who can provide the fruit. The trees from which we source the baobab are the property of the communities who live on the land, and not governments or large organizations. The pulp of the fruit naturally dries out on the tree and turns into an exceptionally nutrient dense powder, which can be mixed into a drink or used as an ingredient for baking.

Why is this mission so important to you?

I spent my early career working in the advertising industry, successfully creating and launching brands for big companies that I didn't truly believe in. In my mid-twenties, I had the opportunity to volunteer in the Gambia, where I worked with small-scale growers of fruits and vegetables. I stayed for four years, and became rejuvenated and inspired by the vibrancy of Africa.

How does Aduna's business model work?

Aduna is a social business, which means that whilst our operations are entirely commercial, our motivations are social. Aduna was created to provide a solution to the failed aid structure in rural Africa whereby cash-crop 'development projects' routinely fail due to lack of market, leaving the targeted producers with little choice but to uproot and return to their subsistence lifestyles, perpetuating a downward spiral of aid dependency. Aduna has pioneered a new model which reverses this structure by creating markets for under-utilised indigenous natural products with high potential in the global well-being market.

What is the key to your marketing strategy?

We create demand by educating consumers and the trade about our super-ingredients, their health and beauty benefits and their social impact potential. We have spent three years working on our campaign to 'Make Baobab Famous', enrolling the press, influencers, bloggers, buyers and consumers in the inspiring possibility of baobab for their health and for rural Africa.

We have successfully taken baobab from complete obscurity to an international best-selling 'superfood' sold in 1,000 stores in 15 countries. This has enabled us to create sustainable income flows for 2,000 women in Upper East Ghana via our added value smallholder supply chain. We are now scaling up to reach 800,000 women in Northern Ghana—and ultimately, 10 million in rural Africa.

The campaign, and the entire Aduna brand, expresses the positivity and vibrancy of Africa, which for so long has been obscured from consumers by the world's clichéd coverage of the continent. Aduna aims to transform perceptions of Africa from 'the Third World', to the place where life all began, full of vibrancy, energy, colour, light.

CASE STUDY:
MAKE BAOBAB FAMOUS *(continued)*

Interview:
Emeka Uzoh, BA (Hons) Animation Student,
London Metropolitan University

A group of student animators were commissioned by Aduna to produce viral material as part of the 'Make Baobab Famous' campaign. The main aims of the brief were to promote the feel good factor of baobab to the metropolitan populace, while avoiding cliché perceptions of Africa by focusing on the contemporary vibrancy of the continent, as well as educating the public about the key nutritional benefits of the fruit and its economic benefits to the communities producing the baobab powder. The interview below with one of the animators illustrates how the brand values of the campaign were applied to the development of an idea for a viral.

How do you feel your own identity helped you to develop a concept that had integrity and authenticity, but also originality? What were your initial sources of inspiration for the imagery and sound?

I have a British and Nigerian heritage. I wanted to make something modern that at the same time paid homage to its African roots. I looked for inspiration from western pop music and comic book superheroes that I have grown up with, that I believe are popular in all cultures, and explored how I could combine this with the colours and patterns typically associated with Africa.

What is the synopsis for your viral?

A giant donut-shaped asteroid threatens all human life on planet Earth. It falls to one lone astronaut to use the power of a giant baoabab fruit floating in space to transform himself into a superhero and save earth from its imminent destruction.

What is the sequence intended to represent?

I wanted to show the transformative effect of the baobab on a human (from fragile astronaut to superhero), and how the superfood could save everyone on Earth from unhealthy food (represented by the superhero destroying the giant donut-shaped asteroid).

What music did you use as the initial temp track for your animation and why?

I tried a range of tracks from very western pop music, including Paolo Nutini, to more contemporary Afrobeat music. In each case I was looking to avoid stereotypes of traditional African music that are often overused, and instead use musical styles that I felt could appeal more to a westernised audience.

5.18

5.18
Production still for an animated viral for the 'Make Baobab Famous' campaign, directed by Emeka Uzoh (2015), which addresses preconceptions of African cultural identity and projects a more progressive world view of Africa.

INTRODUCTION

HAMMERING
IT HOME:
PROPAGANDA
& SOCIALIST
REALISM

THE IDEAL
HOME:
ADVERTISING

WORKBOOK
EXERCISE 5.1

HOME SWEET
HOME: TV
SITCOM &
GAMING

WORKBOOK
EXERCISE 5.2

CASE STUDY:
MAKE BAOBAB
FAMOUS

CHAPTER
SUMMARY
& FURTHER
READING

KEY WORDS,
NAMES & WORKS

What were the core brand values of the campaign and fruit that you wanted to represent, and how did you aim to achieve this?

I focused on the 'Power of transformation', the 'Emotional benefits—feeling more alive', and 'Personality—youthfulness'. I feel my project reflects the positive impact that transformation can have on people on earth; the astronaut feels more alive once he turns into a superhero, and the animation highlights a sense of youth and fun through its comic book style.

To get a sense of 'celebrating the natural vitality, energy, colour, light, vibrancy and positivity of Africa', I borrowed the motifs from the Aduna brand, which are a combination of traditional African batik and western pop art. These colours and patterns feature as planets and as the outfit of the superhero to reinforce the positive spirit of the campaign.

How else did you reinforce the positivity of Africa?

Photos of Earth often place the United States of America at the centre of the image. I decided to put an image of planet Earth with the continent of Africa foremost to represent a more progressive image of Africa as being of present and future world importance, which is often overlooked by depictions of poverty.

Case Study Endnote

Unlike more traditional television commercials, Internet virals are generally used to promote consumer and public goods by minimizing product placement or branding from the content. Other examples of viral campaigns of public goods include the ALS Ice Bucket Challenge mentioned earlier in this chapter. Other examples of a viral campaign for consumer goods include two stop motion projects for Nokia: *Dot* (2010) and *Gulp* (2011), produced by Sumo Science at Aardman.

Dot produced 'the world's smallest stop motion character', a nine-millimeter girl shot on a Nokia N8 using a special microscope attachment used in medicine, while *Gulp* shot a sand animation on a beach using pixilation (stop motion of life-sized objects and real people) by suspending a Nokia N8 from a crane. The two virals demonstrated the capacity and versatility of the Nokia N8 handsets for filming at extreme close up and long range.

In the case of many virals, the brand or organization define the theme and concept, but become incidental in the way they feature (if at all) in the actual content. Where the product does feature, its presence usually does not focus on the brand itself, rather the type of object and/or an activity relating to it or its brand values.

The public usually has the choice to watch and share virals, often through social media. To this end, concept advertising has increasingly superseded the stereotypes and tropes often used historically to promote brands. This engages the viewer by immersing them within a novelty experience or activity, rather than projecting or conditioning an ideology, identity or lifestyle upon them.

In the case of the 'Make Baobab Famous' campaign, the focus was on the fruit and not a brand. In this case study, stereotypes of African identity were challenged by using the anonymous universal figures of astronauts and superheroes. Therefore the only binary notions of otherness used in the viral were positive ones that focused on how the baobab can transform the human condition of mankind as a whole, from its present state to a healthier future one.

CHAPTER SUMMARY & FURTHER READING

In this chapter we have discussed how propaganda, advertising and entertainment have been used to control and manipulate populations. We have explored the power of mass psychology and investigated how the concept of otherness is used to manipulate public opinion and shape the formation of identity. Throughout the chapter the key question that has arisen is to what extent our knowledge and beliefs about others, as well as our knowledge and beliefs about ourselves, is built on factual or fictional information.

It is also important to note that visual propaganda is not unique to the twentieth and twenty-first centuries. As discussed in previous chapters, mankind's understanding of the power of images in the propagation of ideology in the public realm has been around since the earliest cave paintings. Indeed, the Catholic Church, identified in this chapter as the source of the term 'propaganda', has employed some of the greatest artists throughout history to depict passages from the Bible, such as the ceiling frescos in the Sistine Chapel by Michaelangelo, featuring the famous image of the hands of God and Adam from *The Creation of Adam* (c. 1508–1512).

In contrast, what we are witnessing today is how our beliefs, values, identities and way of life have become increasingly shaped and informed not just by the church or state, but also through a consumer culture imposed upon us by large multi-national companies in the digital media. Conversely, it is the same digital technology that is enabling an exponential growth in independent forms of artistic expression, propagating the validity of individual opinions and experiences in a similar way to the printing press during the Enlightenment (see chapter four).

5.19

5.19
The famous image of the hands of God and Adam from *The Creation of Adam* that features in the ceiling frescos of the Sistine Chapel painted by Michelangelo (c. 1508–1512).

INTRODUCTION

HAMMERING
IT HOME:
PROPAGANDA
& SOCIALIST
REALISM

THE IDEAL
HOME:
ADVERTISING

WORKBOOK
EXERCISE 5.1

HOME SWEET
HOME: TV
SITCOM &
GAMING

WORKBOOK
EXERCISE 5.2

CASE STUDY:
MAKE BAOBAB
FAMOUS

CHAPTER
SUMMARY
& FURTHER
READING

KEY WORDS,
NAMES & WORKS

The challenge for the individual and society is to be able to separate knowledge gained through active human experience, reading and debate rather than passively absorbing our identity and understanding of the world through exposure to corporately managed digital media, both in public urban spaces and the privacy of the home.

It cannot necessarily be said that digital technology and mass media is a bad thing. Indeed, this book promotes the benefits of online learning tools, recognizing the advantages brought with the invention of each new technology, without losing sight of the benefit of critical thinking. This book encourages you to integrate processes such as online workbooks with a range of written and practical exercises, with the key aim to develop ways of extending the outreach of collaborative learning and your own animation work with people around the world.

Further, the underlying theme of the human condition in this book may itself appear somewhat propagandist, as each chapter interrogates different aspects of history, cultures, societies and forms of artistic expression. The intention, however, is not to politicize your studies as such, but rather to help you become more aware of the time you live in by comparing events now with events in the past, as well as learning how to absorb relevant artistic influences in order to express yourself and the experiences of others in response to the world around you.

You could also criticize this book for a male sexist bias in its structure, beginning by investigating male-dominated commercial production methods as the historical norm and then interrogating these with other practices as the book progresses. However, I have consciously attempted to counter historical biases in earlier chapters through a careful selection of animators and projects featured in the case studies and interviews. The challenge for all artists and filmmakers is to consider and research subject matter and audience with care, in order to be able to approach sensitive issues responsibly and with empathy and integrity.

While every effort has been made to accurately research and write a text that interrogates how we structure narrative and its content, I will inevitably be subject to the biases of my own culture and era. I will have been shaped by the political events of my own time and society. Therefore, I stress again that you should actively question the validity or accuracy of the views and opinions in *every* book that you read, and in all the media that you watch, and not passively accept what is presented you as absolute knowledge.

In this chapter, otherness has largely been discussed in terms of nationality or ethnicity, built on moral or intellectual superiority of one population over another, i.e., 'us and them', as well as consumer identity built on the demonstration of enviable aspirational lifestyles, i.e., the 'haves and have nots'. Otherness has also been discussed in terms of gender norms from dominant male to female and others. But in each of these cases the focus has largely been on political or corporate values, physical attributes, associated behaviour and actions.

The final chapter goes a stage further in looking at issues of representation, by discussing whether it is possible to actively *experience* the feelings or mindsets of others, rather than passively accept biased representations of them. The importance of the context of the subject matter and the role of the author becomes even more essential in probing deeper into subject matter surrounding ethnicity and gender as well as perceptions of disability. The chapter explores this through the discussion of different forms of documentary and animated documentary and how these enable the viewer to comprehend abstract truths or facts more fully.

FURTHER READING

Propaganda, Advertising & Representation

Baudrillard, J. (Glaser, S. translator, 1994) *Simulacra and Simulation*, University of Michigan Press: Ann Arbor

Benshoff, H. & Griffin, S. (2003) *America on Film: Representing Race, Class, Gender, and Sexuality at the Movies* (New Edition), Wiley-Blackwell: Chichester

Berger, J. (2008) *Ways of Seeing* (Reprint Edition), Penguin Classics: London

Bernays, E. & Crispin Miller, M. (2005) *Propaganda*, Ig Publishing: New York

Boym, S. (2002) *The Future of Nostalgia*, Basic Books: New York

Chomsky, N. (2002) *Media Control* (Second Edition), Seven Stories Press: New York

Chomsky, N. & Herman, E. (1994) *Manufacturing Consent*, Vintage: London

Cullen, J. (2004) *The American Dream*, Oxford University Press: New York

Foucault, M. (1998) *The Will to Knowledge*, Penguin: London

Greer, J. (2012) *The Female Eunuch*, Fourth Estate: London

Hall, S. (2013) *Representation* (Second Edition), SAGE Publications Limited: London

Leslie, E. (2004) *Hollywood Flatlands*, Verso: London

McClintock, A. (1995) *Imperial Leather: Race, Gender & Sexuality in the Colonial Contest*, Routledge: London

Mogen, D. Busby, M. & Bryant, P. (2000) *The Frontier Experience and the American Dream*, Texas A&M University Press: College Station

Rutherford, P. (2004) *Endless Propaganda*, University of Toronto Press: Toronto

Wiedemann, J. (2009) *Advertising Now: TV Commercials*, Benedikt Taschen Verlag: Köln

INTRODUCTION

HAMMERING
IT HOME:
PROPAGANDA
& SOCIALIST
REALISM

THE IDEAL
HOME:
ADVERTISING

WORKBOOK
EXERCISE 5.1

HOME SWEET
HOME: TV
SITCOM &
GAMING

WORKBOOK
EXERCISE 5.2

CASE STUDY:
MAKE BAOBAB
FAMOUS

CHAPTER
SUMMARY
& FURTHER
READING

KEY WORDS,
NAMES & WORKS

Representation, Comedy, Sitcom & Animation

Benshoff, H. & Griffin, S. (2003) *America on Film: Representing Race, Class, Gender, and Sexuality at the Movies* (New Edition), Wiley-Blackwell: Chichester

Buchan, S. (2006) *Animated Worlds*, John Libbey Publishing: Eastleigh

Cohen, K. (2004) *Forbidden Animation*, McFarland & Company, Inc.: Jefferson

Honess Roe, A. (2013) *Animated Documentary*, Palgrave Macmillan: Basingstoke

Jhally, S. & Lewis, J. (1992) *Enlightened Racism*, Westview Press: Boulder

Kirkland, E. (2010) *The Politics of Powerpuff*, Animation: An Interdisciplinary Journal Online 5(1)

Kitson, C. (2005) *Yuri Norstein and Tale of Tales*, John Libbey Publishing: Eastleigh

Lockyer, S. (2010) *Reading Little Britain*, I.B. Tauris: London

Lockyer, S. & Pickering, M. (2009) *Beyond a Joke: The Limits of Humour*, Palgrave Macmillan: Basingstoke

Medhurst, A. (2007) *A National Joke*, Routledge: Abingdon

Mills, B. (2005) *Television Sitcom*, BFI Publishing: London

Mulvey, R. (2009) *Visual and Other Pleasures*, Palgrave Macmillan: Basingstoke

Pinsky, M. (2007) *The Gospel According to the Simpsons*, Westminster John Knos Press: Louisville

Sarkeesian, A. (2014) *Feminist Frequency*, Women as Background Decoration, accessed from http://feministfrequency.com/2014/08/25/women-as-background-decoration-part-2/

Stabile, C. & Harrison, M. (2004) *Prime Time Animation*, Routledge: London

Wells, P. (2002) *Animation Genre and Authorship*, Wallflower Press: London

Wells, P. (2007) *Understanding Animation*, Routledge: London

KEY WORDS

American Dream, The
A national philosophy and belief in social mobility: that anyone can afford a better life and happiness through hard work

Brand Loyalty
Always buying the same brand, often based on the aspirational lifestyle used to sell it rather than its actual value or effectiveness

Class Conflict
When the protagonist behaves in ways uncharacteristic of their new environment, creating a paradox whereby the stereotypical behaviour of each class is both confirmed and also challenged

Commodity Racism
How brands create harmful tropes of race in the promotion of their product

Consumerism
The buying of commodities

Cultural Imperialism
Imposition of values from one dominant culture on others

Holocaust
The mass slaughter of Jews in concentration camps by the Nazis

Hyperrealism
Realistic yet often stylized images that enforce a very clear state ideology on citizens

Islamist
Islamic fundamentalist

Manufacture of Consent
The use of news media by governments and large organizations to filter facts and influence public opinion

Mass Psychology
The conditioning of collective emotional behaviour of large groups of people

Moral Relativism
The self-justification of an act of violence by a dominant organization over the unsubstantiated threats of another, less powerful organization

Otherness
How we collectively project our fears of the unknown onto strangers

Parody
Tongue-in-cheek caricature

Patriarchal Norm
The influence of male authority as the established norm

Propaganda
The spread of exaggerated or false information

Public Goods
The commodification of moral values

Public Relations
A term used in advertising and politics in place of the word propaganda

Soyuzmultfilm
Famous Russian animation studio

Trope
An overused stereotype or cliché

Viral
A video rapidly circulated via the Internet

KEY NAMES

Roland Barthes
John Berger
Edward Bernays
Margaret Bourke-White
Noam Chomsky
Jacques Derrida
Germaine Greer
Winsor McCay
Walter Lippman
Anne McClintock
Michelangelo
Laura Mulvey
Yuri Norstein
Yarbusova Norstein
Lyudmila Petrushevskaya
Anita Sarkeesian
Henri Toulouse Lautrec
Joy Van Fuqua

KEY WORKS

Aduna
Betty Boop
Boondocks, The
Charlie Hebdo
Cosby Show, The
Creation of Adam
Dot
Family Guy
Fresh Prince of Bel Air, The
Good Times
Gulp
Incredibles, The
Kentucky Flood
Lara Croft Tomb Raider: The Cradle of Life
Les Demoiselles d'Avignon
Pears' Soap
Powerpuff Girls, The
Scrub Me Mamma with a Boogie Beat
Sinking of the Lusitania, The
Tale of Tales
Tokio Jokio

CHAPTER SIX
ANIMATED DOCUMENTARY: OBJECTIVE FACT VERSUS SUBJECTIVE EXPERIENCE

CHAPTER OVERVIEW: REDEFINING NARRATIVE STRATEGIES

In this chapter, you will learn:

- How the work of independent, contemporary, female artists and filmmakers has confronted the prejudiced stereotypes of identity often presented in mainstream media.

- How alternative approaches to animation have freed both female and male animation directors from the more formulaic approaches of mainstream commercial animation.

- How a range of directors have focused on representing nonfictional knowledge in ways that avoid stereotyping and that challenge preconceptions about the role of documentary.

6.1

6.1
Reenactment of the Battle of Waterloo, 1815. More
conventional forms of documentary often include
reenactments, such as battles, to illustrate things
that could not be filmed.

INTRODUCTION

In the last chapter, we introduced feminist critique of advertising, cartoon series and video games and discussed how exposure to these affect our individual identities as well as our perception of others. In this chapter, we will start by looking at how the work and methods of *independent*, contemporary, female artists and filmmakers has been addressing the binary tropes and prejudiced stereotypes of identity often presented in more mainstream media.

However, as with the last chapter, the focus here is not specifically about feminism. Discussion about identity centres upon the representation of knowledge and fact in live action documentary film and analysis of the genre known as animated documentary. In exploring the differences and similarities between live action film documentary and animated documentary, this chapter looks at how female filmmakers have directly and indirectly challenged preconceptions about the narrative content, function and form of animation.

This chapter also looks at how developments of alternative approaches to animation apply more generally to the work of both female and male independent animation directors, who are free from the more formulaic approaches of mainstream commercial animation. The selection of case studies revisits *The Sinking of the Lusitania* and contrasts this with analysis of the feature length animation *Persepolis* and *Waltz with Bashir* as well as the animated shorts *Hysteria*, *Crying & Wanking*, *Parada*, *A Is for Autism* and *Snack & Drink*.

These animated films have been chosen as they illustrate how a range of female and male directors have focused on presenting the audience with nonfictional knowledge that often reveals more personal abstract truths and aspects about the human condition, in ways that avoid stereotyping, delve deeper into the human psyche and challenge our preconceptions about the function and purpose of *all* forms of documentary. Ultimately, this chapter reveals a point at which the realism of genre and abstraction of modernism meet.

The chapter concludes with a workbook exercise on documenting and visualizing synesthesia. This is a neurological phenomenon in which some people's senses, such as sight, taste, smell and hearing, cross over with one another. The result for some is that sounds, words and letters may be perceived as being of a certain colour or even having a particular smell or taste. The exercise is intended to help you explore ways in which you can define other animation strategies, for accurately representing knowledge about subjective abstract experiences, feelings and memories.

INTRODUCTION

FEELING THE
FACTS: FROM
DOCUDRAMA   CASE STUDY: POETIC TRUTHS:
TO ANIMATED   SEXUALITY &   WHERE FILM   CASE STUDY: A   WORKBOOK
DOCUMENTARY   MENTAL HEALTH   & ANIMATION   IS FOR AUTISM   EXERCISE 6.1
                                      MEET

                                                                           CHAPTER
                                                                           SUMMARY
                                                                           & FURTHER   KEY WORDS,
                                                                           READING   NAMES & WORKS

RECOMMENDED VIEWING

A Is for Autism, directed by Tim Webb, Fine Take
Productions (1992)

Crying & Wanking, directed by Alys Scott-Hawkins,
Royal College of Art (2002)

Girls' Night Out, directed by Joanna Quinn,
Channel 4 Television Corporation (1998)

Going Equipped, directed by Peter Lord,
Aardman Animations (1990)

Hysteria, directed by Alys Scott-Hawkins,
Royal College of Art (2001)

Monty Python's Flying Circus, created by
Graham Chapman, Eric Idle, Terry Jones, Michael
Palin, Terry Gilliam & John Cleese, BBC (1969–1974)

Parada, directed by Jerzy Kucia, Studio Filmów
Animowanych w Krakowie (1987)

Persepolis, directed by Marjane Satrapi & Vincent
Paronnaud, 2.4.7. Films (2007)

Snack & Drink, directed by Bob Sabiston,
Flat Black Films (2000)

The Sinking of the Lusitania, directed by Winsor
McKay, Universal Film Manufacturing Company
(1918)

Triangle, directed by Erica Russell, Ginco (1994)

Waltz with Bashir, directed by Ari Folman
& Bridgit Folman, Film Gang (2008)

FEELING THE FACTS: FROM DOCUDRAMA
TO ANIMATED DOCUMENTARY

6.2

6.2
A scene from the animated feature film *Persepolis*,
directed by Marjane Satrapi and Vincent
Paronnaud (2007). The film was not designed as
a documentary, but it is important for the way
it represents the human side of political conflict
through the life of a young girl.

❝Generally, the action genres—adventure, war, gangster,
detective, horror, science fiction and, of course, the western—
were addressed to a male audience, while musicals and romantic
melodramas (known as 'weepies') were marketed as 'women's
films'. This distinction bespeaks wider patriarchal assumptions
about gender difference in the real world.**❞**
Barry Keith Grant (2007), *Film Genre: From Iconography to Ideology*, p. 80

Representation of Conflict: Memory, Humor & Identity

Persepolis (2007), directed by the comic book artist and filmmaker Marjane Satrapi, marks a significant moment in the development of feature length animation. Releasing a film about the Islamic Revolution in Iran does not seem a likely subject for an animation that has had such widespread appeal. It is also fairly unusual for a female to direct such subject matter, which is still more often associated with male filmmakers, and furthermore that it has a female lead character.

Although there is a historical context, this becomes the backdrop to a film that in many ways acts as a memoir documenting the rite of passage of the director (known in the film as Marji) from childhood through adolescence to adulthood. The context is still hugely important to the story of the main character, sent to Austria by liberal parents to shelter her from the effect of the events and propaganda of the Islamic Revolution, in which her uncle is murdered, and continue with an education outside Iran that would otherwise have become stifled by the change in political regime.

However, things do not work out for Marji in Europe, where she is faced with the hypocritical ideological prejudices of her fellow students, whose beliefs highlight various double standards of the society they live in. She also struggles with a personal sense of helplessness and guilt as she witnesses the troubles in Iran from a distance. She later leaves her lodgings after a falling out over the prejudices of her landlady and then falls foul of the dogma (a set of principles believed to be absolute truth) at the convent where she subsequently shelters, rendering her homeless.

After finding herself in hospital with pneumonia caused by living on the street, Marji returns to Iran. But after only a short period back home, her time away gives her a new more objective and critical perspective on people and events in her own country, and she is left feeling as equally outcast as when she was in Austria. The film concludes with her leaving a failed marriage behind in Iran, this time heading for a new life in Paris.

Despite such challenging subject matter, *Persepolis* is intended neither specifically as a polemic (controversial attack or statement) on politics or war nor as a feminist film. The key to its success is that it manages to take serious historical events and find a comfortable middle ground that identifies with universal human experiences. Satrapi prioritizes humor over an aggressive stance to document and dramatize the absurdities and prejudices a young woman faces growing up in three very different cultures, pre- to post-revolution Iran and Austria.

In one scene the ban on western culture and commodities in Iran is humorously likened to prohibition of drugs, with men in trench coats secretively dealing albums of pop musicians from Julio Iglesias to 'Jichael Mackson'. Subtle reference is also made to gender stereotyping as Marji ignores one man trying to sell make-up, but turns in delight to another man who has Iron Maiden albums to sell. She then haggles furiously with him, succeeding, before the dealers are frightened away by two older women fully covered in Muslim headwear and garments, who question Marji's westernized appearance with the sense that they are about to report her to the authorities.

"A younger generation has felt free to explore a range of subjective experiences in a sense taking feminism for granted. Some reject an explicitly feminist stance, preferring to address women's experiences through humor and aim for the widest possible audience."
Jayne Pilling (1992), *Women & Animation*, p. 5

Satrapi has stated in various interviews that *Persepolis* is neither fully autobiographical nor a documentary. She emphasizes that like many people living in exile, memories and associated feelings became increasingly important to her work. She insisted that the animation be hand drawn such that its stylization gave the film a level of abstraction that minimized any particular preconceptions or prejudices around the ethnicity of characters and location of the story. This also enables the audience to engage with moments of fantasy that focus purely on understanding the character's mental state, such as a dream-like sequence when Marji is on medication for clinical depression.

6.3

6.3
A recurring dream sequence from *Waltz with Bashir* directed by Ari Folman (2008). The use of a semi-realistic visual style, combined with dream sequences and flashbacks linked together by interviews with the real people upon who the characters are based, enables the audience to empathize with the protagonist's real inner feelings and experiences.

INTRODUCTION

FEELING THE FACTS: FROM DOCUDRAMA TO ANIMATED DOCUMENTARY

CASE STUDY: SEXUALITY & MENTAL HEALTH

POETIC TRUTHS: WHERE FILM & ANIMATION MEET

CASE STUDY: *A IS FOR AUTISM*

WORKBOOK EXERCISE 6.1

CHAPTER SUMMARY & FURTHER READING

KEY WORDS, NAMES & WORKS

Waltz with Bashir (2008), directed by the Israeli filmmaker Ari Folman, is another highly successful feature length animation documenting conflict, in this case the war between Israel and Lebanon in 1982. Like *Persepolis*, the film resembles a form of comic book or graphic novel. *Waltz with Bashir*, however, is rendered in a semi-realistic style and focuses much more on a male experience of combat. This is perhaps more typical of westernized war films than is the focus on the everyday lives of civilians caught up in conflict, as seen in *Persepolis*.

Waltz with Bashir is also a more polemical or politically charged interrogation of the events and experiences that shaped and traumatized the subsequent lives of a group of naïve young Israeli soldiers. The protagonist tries to remember and make sense of confused and repressed memories by piecing together the recollections of other veterans from his military unit.

Both *Persepolis* and *Waltz with Bashir* have a strong sense of catharsis (the psychological healing process of release from repressed emotions or memories). Each director places her or himself in the frame as the main character, but also uses personal memories and traumas from a range of real characters to weave together the history of actual political events.

Whereas *Persepolis* takes the form more of a docudrama (a dramatization of real events), *Waltz with Bashir* essentially functions as a documentary about post-traumatic stress disorder (the delayed effect of extreme events on peoples' mental health). The film achieves this through its semi-realistic style and dialogues based on actual interviews with various war veterans, combined with often surreal animated flashbacks representing memories of real events. The film concludes by revealing shocking real footage of the aftermath of the massacre of innocent Lebanese civilians by Israeli forces—and therefore the suppressed memories of the film director.

In both animations, we also see how the events of war shape the identities of young adults. This helps the audience to see through stereotypes of nationality, ethnicity or gender associated with particular cultures and empathize with the individual or subjective experience instead. It is this idea of the subjective experience that can be uniquely expressed through the genre of animated documentary.

❝Animation is especially persuasive in depicting such states of consciousness—memory, fantasy, dream, and so on—because it can easily resist the conventions of the material world and the 'realist' representation that characterises live-action cinema. Interestingly, this capability is highly enabling because it can illustrate both states of consciousness and the visual conceptualisations of psychological and emotional conditions.❞
Paul Wells (2002), *Animation, Genre and Authorship*, p. 49

Documentary & Discourse:
Defining Fact

In chapter four we discussed the concept of realism and how for several centuries art followed the same principle as mimesis, established by the ancient Greek philosopher Aristotle—to represent knowledge and aspects of our external reality as accurately as possible. We also looked at how in the twentieth century modernist artists began to focus on personal and more abstract sensory experiences, internal spiritual feelings or states of mind instead.

In recent decades the emergence of the increasingly popular film genre of animated documentary has challenged established preconceptions about documentary filmmaking in general, as something that need no longer present real imagery or be factually driven as such. The animated documentary is something that can be more abstract and place greater emphasis on active experience, offering a deeper level of insight into a particular area of knowledge than live action.

In order to understand the unique qualities of animated documentary we will first consider some of the defining characteristics of film or live action documentary and how animation is sometimes used within it. The American film critic and theoretician Bill Nichols divided live action documentary film into six main categories. Of these, we are probably all familiar with two of the most dominant forms, known as observational and expository documentary.

6.4

6.4
A political map of Europe from 1876. Animated political maps are commonly used in historical expository documentaries to illustrate changing national borders after wars or changing political unions.

Observational documentary, also frequently referred to as 'fly on the wall', is used to describe a mode where the filmmaker has limited if any interaction with the subject or environment that is being filmed. This is in order to record and document subject matter as objectively as possible. This could include investigating the reality of subject matter that is often quite challenging, such as a day in the life of a drug rehabilitation or young offenders centre. This approach often results in footage that is more hard-hitting, raw and unpolished in the way that it is presented.

Expository documentary tends to be narrated or presented by an authoritative figure as an objective (fact-based, not personal), accurate, educational and/or moral account on a particular topic. Subject matter might include description and analysis of historical periods or events, e.g., the dynasties of monarchies or wars that changed the political maps of geographical regions.

This form of documentary is usually illustrated and edited together using indexical images, such as film footage of real historical locations or artifacts and interviews with experts. These act as a direct or causal link to the subject matter being discussed, and therefore reality, truth and facts. This concept essentially builds on Pierce's 'indexical mode' discussed in chapter one, whereby a footprint for example signifies the presence or action of a real person who, though not in shot, clearly exists.

Other content might include the explanation of scientific knowledge, such as natural history phenomena or space exploration. It is here that authenticity of expository documentary becomes more problematic, when presenting things that *cannot* necessarily be filmed, and that depend upon animated reconstructions or simulations of historical events or scientific phenomena.

English academic Annabelle Honess Roe has dedicated a book to the study of animated documentary. She uses three key terms to explore its range of functions. The first function, mimetic substitution, incorporates the Aristotelian principle of mimesis and describes the more conventional use of animation in expository documentary— to recreate things or events that could not otherwise be filmed, often as realistically as possible. Examples include computer-generated dinosaurs or historical events such as *The Sinking of the Lusitania* (see chapter five).

Mimetic substitution and expository documentary in general are problematic in so far as they are dependent on the accuracy of the material sourced by the animator and filmmaker, as well as the quality of their interpretation of it. Further, the reality is that content is often created or edited to suit a particular bias, such as allied propaganda in the case of *The Sinking of the Lusitania*, which in many senses also qualifies as a form of documentary as it is essentially a historical record of a real war time event.

Even if it had been possible to actually film the plight of the Lusitania and edit it from a politically impartial viewpoint, simply editing the footage together would affect the audience's comprehension of the event in a different way than if they had witnessed or experienced it for themselves. It can be argued therefore that no expository or observational documentary can be a totally authentic, accurate account of events, as what we learn will always have been mediated in some way by someone else.

Discourse & Context

French Constructionist theorist Michel Foucault (1926–1984) believed that knowledge is produced through discourse and that nothing exists meaningfully within itself without being defined as a topic for discussion. Further, it is the context within which something is discussed, in other words the era or culture in which the subject is discussed, that defines the nature of its very being. Above all, at any period in history, it is the views of those in particular positions of power that determine commonly held knowledge and beliefs.

From the point of view of expository documentary, the discussion of the nature of the existence, evolution and extinction of dinosaurs, for example, changes periodically as new scientific discoveries are made. With each new decade improvements in carbon dating technologies enable us to analyse the age of a dinosaur bone more accurately, which combined with fossilized remains discovered in deeper rock layer samples or at new locations, helps us understand the environment in which the dinosaur existed, what it ate, the factors that determined its extinction and so on.

With advances in 3D computer simulations we also are able to calculate the probable way in which a creature moved, for example, changing the belief that the tail of a diplodocus did not hang near the ground, but rather it was raised up in the air. In such cases it is the selection of experts by editors of science journals and/or the documentary maker that confirm the nature of the existence of a subject. Moreover, it is the edited discussion of the experts within the documentary that determines the knowledge that is formed and commonly believed by society.

In the book *Representation*, Stuart Hall summarizes how Foucault's works (including *Madness & Civilization* and *The Will to Knowledge*) looked extensively at the important implications of context on knowledge regarding more abstract issues surrounding mental health and sexuality. Hall focuses in particular on how forms of mental illness such as hysteria in female patients have been diagnosed and treated during different periods throughout history.

Until the period of the Enlightenment, the cause of mental illness in Europe would sometimes be attributed to the soul being possessed by demons, with religious practices such as exorcism used in some cases to cure the afflicted person. By the nineteenth century greater emphasis was placed on using medical science to cure the nervous system with often-brutal mutilation of the body through surgery.

6.5

6.5
A CGI impression of a diplodocus herd illustrates the dinosaur species in motion with their tails raised, in contrast to nineteenth century illustrations that depict them with their tail hanging near the ground. The use of hyper-real visual effects is problematic, as audiences may perceive what is depicted as absolute truth.

By the turn of the twentieth century the treatment of conditions such as hysteria in female patients involved methods including hypnosis and psychoanalysis. Pioneering psychiatrists, such as Sigmund Freud, identified the root of the psychological symptoms of hysteria to be caused by heavily repressed feelings stored within the unconscious mind, which once revealed to the conscious mind could help recovery of the patient.

Over time medical advances have revealed other biological or neurological factors affecting mental illness. Today psychiatry is often used in conjunction with prescription drugs to help patients recover from a range of mental health issues. In the case of conditions such as post-traumatic stress disorder, the root cause of apparent epidemics of mental health problems may only be identified decades later as being caused by society or mankind's own actions, such as prolonged exposure to the emotional stress of war.

Mental illness is also often still revered in many cultures as a spiritually transformative process. In this instance and in the case of post-traumatic stress disorder, we can see how the discourse described by Foucault is essential to perception of psychological condition and the development of knowledge that results within a particular society or cultural context.

6.6

6.6
An image of an Eskimo medicine man exorcizing evil spirits from a sick boy (circa 1900–1930) illustrates how perceptions of illnesses and their treatments vary from one culture and/or time period to another.

Animated Documentary:
The 'Feminine Aesthetic'

Indeed, feminist academics such as Germaine Greer have argued that using methods of psychoanalysis for the treatment of hysteria in female patients are flawed, due to the fact that Freud's theories assume that the female psyche (mind or spirit) is defined as being a castrated (sexually disempowered) version of the male psyche. In other words, within the context of psychoanalysis it is impossible to 'fix' a hysterical female patient, if her very identity is defined from the outset as being a 'broken' version of the patriarchal (dominant male) norm.

Therefore, Greer points out that in actual fact you need to change the sexist society in order to mend the hysteria of the female patient, as society constructs both the norm and therefore the 'maladjusted' exception to it. Here again we see the effect of the concept of otherness, introduced in the last chapter, on our sense of self and understanding of others.

Thus, we can see that conveying issues such as mental health in expository documentary can be more problematic than, say, presenting an account of a particular historical event—especially if we follow Foucault's approach to the representation of knowledge of a subject as the product of discussion by a particular culture or society.

We might be presented with facts about chemical imbalances or images of scans of the electrical activity in the brain of those suffering from a particular condition and how this can affect human behaviour. Interviews with doctors, psychiatrists and patients may even be presented to us describing symptoms, treatments and the impact of these on day-to-day life.

But despite all this discourse and resulting knowledge there is still something fundamentally missing. In order to fully comprehend any mental illness or psychological condition and represent it truthfully, we must know what it is like to actually *experience* it. If this is the case, then Foucault's argument starts to fall down, as only the person with the condition (the subject themself), or possibly someone very close to them, can communicate how something so abstract actually *feels*.

Jayne Pilling, Paul Wells and Annabelle Honess Roe all explore the unique capacity of animation to communicate knowledge of abstract human experience through expressive techniques that reject realism but are seen as of equal value to the indexical links (real footage) or mimetic substitution (recreated animated footage) used in expository documentary (narrated fact).

Pilling highlights how the abstract qualities and possibilities of animation enabled independent female animators in particular to explore highly personal subject matter that they would not have otherwise felt safe to explore, or even able to express, through the more traditional methods of mainstream animation studios.

The notion of the 'feminine aesthetic' used by Wells characterizes the steady increase since the 1970s in the number of female animators exploring subject matter using a range of expressive techniques including visual metaphors, heightened colours, rhythms, sounds and internal monologues, that enable the audience to subjectively recreate the state of mind in question for themselves.

❝Psychologists cannot fix the world so they fix women. Actually they don't even manage that.❞
Germaine Greer (1970), *The Female Eunuch*, p. 104

Some female animators, such as Joanna Quinn, use more realistic drawing techniques and humor to challenge tropes of female identity (*Girls' Night Out*, 1987). Other filmmakers explore female sexuality with the vibrancy and abstraction of modernist painting, such as Erica Russell mentioned in chapter four (*Triangle*, 1994). There are also female animators who have turned to animated documentary to express knowledge about subjective aspects and abstract experiences of the human condition.

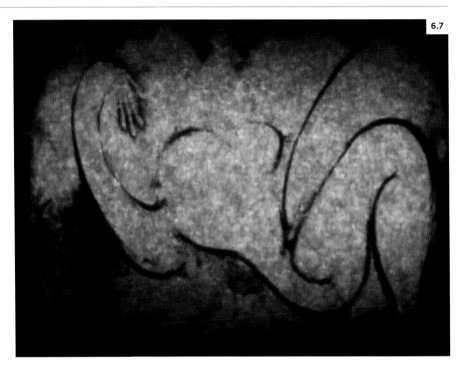

6.7

"If men, in general, have used animation to echo and extend the premises and concerns of men in live-action film-making, then women have used animation to create a specific *feminine aesthetic* which resists the inherently masculine language of the live-action arena, and the most dominant codes of orthodox hyper-realist animation which also use its vocabulary."
Paul Wells (1998), *Understanding Animation*, p. 198

6.7
The animated documentary *Hysteria* directed by Alys Scott-Hawkins (2001) uses a range of animation techniques including sand animation to illustrate male attitudes towards women and supposed treatments for female mental health in Victorian Britain.

"Animation is uniquely capable of taking an idea, an emotion, a set of observations—anything at all, for a walk to see what emerges—and take the audience along with it. Ideas, feelings, issues can be presented not as linear arguments—to be accepted or rejected by the viewer—but imaginatively embodied, enacted, literally played around with for the viewer to experience and interpret for themselves. Serious issues such as incestuous sexual abuse or women and the law can be explored in ways unthinkable in feature or documentary film and often far more imaginatively and accessibly."
Jayne Pilling (1992), *Women & Animation*, p. 6

CASE STUDY:
SEXUALITY & MENTAL HEALTH

Over the last two chapters we have seen in films such as *The Sinking of the Lusitania*, *Tale of Tales*, *Persepolis* and *Waltz with Bashir* how recreations of real events, memories and mind states are used to document historical facts and human experiences. We will now explore some of the defining features of animated documentary in more detail through an interview with BA and MA animation lecturer, artist and animation director Alys Scott-Hawkins. This student case study looks at two animated shorts she made during her own MA animation studies: *Hysteria* (Royal College of Art, 2001) and *Crying & Wanking* (Royal College of Art, 2002). The two projects look at issues of representation around female sexuality.

Hysteria

Hysteria investigates mental health care in Victorian Britain (1837–1901) and the seemingly brutal, even absurd, methods used to 'treat' female hysteria. The animation can be described as an animated documentary due to a range of techniques used by the director. These techniques are broken down using a range of terms, including two further functions defined by Honess Roe.

Hysteria contains various sequences of animated medical diagrams and text definitions. These diagrams illustrate how masturbation was genuinely seen as the cause of serious physical and mental illness, and how the use of a surgical cure was seen as the preferred method of treatment for any mysterious or debilitating condition in the Victorian era.

There is an element of parody in sequences such as this, in which the diagram features macabre *Monty Python* style cut-out animation of surgical scissors accompanied by grotesque sounds. The use of parody highlights the absurdity of the official beliefs of early Victorian society and medical science, and also subverts some of the methods used for direct representation of factual discussion in expository documentary.

There are also sequences in the film that use partially rotoscoped old photographs of women writhing in sudden fits, which was seen to define hysteria in the Victorian era. The adaption of these images and juxtaposition with mechanical, electronic and medical sounds suggests how dehumanizing the treatment of hysteria might have felt to patients.

This type of approach to animation may be defined as non-mimetic substitution. This differs from *mimetic substitution* in that it is *not* the animated production of footage to recreate unfilmable events. Rather, it can be the embellishment of existing footage, or creation of new and sometimes hyper-real animated footage (such as the animated interviewee in *Going Equipped*, discussed in chapter one), in order to add or emphasize something about the experience (see fig. 6.8).

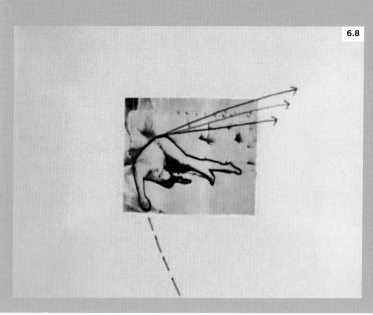

6.8

6.8
An example of non-mimetic substitution used in the animated documentary *Hysteria* directed by Alys Scott-Hawkins (2001). The method uses rotoscoping to embellish an image to emphasize the cold, clinical nature of various treatments for female hysteria.

FEELING THE
FACTS: FROM
DOCUDRAMA
TO ANIMATED
INTRODUCTION   DOCUMENTARY   CASE STUDY:
SEXUALITY &
MENTAL HEALTH

POETIC TRUTHS:
WHERE FILM
& ANIMATION
MEET

CASE STUDY: A
IS FOR AUTISM

WORKBOOK
EXERCISE 6.1

CHAPTER
SUMMARY
& FURTHER
READING

KEY WORDS,
NAMES & WORKS

Finally, there are sequences that reject realism altogether (see fig. 6.7). Instead, they focus on semi-abstract, expressive and dream-like sand animation of a nude female masturbating, which is used to help give further psychological insight to, or evoke a feeling of the state of mind of the subject. Honess Roe would more closely define this as evocation, which like the concept of the 'female aesthetic' focuses on more abstract stimuli such as colours, textures, rhythms, sounds and so forth.

This short film is therefore a relatively simple example of a more typical animated documentary that largely resists the indexical use of real film footage seen in expository documentary. This animated documentary also does not need to make use of mimetic substitution, the animated recreation of real events that could not have been filmed. This is because more than anything, this short animated documentary gives the viewer a closer insight into the field and treatment of hysteria from the perspective of the female subject, as well as documenting developments in medical science and Victorian social attitudes towards female sexuality.

Crying & Wanking

Crying & Wanking is an animation film about female sexuality. It explores the sexuality of the female body, the personal guilt of exploiting one's own body for sexual pleasure and emotional release. It also interrogates harmful negative male attitudes towards women and the exploitation of the female body by men.

This documentary is an interesting example of non-mimetic substitution. The whole piece essentially inverts conventions of animated and live action documentary. In this instance, animation is used as a subjective representation of the 'real' world, emphasizing the state of mind of the subject, whereas live action film, embellished with superimposed animated elements, is used as a means of visualizing the dream states of the subject.

The majority of the animated shots are from the first person point of view. Combining this with a narration and poem has the effect of an intense internal monologue or personal thoughts, evoking in the audience a full sense of what the subject is feeling. The live action, close-up footage of the female subject's naked body, with animated visual metaphors apparently drawn onto it by her lover, also reinforce the sense of a first person experience (see fig. 6.9).

The very human traces of the expressive hand drawn techniques often used in making animated documentary can also help the audience to feel even more fully connected with the subject's internal state of mind, in a similar way to how the expressive paint marks and vivid colours of Van Gogh's post-impressionist paintings help us comprehend his unfolding madness.

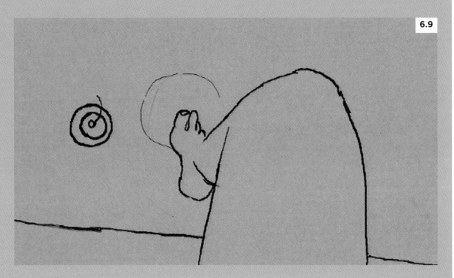

6.9

6.9
An example of not only non-mimetic substitution, but also how the indexical reference in this animated documentary is inverted, i.e., animation is used instead of live action film to refer to the real world. *Crying & Wanking*, directed by Alys Scott-Hawkins (2002).

CASE STUDY:
SEXUALITY & MENTAL HEALTH *(continued)*

**Interview with Alys Scott-Hawkins
on Animated Documentary**

To what extent would you agree that the nature of the subject matter and processes you used for making these two projects, and indeed many of your subsequent projects, define them as animated documentary, documentary or something else altogether?

In terms of subject matter—*Hysteria* for me felt like making a documentary in that I was given a starting point—the word 'bedlam', which led me to research mental health care in Victorian Britain and from which I discovered the histories of hysteria and its treatments. I got completely absorbed in the research—finding far more juicy material than I could cram into such a short film—the brief was for one minute!

The processes were attempts to explore the material and to represent it to the audience in different ways. Some of that was purely experimental: How can I work from this set of reference images? If I use that technique how will it interpret this feeling? But it was also part of my agenda for the film to expand: 'social extension', enlarging the range of what's acceptable on screen. Looking back at the time in which the film was made (2001), there had been an extending of the range of acceptable roles for young women, especially as a part of Riot Grrrl and 'ladette' culture, and yet the subject of female masturbation was still most definitely a taboo. Arguably, it still is—outside of the realm of pornography.

In some ways *Crying & Wanking* is a development of the themes in *Hysteria*, in that I was seeking to explore in more depth female sexuality on screen. I suppose that—inside a package of what I tend to consider now as a rather miserable film—*Crying & Wanking* is 'pushing boundaries' in that it represents female sexuality, partially, on its own terms rather than as something always dependent on a (male) partner. At least that sexuality exists even outside of the sexual encounters with a partner. A woman is trying to resolve her vulnerabilities and desires on her own terms. The original idea for the film was far more 'straight' a documentary, about the hormonal fluctuataions of menstruation and emotional rollercoaster of the monthly cycle.

Your second MA project uses a combination of digital drawn animation and live action. Why did you decide to use this combination? For example, did the different mediums enable you to communicate some ideas more explicitly and leave others more open to subjective interpretation?

I knew I wasn't getting the best out of my work shooting on film. I wanted to try working digitally, to make a drawn film, and I had discovered the thrill of drawing into Photoshop with a Wacom tablet. It made perfect sense to me that a film in which the 'reality' was drawn needed a dream sequence shot in live action. But in addition to that reasoning, I knew that I wanted to animate the partner drawing onto the woman's body, and when I drew that it just didn't look right (see fig. 6.10).

6.10

6.10
Another example of how the idea of indexical footage is challenged. Animated documentary often makes reference to the presence of the directors themselves. *Crying & Wanking*, directed by Alys Scott-Hawkins (2002).

INTRODUCTION

FEELING THE
FACTS: FROM
DOCUDRAMA
TO ANIMATED
DOCUMENTARY

CASE STUDY:
SEXUALITY &
MENTAL HEALTH

POETIC TRUTHS:
WHERE FILM
& ANIMATION
MEET

CASE STUDY: A
IS FOR AUTISM

WORKBOOK
EXERCISE 6.1

CHAPTER
SUMMARY
& FURTHER
READING

KEY WORDS,
NAMES & WORKS

What do *you* think distuinguishes animated documentary from other forms of animation production? Does there need to be a clear set of issues or questions to be investigated, with some form of interview for example as a starting point? Or for you is the whole nature of an animated documentary that it follows a more intuitive process?

Personally, I define animated documentary as any film based on nonfiction which uses animation techniques. For me (particularly in my role as cocurator of the animateddocumentary.com blog) that definition works well, as it doesn't exclude autobiography nor live action documentaries with animated segments.

There is certainly a heritage of interview or 'survey' based animated documentaries, where a range of voices are heard offering experiences on a shared subject (for example *A Is for Autism* by Tim Webb, or *Camouflage* by Jonathan Hodgson). But I don't consider an interview essential, or that there has to be verification or evidence presented within the film's soundtrack. Animated documentary can successfully function without language and operate in the realm of sensation and emotion, where the subject matter is appropriate.

Ultimately, who decides what is an animated documentary and what is not? Is it a conscious decision on the part of the director, or is it up to the audience? Does it even matter, and if so why?

That's a tricky question to answer. A film will always be open to interpretation by its audience. That's something I really encourage students to be aware of. As the director you have to take responsibility for every interpretation, and potential misinterpretation, of what you make.

As audiences it's good if we can come to a documentary with a sense of scrutiny, questioning who has made this film, what is the standpoint and increasingly these days what is actual footage and what is reconstruction? The difference often becomes almost imperceptible. Of course it matters whether or not the director defines a work as documentary, but I suppose its always the responsibility of the audience to examine that and question it as they watch.

There are various themes around female identity that run through several of your subsequent projects. On the basis of your own filmmaking experience and in your role as an animation lecturer, what advice would you give other animators when identifying challenging subject matter—for it to work, should it ideally be something that they have personal experience of themselves?

No, I don't think there should be any limitation on which subjects or stories are or are not yours to explore but, especially in terms of documentary, there are always questions for the filmmaker to answer about whose story it is that's being presented, and how. The lines between documentary and fiction become ever-increasingly blurred, but nonetheless documentary ethics and questions about representation still apply, just as much to animation as to live action productions.

I can say though that the films I've made which have come from a personal perspective or feeling are probably the ones which have had the most success with audiences. I encourage my own students to examine their own preoccupations and passions as a starting point for film ideas but that certainly doesn't mean that I discourage making films about experiences you don't know. I'd say that animated documentary, in particular, lends itself to films which are a journey of discovery or make an enquiry.

POETIC TRUTHS: WHERE FILM & ANIMATION MEET

The final case study in this book, the BAFTA award-nominated film *A Is for Autism*, directed by Tim Webb (1992), is in many ways both an animated documentary and live action documentary film all in one. The case study highlights how we need not think of animation or live action film as separate forms, rather as interchangeable or combinable means of understanding both tangible facts and abstract experiences. But before discussing *A Is for Autism*, we will first look at some of the parallels in the definitions of animated documentary and more expressive forms of live action documentary film in order to understand the grey area between them.

Performative and Poetic Modes of Documentary

The terms Honess Roe uses to describe the range of techniques that define animated documentary are not dissimilar to features that Bill Nichols uses to define some of his other live action documentary categories. These include performative and poetic modes. Unlike the expository mode that Nichols defines as an authoritative, objective, accurate and factual account of real events, the *performative* and poetic modes explore documentary as more subjective interpretations of the human experience.

The performative mode has parallels with *non-mimetic substitution*. It focuses on representing a 'direct experience' (Nichols, 2010, p. 210) of the subject or main person in the documentary. Nichols includes the animation *Waltz with Bashir* as an example that, like *Crying & Wanking*, focuses on representing the intense internal thoughts, feelings, memories and voice of the subject, who may be the director himself. Nichols stresses the importance of experiencing the moral or 'emotional complexity' of the subject (Nichols, 2010, p. 202), rather than being presented with rigid facts and binary arguments.

The poetic mode has parallels with *evocation*. The intention here is also to create a subjective experience for the viewer, but one that is not influenced directly by the voice of the director or the individual identities of any of the people that may feature within the film, but experienced wholly in the first person by the viewer. Here, historical or cultural knowledge is represented by the way in which film footage is distorted or exaggerated to create an aesthetic experience. Film footage is often edited together rhythmically or embellished through the juxtaposition of different spaces or shapes, essentially often using the same modernist filmmaking methods of montage introduced in chapter four.

The poetic mode can be illustrated by the work of the Polish painter, filmmaker and animation director Jerzy Kucia. His film *Parada* (1987) mixes the traditions of film montage with complex animation techniques resembling rotoscoping. His films often involve multiple exposure of live action film footage that has been laser copied or redrawn.

❝It is something of a myth that animation is a mode that somehow cannot be used by documentary practitioners. Such a way of thinking is based in naïve and simplistic notions of how documentary functions, and in a misguided belief that documentary is somehow 'capturing' reality rather than offering an *analysis* of it. Animation can do this just as well as live-action; in some cases, animation is in fact better suited to the job.❞
Paul Ward (2006), *Animated 'Worlds'* (Edited by Suzanne Buchan), chapter 8, p. 114

INTRODUCTION

FEELING THE
FACTS: FROM
DOCUDRAMA
TO ANIMATED
DOCUMENTARY

CASE STUDY:
SEXUALITY &
MENTAL HEALTH

POETIC TRUTHS:
WHERE FILM
& ANIMATION
MEET

CASE STUDY: A
IS FOR AUTISM

WORKBOOK
EXERCISE 6.1

CHAPTER
SUMMARY
& FURTHER
READING

KEY WORDS,
NAMES & WORKS

> **"Feelings in opera are, ultimately, like axioms in mathematics, which cannot be concentrated and cannot be explained any further. The axioms of feeling in the opera lead us, however, in the most secret ways, on a direct path to the sublime . . . But in the fine arts, in music, literature, and cinema, it is possible to reach a deeper stratum of truth—a poetic, ecstatic truth, which is mysterious and can only be grasped with effort; one attains it through vision, style, and craft."**
> **Werner Herzog, *On the Absolute, the Sublime, and Ecstatic Truth***
> **Boston University, College of Arts & Sciences—Arion**

Parada is formed from a montage made up of semi-abstract close-ups of the activities traditionally involved in harvesting farm crops, edited together rhythmically with evocative sounds of tools, animals and folk music, but there is no narration. The sequences are all shot from a point of view that makes us feel as if we are experiencing them in the first person. The techniques used to render the shots also give the film footage the dreamlike quality of memories. These methods create a subjective sensation or experience for the viewer, who can fully comprehend the cultural context of the subject matter as if it was from their own memory, without the need for any kind of rational description or explanation to make sense of what is happening. To paraphrase Kucia, he essentially describes many of his films involving such techniques as 'emotional documentaries', which embodies notions of the poetic mode.

The fact that animations can be used instead of live action film as examples of the performative and poetic modes of documentary reinforces the point that aesthetic experience can be as meaningful as any kind of factual discussion. *Parada*, therefore, illustrates how any sense of division between the processes and qualities of animation and live action film becomes blurred, even irrelevant—particularly when the director is both an animator and live-action filmmaker.

In his essay *On the Absolute, the Sublime, and Ecstatic Truth*, German filmmaker Werner Herzog wrote that we can never reach or represent an absolute truth about anything, but he refers to the arts as a means of representing sublime or ecstatic truths. To explain this, he compares the abstract artistic experiences used to understand the human condition with the most abstract mathematical equations used to define the nature and being of our universe—and how at a certain point our understanding of art or science can no longer be broken down any further.

Herzog defines this as the sublime experience, one that needs no further explanation. He goes on to define a poetic or ecstatic truth as the deeper understanding that is reached through our subjective interpretation of this experience. In many ways Herzog's analogy reinforces the idea that there is a limit to the level of truth that can be conveyed in any given mode of documentary, and beyond that it requires the effort of the viewer to make a purely subjective decision about what has been presented to them.

CASE STUDY:
A IS FOR AUTISM

So far we have seen how poetic, expressive and abstract representations of knowledge and human experience are common in both live action film documentary and animated documentary. It is also important to recognize that although the expressive practices frequently used in animated documentary may be more commonly associated with the work of female directors, many of the examples we have looked at illustrate that these practices are commonly used by men as well.

However, our final case study—the documentary *A Is for Autism*—looks beyond the gender of the director altogether. It illustrates how the subjective experience, in this case the experience of autism, can be presented to an audience through the collective authorship of a film by the actual subjects of the film themselves.

'Autism' is a term used to describe a broad range of cognitive, emotional and behavioural patterns. Some of the most common of these may include highly focused interests or an affinity for repetitive activities, which may result in specialized talents from memorizing facts to drawing complex and detailed images from memory; having hypersensitivity to noise or emotions, often avoiding crowded spaces, eye contact or bodily contact; or difficulties in following instructions, engaging in fluid conversation or interacting in social situations.

The documentary *A Is for Autism* was directed by Tim Webb, but made by using the interviews of a group of adults and children who describe their introspective (self-examination of personal emotions and mental processes) recollections of growing up with autism. The film is unique in that drawings made by its subjects are used to create the animation that illustrates their narration. The animation is intercut and also combined with live action as well as pixilation (stop frame animation of real people and objects).

It is perhaps less relevant for us to try and define *A Is for Autism* as an animation or film, as it is yet another example of a documentary that combines modes and functions from both media. These are discussed below, with a view to then being able to apply a range of them to the final exercise in this book. The exercise maps out an idea on how to make a documentary that connects its audience with some of the more abstract feelings, sensations and memories of people who have synesthesia.

INTRODUCTION

FEELING THE
FACTS: FROM
DOCUDRAMA
TO ANIMATED
DOCUMENTARY

CASE STUDY:
SEXUALITY &
MENTAL HEALTH

POETIC TRUTHS:
WHERE FILM
& ANIMATION
MEET

CASE STUDY: A
IS FOR AUTISM

WORKBOOK
EXERCISE 6.1

CHAPTER
SUMMARY
& FURTHER
READING

KEY WORDS,
NAMES & WORKS

6.11
A Is for Autism, directed by Tim Webb (1992), is the product of collective authorship. The subjects of the film create much of the artwork, animation and narration in the piece. The result is a film that combines animation, pixilation and live action to produce a closer insight into the subjective experiences of people with autism. Drawing by Daniel Sellers.

6.11

❝The current mushrooming of animated documentary and autobiographical films—by authors of both sexes—makes it necessary to question the validity of generalist assumptions made about women, and animation by women, such as the opinion that women tend to be more able than men to explore and share personal experience.❞
Maria Lorenzo Hernández (2010), *A Film of One's Own: The Animated Portraits of Young Contemporary Female Animators*, Animation: An Interdisciplinary Journal, p. 84

CASE STUDY:
A IS FOR AUTISM (continued)

**Use of Different Modes and
Functions of Live Action and
Animated Documentary**

A Is for Autism might be loosely defined as a performative documentary. Rather than presenting a factual account as such, it explores the 'emotional complexity' of autism through some of the more common, intense internal thoughts, feelings and memories of its subjects. The narration gives it a strong personal feel that also helps the audience piece together their understanding of an initially seemingly random sequence of self-portraits and drawings of trains.

As the film unfolds the viewer builds up a web of scenarios in their mind, which reveal personal facts and experiences that help to humanize autism, rather than present factual data or information about it as a condition that is all too often misunderstood. We frequently see indexical links to the 'real world' and the subjects themselves in the film. These links include footage often revealing the hands of the participants creating the images and regular cutaways of close-ups of hands involved in repetitive actions such as turning light switches on and off, opening and closing doors, tearing strips of paper, spinning coins and so on.

The use of these almost first person, live-action, close-up shots of repetitive actions reinforces the realness of the experience, which juxtaposed against the more abstract drawn imagery helps us more fully comprehend both the behavioural and emotional aspects of autism. We are therefore able to connect the more abstract internal feelings or thought processes represented by the animated drawings to real life. This presents the audience with a body of valid and authentic information that could not be communicated purely through the expository documentary mode.

To this end, *A Is for Autism* in some ways also reflects the poetic mode. Sometimes the shots or sequences become a more expressive representation that evokes certain feelings or sensations, particularly when the audience is left to experience the film in the first person. Examples include chalk text on a blackboard becoming scrambled or nonsensical doodles that rotate, fragment, morph and reconfigure.

These sequences illustrate how autism can make it difficult to follow conversation or cause a struggle to be able to pick out or notice things that others can spot easily in the everyday world. Our sensory experience is also often heightened with expressive sound effects such as road traffic or noise from the playground that grow in intensity before fading away.

The animated documentary *Snack & Drink* by Bob Sabiston (2000) also attempts to create the inner world of a young teenager who has autism. To do this, Sabiston rotoscopes over live action footage of a boy walking to the local store and explaining the specifics of this daily routine. The rotoscoping uses an expressive range of vivid colours and distorted shapes to embellish the original footage, which suggest the disorientation that can be experienced by people with autism.

What is interesting is that while both Sabiston and Webb use expressive techniques, *Snack & Drink* is more dependent on the director's subjective interpretation or supposition of how it might be to experience autism. *A Is for Autism* enables the viewer to more fully comprehend the condition through the expressive drawings and explanations from the subjects themselves.

INTRODUCTION

FEELING THE
FACTS: FROM
DOCUDRAMA
TO ANIMATED
DOCUMENTARY

CASE STUDY:
SEXUALITY &
MENTAL HEALTH

POETIC TRUTHS:
WHERE FILM
& ANIMATION
MEET

CASE STUDY: A
IS FOR AUTISM

WORKBOOK
EXERCISE 6.1

CHAPTER
SUMMARY
& FURTHER
READING

KEY WORDS,
NAMES & WORKS

6.12

6.12
Snack & Drink, directed by Bob Sabiston
(2000). Rotoscoping is used here to embellish
real footage to the extent that it becomes an
expressive representation or sense of the way
the world might feel to the autistic teenager who
features as the subject of the film.

CASE STUDY:
A IS FOR AUTISM (continued)

**Interview with Tim Webb
on Animated Documentary**

What prompted you to make a film about autism, and how did you get started on it?

I had been trying to work out how I fitted into the animation industry after graduating from my BA in animation. A new fund for independent shorts 'Animate' was advertised in the late 1980s and I thought I really should submit a proposal.

I had never really thought of making a film about autism. My idea came from my admiration for an artist's drawings. This artist, Stephen Wiltshire, just happened to be autistic and only nine years old. I had first seen his work on a BBC television programme *QED* (1987). The programme focused on the genius qualities of three autistic savants: musical, mathematical and artistic.

I bought three of Stephen's prints and his book. He has amazing ability in expressive perspective drawing; he draws in mirror form and from memory. My initial idea was to make a film about London, in collaboration with Stephen. My partner suggested including something about autism. I found a book by Lorna Selfe that contained a list of common autistic traits. My initial idea aimed to draw parallels of autistic traits with behaviour we all exhibit living in the city environment.

This idea was shortlisted, mainly as the 'Animate' board liked the collaborative element to the film. Also my BA film, a diatribe about the politics of smoking based on Peter Taylor's book *The Smoke Ring*, indicated a possible direction in which I could take the idea. Claire Kitson, the commissioning editor of Channel Four, was part of the animate board and liked my idea.

I tried to contact Stephen, who by now had an agent who was in the process of publishing a second book alongside an accompanying second BBC programme. As I remember, the agent would not allow me any contact with Stephen, which turned out to be my big break. Clare Kitson thought the film would fit into a disability season of films planned by Channel Four and offered me development money to rethink the idea, research it properly and establish new collaborations.

Part of my development period included finding a producer and I asked Dick Arnall, who was working as an advisor for the 'Animate' scheme, who accepted. His input went far beyond the producer role and was crucial to the final outcome. Dick steered the film toward the deadline, but also initiated ideas that became part of the film content and communicated brilliantly with the numerous escalating numbers of potential leads and collaborators.

What initial research or consultation was involved or required in developing the idea, content and structure? What challenges did you face in securing subjects or other participants?

My BA film was constructed more along the lines of a live action documentary—with almost no storyboarding and making the postproduction stage part of the creative process where new ideas emerge. I wanted to follow this model for this commission and Clare Kitson allowed me great freedom in this approach. The multi-voice interview approach was a result of extensive research. The length of the film was limited to eleven minutes, the time between two advertisement breaks. The content and structure, the amount of artists and voices used was really dictated by the research period, the production period and the broadcast deadline.

There are not a great deal of people who express what it's like to be autistic as this is very 'un-autistic' and there are not that many autistic artists. This development period doubled, as researching and contacting potential collaborators, as well as building up trust with the autistic community, took a great deal of time and had to be done with care. One of my biggest fears was of exploitation.

INTRODUCTION

FEELING THE
FACTS: FROM
DOCUDRAMA
TO ANIMATED
DOCUMENTARY

CASE STUDY:
SEXUALITY &
MENTAL HEALTH

POETIC TRUTHS:
WHERE FILM
& ANIMATION
MEET

CASE STUDY: A
IS FOR AUTISM

WORKBOOK
EXERCISE 6.1

CHAPTER
SUMMARY
& FURTHER
READING

KEY WORDS,
NAMES & WORKS

As my deadline loomed, I had thought it was a film that could not be made, as I had not found any collaborators. The National Autistic Society, one of my first contacts, were very wary about exploitation and misrepresentation and they saw potential for both in my film, and they were not helpful. The irony is that they now list the film as suitable watching material.

I asked Channel Four for an extension to my development period. At this point I got one of my first positive contacts from Temple Grandin, a highly successful autistic person, who had written about her experiences, who was willing to let me use her quotes. Temple had advised Dustin Hoffman, who played an autistic person in the film *Rain Man*.

Not long after this I had a positive response from Professor Elizabeth Newson from the Child Development Unit in Nottingham University. Newson worked with autistic children and also had a daughter who works in the media. She was very enthusiastic and cooperative and gave me contacts with the autistic community and at least half the contributors to my film. These included Darren White and Daniel Sellers, both significant contributors and in Daniel's case a true collaboration. Elizabeth became consultant for the film.

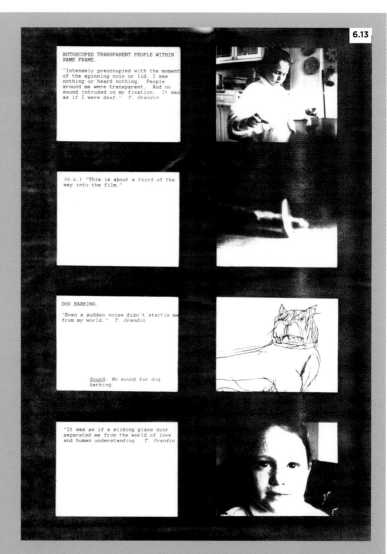

6.13

6.13
Initial storyboards for *A Is for Autism*, directed by Tim Webb (1992), were based on interviews with a number of people with autism and provided a loose structure that could be refined at the editing stage of production. This enabled the subject matter to speak for itself, rather than be determined by any preconceptions of the subject by the director.

CASE STUDY:
A IS FOR AUTISM (continued)

What were the starting points for actually visualizing the film, and how did you decide on the order of the final edit? Did you work intuitively or take a more thematic approach to this? To what extent as director did you steer the content and structure of the film?

As my film developed from the idea to draw a parallel between living in a city and autism, I abandoned the idea to visualize and illustrate. On finding brilliant artists and securing the rights to use their drawings, I then only wanted use these to illustrate the interview/narration sequences. It seemed more authentic and important to convey the idea that the images were people's drawings and not a visualization or illustration of the voice. Connections between voice and image would be created in the editing process.

Clare Kitson has a great claim for enhancing the reputation of British animation through her commissioning period. She encouraged individual approaches to animation filmmaking and allowed great freedom and she commissioned my film based on a very loose storyboard and the idea of collaboration. Animation films are usually commissioned with scripts and tight animatics—a storyboard, on a timeline with sound.

My initial storyboard included quotes from the autistic community, parents and experts. I also had a number of potential collaborators who might work on the film. One of the experts I showed the storyboard, Dr. Neil O'Conner, thought the quotes from the autistic people were most poignant and made the suggestion I only include their voice. I knew this was a good idea and stole it. The film I had been proposing was attempting to be a definitive take on the subject in eleven minutes. By simplifying the point of view to concentrate on the voice of the autistic person the film became more focused.

The freer approach which Clare Kitson encouraged allowed me to make a film in such a way that I was not fully aware of what I was making until the final edit deadline. Structural ideas, which were in the initial storyboard, did remain in the final edit, but new ideas also emerged. However, when compared to the commissioned storyboard, the finished film is very different.

In the initial storyboard and finished film, the start of the film aimed to compare so-called 'normal' thinking with that of autistic thinking, by contrasting 'normal' drawing development with that of an autistic person (I'm never really sure this point is clear). I had also always wanted to punctuate the different themes in the interviews/quotes with a series of edited obsessions using live action. But the rest of the order was really decided in the editing room.

I was only able to initiate one animated collaborative partnership and this was with Daniel Sellers; I did not know what the outcome of this would be or where in the film his section would go. But this collaboration proved to be quite brilliant. I have been lucky to work with Daniel, who I think is a 'genius'. Daniel was nine years old when I worked with him, visiting him about nine times in Chesterfield.

I took Daniel a light box and showed him how to animate. He took to it very naturally and every bit of animation that he made is in the film. He was able to visualize very sophisticated viewpoints though a train-cab window and other moving camera shots. He became a key animator, and Ron MacRae and myself became his 'inbetweener' assistants, slowing down his animation back in London.

On one of the trips, for a change, I had asked Daniel if he would like to go out and draw, and he chose a railroad siding, next to a supermarket car park in the town of Worksop. This remarkable sequence was initiated by thirty key drawings by Daniel. When we got there and on completing his first drawing, which looked down on the siding and passing trains, I asked him if he could draw the siding in front of us as if he were sitting on top of the building on the other side of the railway.

INTRODUCTION

FEELING THE
FACTS: FROM
DOCUDRAMA
TO ANIMATED
DOCUMENTARY

CASE STUDY:
SEXUALITY &
MENTAL HEALTH

POETIC TRUTHS:
WHERE FILM
& ANIMATION
MEET

CASE STUDY: A
IS FOR AUTISM

WORKBOOK
EXERCISE 6.1

CHAPTER
SUMMARY
& FURTHER
READING

KEY WORDS,
NAMES & WORKS

He did this without seeming to even think about how to do it. I'd remembered an idea lifted from an exercise Dr. Neil O'Conner, who researched into genius autistic artists. He had tested their ability to visualize from different positions, by asking artists to draw a toy farmyard set up, viewed from one point of view and asked them to visualize as if from seen from a different point of view.

I asked Daniel if he could draw the same railway, from other points all around the three hundred and sixty degrees of the siding. He did all of these, with seemingly little effort of thought on how to visualize them. He also did one drawing from a bird's eye point of view, which I had not requested.

Upon viewing the finished scene, complete with all the in-between drawings added, the scene not only conveyed an accurate portrayal of the environment through a sweeping 360-degree camera movement, but Daniel had also made an accurate record of time, as the sequence documented each of the passing trains while we were there. I had not realized he had done this until working on the sequence in London and it is truly remarkable.

What do you feel were the main things that you learned by making a film about the abstract experiences of others? For example did it make you more sensitive to subject matter that is personal to others, or did it help think about narrative in a less linear and less literal way perhaps?

I undoubtedly learnt a great deal about the spectrum of autism, drawing development and true genius. An important point about content was that although nearly all of my contributors were high achieving and from a very small percentage of the autistic community, my film did not focus on this. The film evolved into a project, which tried to give a voice to autism from the point of view of autistic people.

End Note on A Is for Autism

The filmmaking methods and techniques used by Tim Webb reveal a number of complexities in making animated documentary. Research can be essential in understanding the nature of your subject matter if it involves sensitive issues for discussion. Finding participants may be more challenging than you think, but by involving them as active contributors you can enrich the filmmaking process in ways that cannot be predetermined.

The process of animated documentary may also often work better if there is a degree of spontaneity by the director, responding to developments and not necessarily imposing a highly rationalized, fact-driven structure. Identifying and applying to film schemes or funding bodies such as national art councils or charitable startup schemes can also be really helpful for gaining access to support from industry experts, as well as ensuring exposure for your work—especially as such projects are often more difficult to pitch to commercial clients or sponsors.

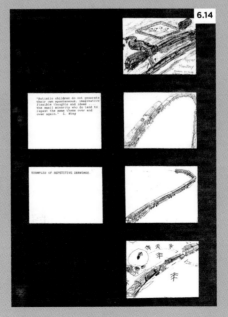

6.14
The talented key frame drawing of trains by one of the main interviewees, Daniel Sellers, provided the basis for full artistic collaboration with one of the main subjects of the film.

WORKBOOK EXERCISE 6.1:
DEVELOPING ANIMATED DOCUMENTARY TECHNIQUES

This final exercise is intended to help you explore ways in which you can apply some of the alternative narrative strategies covered in this chapter to the representation of subjective abstract experiences, knowledge and facts.

The exercise proposes various ways in which you might research, document and visualize the neurological phenomenon synesthesia, in which people's senses, such as sight, taste, smell and hearing, cross over with one another. The result for some is that sounds, words and letters may be perceived as being of a certain colour or even having a particular smell or taste. One of the most common forms is known as *colour synesthesia*, where each letter of the alphabet has an automatic colour association in the mind, such as the letter 'A' being red.

A list of further reading has been suggested to help you research and represent the condition, which is not uncommon amongst artists and musicians, and also features or reveals itself in their work. Famous composers and artists with synesthesia include Olivier Messiaen (1908–1992), David Hockney (1937–) and potentially Kandinsky (the expressionist painter covered in chapter four).

6.15
An example of the sensory condition known as colour synesthesia, where each letter or number is automatically perceived as having its own colour.

6.15

226

INTRODUCTION

FEELING THE
FACTS: FROM
DOCUDRAMA
TO ANIMATED
DOCUMENTARY

CASE STUDY:
SEXUALITY &
MENTAL HEALTH

POETIC TRUTHS:
WHERE FILM
& ANIMATION
MEET

CASE STUDY: A
IS FOR AUTISM

WORKBOOK
EXERCISE 6.1

CHAPTER
SUMMARY
& FURTHER
READING

KEY WORDS,
NAMES & WORKS

1. Research the topic

- Cytowic, R., Eagleman, D. & Nabokov, D. (2011) *Wednesday Is Indigo Blue: Discovering the Brain of Synesthesia*, MIT Press: Cambridge

- Cavallaro, D. (2013) *Synesthesia and the Arts*, McFarland & Co Inc.: Jefferson

- Numerous articles and short documentaries on synesthesia can be found online, including *Correspondences in Cinema: Synaesthetic Film Reconsidered* by Paul Taberham (online article) and *An Eyeful of Sound* by Sam Moore (animated documentary).

2. Identify your subject and devise a set of questions you aim to answer

- You could research a famous artist or composer and/or perhaps interview someone you know who has synesthesia.

- Put together a list of key words to help you research the indexes of various books or words that you commonly come across in the texts that help you research your film further, e.g., Olivier Messiaen, music, sound, chromesthesia (sound-to-colour synesthesia).

- Think about what you might want to know, e.g., how common is synesthesia; how does it affect everyday life; is it possible to describe how it feels; is it perceived as a disability or a talent; how does it manifest in a particular painting or musical score etc.?

3. Think about how the various modes of live action film documentary and animated documentary could be used to visualize the experience of synesthesia

- Direct representation: The word 'synesthesia' could be used as the title of the film and presented as piece of diagrammatic text, with each letter changing in colour to illustrate the narration.

- Expository mode: A factual account about synesthesia by an interviewee can be illustrated by filming real footage of them at work as an artist or going about everyday life, as well as cut away shots to their studio space and artwork.

- Performative mode and non-mimetic substitution: Film footage of the interviewee could be embellished by partially rotoscoping it with digital drawing to emphasize certain sensations manifested by synesthesia or emotions associated with it (think of the methods used in *Snack & Drink* by Bob Sabiston).

- Poetic mode and evocation: The images made and supplied by the artist could be used as the starting point for abstract animation combined with the sounds he/she has described, but without any narration or explanation.

Other topics: A particular topic has been put forward here, but the process could of course be applied to research into any number of other common abstract experiences or conditions, such as depression, and illustrated through public accounts of the lives and work of artists or comedians, for example. You might even be brave enough to put yourself in the frame and make a film about your own personal and abstract experiences.

CHAPTER SUMMARY & FURTHER READING

In this chapter, we have compared and contrasted more traditional methods used in factual film documentary with some of the unique qualities of animated documentary. This has enabled us to discuss some of the most abstract experiences of the human condition. However, we must be careful not to conflate (combine and confuse) these experiences in our analysis of different forms of documentary. For example, direct parallels should not be drawn between the subject of clinical depression represented in *Persepolis* and the experience of autism explored in the animated documentary *A Is for Autism*. Neither is the subject of hysteria covered in the animated documentary *Hysteria* directly comparable with the condition synesthesia explored in the last exercise.

The key point of exploring such diverse and sensitive topics is to help you think about how you might begin to express personal truths of your own through more expressive means and also think carefully about how to author films about the abstract personal experiences of others. This final chapter brings us not to an end point therefore, but hopefully a starting point for delving deeper into the kind of subject matter that it is possible to express through animation.

What we have seen, in each separate case study, is how experiences and memories can be as important as concrete knowledge and facts. For example, the films *Persepolis* and *Waltz with Bashir* illustrate how the context of historical events can be used as a platform to represent and understand conditions such as depression or post-traumatic stress disorder and how they can be triggered.

We have also explored a grey area between fact and fiction in both live action filmmaking and animation, with a view to opening up the range of techniques that you can combine from the two mediums. As with other chapters, this chapter will hopefully encourage you to broaden the range of sources of inspiration from documentary filmmakers to expressionist painters and composers. More expressive practical methods covered have once again included rotoscoping, montage, monologue narration, layered sound effects and leitmotifs.

Despite any quest for expressing deeper internal truths, in every case we are also aware that the very process of capturing an image or editing a sequence of images creates a selective interpretation of events. From the *Sinking of the Lusitania* or *Waltz with Bashir*, to *A Is for Autism*, events, interviews, memories and experiences have all been mediated through a director and the media used by them to record and communicate their subject matter.

6.16

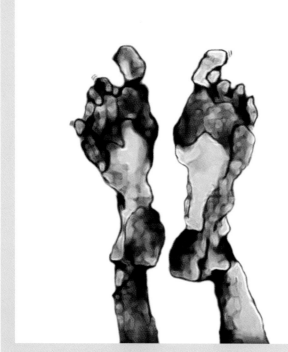

6.16
A film still from the animated documentary *Test Strip* by the author Mark Collington, Royal College of Art (2000). The film explores the experience of being a life model. In one sequence a life model expresses how, if her feet are warm, then she does not feel undressed.

INTRODUCTION

FEELING THE
FACTS: FROM
DOCUDRAMA
TO ANIMATED
DOCUMENTARY

CASE STUDY:
SEXUALITY &
MENTAL HEALTH

POETIC TRUTHS:
WHERE FILM
& ANIMATION
MEET

CASE STUDY: *A
IS FOR AUTISM*

WORKBOOK
EXERCISE 6.1

**CHAPTER
SUMMARY
& FURTHER
READING**

KEY WORDS,
NAMES & WORKS

Once again we can challenge the integrity of this book or any textbook in the same way we can challenge the authority of the expository documentary. In many senses this book is a printed equivalent of the expository documentary, in so far as it has been designed upon a particular selection of topics or themes, inclusion of particular current affairs and historical events, interviews, quotes by experts and so on. The book is by definition also limited to a particular set of arguments, as it is simply not possible for any single textbook to cover 'everything'.

The intention of this book is to provoke its audience to challenge that which has been documented by the author by responding to the series of workbook exercises that encourage critical thinking on your part. This brings attention to one of the key subjects that form the starting point for the concluding chapter: how the process of reading in itself is a form of authorship, as you edit together knowledge and opinions in your own mind as you read this book.

The concluding chapter will also explore the concept of the essay film, which is in many ways an extension or alternative to the more expressive modes of documentary explored in this chapter. The essay film will be introduced as a means of weaving together your own selection of the workbook exercises in this book, as a starting point to explore and express your own experience and thoughts about the impact of present day events on you or others in the world around you.

FURTHER READING

Genre, Documentary & Female Authorship

Buchan, S. (2006) *Animated Worlds*, John Libbey Publishing: Eastleigh

Foucault, M. (1988) *Madness & Civilization*, Vintage Books: New York

Foucault, M. (1998) *The Will to Knowledge*, Penguin: London

Grant, B. (2011) *Film Genre: From Iconography to Ideology*, Wallflower Press: Brighton

Greer, J. (2012) *The Female Eunuch*, Fourth Estate: London

Hall, S. (2013) *Representation* (Second Edition), SAGE Publications Limited: London

Herzog, W. *On the Absolute, the Sublime, and Ecstatic Truth*, Boston University, College of Arts & Sciences—Arion (online)

Honess Roe, A. (2013) *Animated Documentary*, Palgrave Macmillan: Basingstoke

Lacey, S. (1995) *British Realist Theatre: The New Wave in Its Context 1956-1965*, Routledge: London

Lorenzo Hernández, M. (2010) *A Film of One's Own: The Animated Portraits of Young Contemporary Female Animators*, Animation: An Interdisciplinary Journal (online)

Nichols, B. (2010) *Introduction to Documentary* (Second Edition), Indiana University Press: Bloomington

Pilling, J. (1992) *Women and Animation: A Compendium*, British Film Institute: London

Wells, P. (2002) *Animation Genre and Authorship*, Wallflower Press: London

Wells, P. (2007) *Understanding Animation*, Routledge: London

KEY WORDS

Animated Documentary
A form of factual animation, often concerned with expressive rather than realistic representation of knowledge

Autism
A broad range of cognitive, emotional and behavioural patterns that can include highly focused interests, an affinity for repetitive activities, hypersensitivity to stimuli and difficulties with social situations

Catharsis
The psychological healing process of release from repressed emotions or memories, often as the result of creating or experiencing art, film or music

Discourse
The process by which discussion and context define the meaningful existence of something

Docudrama
A film that dramatizes real events

Dogma
A set of principles believed to be absolute truth

Ecstatic Truth
The deeper understanding that is reached through our subjective interpretation of a viewing experience, i.e., there is a limit to the level of truth that can be conveyed in any given mode of documentary and results in a purely subjective decision by the viewer

Evocation
The focus on more abstract animated stimuli, such as colours, textures, rhythms and sounds, to evoke a feeling of the state of mind of the subject and thus knowledge of the experience being documented

Expository Mode
Documentary that tends to be narrated or presented by an authoritative figure as an objective, fact based, accurate, educational and/ or moral account on a particular topic

Feminine/Female Aesthetic
Like the function of evocation, the female aesthetic is used in animation in general to explore more sensitive or more abstract subject matter using a range of expressive techniques

Hysteria
A disorder whereby psychological stress results in physical symptoms and extreme emotional behaviour

Indexical Links
Real film footage that acts as a direct or causal link to the subject matter being discussed and therefore reality, truth and facts

Live Action Documentary
A form of factual filmmaking, usually focused on presenting knowledge as fact using real film footage of subject matter

Mimetic Substitution
The more conventional use of animation in expository documentary—to recreate things or events that could not otherwise be filmed, often as realistically as possible

Non-Mimetic Substitution
The embellishment of existing documentary footage (using methods such as rotoscoping) or creation of new and sometimes hyper-real animated footage, in order to add or emphasize something about the experience

Observational Mode
Frequently referred to as 'fly on the wall', a documentary method where the filmmaker has limited if any interaction with the subject or environment that is being filmed

Performative Mode
Live action documentary that focuses on representing a direct experience of the subject or main person in the documentary, e.g., intense, complex, internal thoughts, feelings and memories of the subject, not necessarily being presented with rigid facts and binary arguments

Poetic Mode
Documentary similar to the performative mode, though not influenced directly by the voice of the director or the subjects, but experienced wholly in the first person by the viewer; like evocation, historical or cultural knowledge, it is represented by film footage that is distorted, exaggerated and edited to create an aesthetic experience

INTRODUCTION

FEELING THE
FACTS: FROM
DOCUDRAMA
TO ANIMATED
DOCUMENTARY

CASE STUDY:
SEXUALITY &
MENTAL HEALTH

POETIC TRUTHS:
WHERE FILM
& ANIMATION
MEET

CASE STUDY: A
IS FOR AUTISM

WORKBOOK
EXERCISE 6.1

CHAPTER
SUMMARY
& FURTHER
READING

KEY WORDS,
NAMES & WORKS

Polemic
A controversial attack or statement, often in the form of a film or written document

Post-Traumatic Stress Disorder
The delayed affect of extreme events on peoples' mental health

Rotoscoping
Drawing or painting over live action footage

Social Extension
Expanding the range of subject matter that is acceptable on screen

Sublime Experience
A viewing experience that needs no further explanation

Synethesia
A neurological phenomenon in which people's senses such as sight, taste, smell and hearing cross over with one another

KEY NAMES
Ari Folman
Michel Foucault
Terry Gilliam
Stuart Hall
Werner Herzog
David Hockney
Annabelle Honess Roe
Jerzy Kucia
Peter Lord
Olivier Messiaen
Winsor McCay
Sam Moore
Bill Nichols
Jayne Pilling
Joanna Quinn
Erica Russell
Bob Sabiston
Marjane Satrapi
Alys Scott-Hawkins
Paul Ward
Tim Webb
Paul Wells

KEY WORKS
A Is for Autism
An Eyeful of Sound
Crying & Wanking
Girls' Night Out
Going Equipped
Hysteria
Monty Python's Flying Circus
Parada
Persepolis
Sinking of the Lusitania, The
Snack & Drink
Triangle
Waltz with Bashir

CONCLUSION

PULLING IT ALL TOGETHER

From *memories* of the *past*, to *hopes* or *fears* for the *future*, this book has been designed in response to a selection of particular topics or themes relating to the *human condition* and for *understanding* the world we live in *today*. These have included the right of passage of a child or journey of the *everyman*, the impact of *technology* on society and how the *media* shapes and controls identity.

The inclusion of certain historical events and current affairs has been essential for understanding the selection of case studies, ranging from European colonization of America to American cultural imperialism, as well as historical treatment of mental illness to representation of gender and ethnicity in advertising. These case studies will have hopefully provided you with a range of potential starting points for your own subject matter.

This book began by introducing semiotics, semantics, monoscenic and synchronic narratives and how to read an individual image, as well as exploring symbolism contained in myths, breaking down the formalist structure and archetypes of the folk tale and applying this formula to understanding other genres. Myth, folk tale and genre have all been discussed in terms of how they are used to understand the world around us.

We then looked at how these more conventional ways of reading images and narrative sequences can be challenged through more abstract modernist art movements, such as expressionism and the editing technique montage. Different modernist approaches to narrative have also been discussed in terms of how they have been used by artists to make sense of the world we live in.

In discussing realism and propaganda, we have seen how hyper-real images and text can be used to control and influence our behaviour and identity. Finally, we explored how certain modernist techniques can be used within the various modes of documentary and animated documentary to challenge more conventional notions of how to represent facts and truths. Once again we have seen how propaganda and documentary are used to define our knowledge of the world.

Perhaps most importantly, we have explored the difference between passively accepting the story presented to us in a fairy tale, propaganda or traditional documentary and how modernist film movements such as German expressionism or contemporary documentary evoke a more subjective, emotional or psychological reaction in the audience.

In all cases, the purpose of this book and the exercises included in it has been to help you develop an initial idea into an animation project that is enriched directly by a framework of concepts commonly introduced through critical, cultural and contextual studies programmes. This concluding chapter summarizes how you might combine a range of these exercises into the production planning and development of two key types of animation project.

RECOMMENDED VIEWING

Frank Film, directed by Frank Mouris, Frank Mouris Productions (1973)

Letter from Siberia, directed by Chris Marker, Argos Films (1957)

Man with a Movie Camera, directed by Dziga Vertov, VUFKU (1929)

PULLING IT ALL
TOGETHER

FROM ANIMATED
SHORT TO
ESSAY FILM

CROSS-
DISCIPLINARY
PRACTICE

READING AS
REWRITING &
INTERTEXTUALITY

FURTHER
READING

KEY WORDS,
NAMES & WORKS

7.1

7.1
Work-in-progress film still from *A Life
Ephemeral*, essay film-animation by the author,
Mark Collington (2015–2016). The sequence
depicted here uses the signs and structures
of the motorway to explore the concepts of
semiotics and semantics. The sequence is also a
reinterpretation of the journey into the forest in
the fairy tale, and acts as a visual metaphor for
the journey into the unknown of adult life.

FROM ANIMATED SHORT
TO ESSAY FILM

You could on the one hand apply the exercises to the development of a more traditional animation. For example, you could work on developing a narrative context, beat board and layout designs from the exercises and material on monoscenic and synchronic narrative in chapter one, in conjunction with the narrative stages of the folk tale outlined in chapter two and deciding on a genre and deeper topical theme for your animation covered in chapter three.

On the other hand, you could explore the concept of the essay film, which is in many ways an extension or alternative to the more expressive modes of documentary explored through the final workbook exercise in chapter six—a means of expressing your experience, knowledge and opinions about the impact of past, present or future events on you or others in the world around you.

Dziga Vertov and Chris Marker are frequently referred to as key filmmakers whose work can be used to define the often-disputed form of the essay film. The film *Man with a Movie Camera* by Dziga Vertov (1929) is often regarded as the precursor or prototype for the essay film. This film ignores literary conventions, using a montage of self-conscious camera angles and semi-abstract compositions to document the dynamics of metropolitan societies.

The message of the film is open to subjective interpretation, juxtaposing images glorifying industrial labour and its benefits to society on the one hand with working class living conditions and images of the lifestyle of high society on the other. The reality of what is being filmed is also brought into question by revealing the cameraman in many of the shots, and also through the use of stop motion and slow motion.

Subsequent essay films by Chris Marker have added narration to montage, which is both a factual-political and poetic commentary on footage that clearly exposes the reality of Soviet life in *Letter from Siberia* (1957). Again we see animated visuals used to question reality and the representation of it. But while there is a clear aesthetic, it is cruder and less contrived in its execution.

Frank Film, directed by Frank Mouris (1973), is an animation that continually and rapidly adds new layers of magazine cuttings on top of one another. This creates the effect of a montage, with a monologue of overlapping descriptions of the director's childhood. The result is open to subjective interpretation of consumer culture and Mouris' autobiography.

While this might not necessarily be described as an essay film it shares many of the same characteristics and is a useful starting point for thinking about a completely animated essay film. In particular, it challenges preconceptions about the aesthetics of animation, as something that need not be beautiful to look at, but still presents a poetic and thought-provoking aesthetic.

Further, like an academic essay, the essay film can also be a visual means of exploring and weaving together the range of concepts and techniques used by other artists and filmmakers. You can illustrate your understanding of concepts and techniques by recreating or reinterpreting your own version of the work of others, potentially adding critical commentary (a narration) on what you have learned about techniques applied to the treatment of specific subject matter.

7.2

7.2
Frank Film, directed by Frank Mouris (1973), uses techniques that resemble aspects of essay films by Vertov and Marker, such as use of montage and narration.

PULLING IT ALL
TOGETHER

FROM ANIMATED
SHORT TO
ESSAY FILM

CROSS-
DISCIPLINARY
PRACTICE

READING AS
REWRITING &
INTERTEXTUALITY

FURTHER
READING

KEY WORDS,
NAMES & WORKS

CROSS-DISCIPLINARY
PRACTICE

In the discussion of modernism in chapter four, we concluded by highlighting how animation was partly born out of experimentation with a range of expressive art forms, such as shadow puppetry, and also the technology of optical toys. We have also witnessed how animation very quickly became an industrialized form of highly stylized mainstream entertainment.

This book has made the case that the visual techniques used in the most meaningful animations are not driven by technology or style, but are the result of narrative form and function. Many *independent* animators continue, therefore, to work with a range of experimental and expressive techniques inspired by practices in other film, art and design disciplines to enhance their storytelling skills. This is known as cross-disciplinary practice.

As far as possible, this book is the product of a response to the material produced by a diverse range of professional animators, artists and filmmakers working across a range of disciplines. The final intention of this book is to encourage you to revisit the concept of animation as a cross-disciplinary or hybrid process rather than a specialist discipline. Hopefully this book will therefore have equal relevance to filmmakers or sculpturers, for example, as it will to animators who wish to sustain a more versatile career.

To that end, the practical methods and theoretical subject matter covered in this book could be as readily applied to creating a narrative sequence of paintings in a gallery (like the church frescos or triptychs discussed in chapter two), making an animated museum installation (such as the 3D zoetrope produced for the Museum of London discussed in chapter two) or projection mapping a more immersive experience within a public space (see fig. 7.3) as they could to developing an animated short or viral.

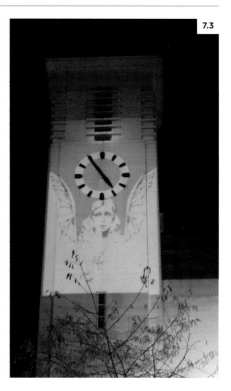

7.3

7.3
Projection mapping of an animated Christmas narrative onto Surbiton Station, created by the author, Mark Collington (2013).

READING AS REWRITING & INTERTEXTUALITY

In watching different types of film or animation, we have discussed the idea of passive and active audience experience. The more conventional expository documentary, for example, requires little effort on the part of the audience to absorb and understand what is presented to them. The poetic mode of documentary, however, requires an active response from the audience, whereby each person subjectively interprets and absorbs a more abstract body of visual information.

Semioticians treat film as being of the same function and status as a literary text, in other words, as a film text. Roland Barthes described the kind of linear, realistic text that requires a passive audience (such as the expository documentary) as a 'readerly text', and the more abstract, subjective kind of text that requires an active response as a 'writerly text'. What Barthes proposed is a post-structuralist concept, that reading is a form of writing (or rewriting) in itself. The writerly text therefore 'stimulates and provokes an active reader' (Stam, Burgoyne & Flitterman-Lewis, 1992, p. 192).

Thus, the intention here is to open up a dialogue between myself, contributors to this book and you through the case studies and exercises in each chapter. These are designed to encourage critical thinking on your part and create understanding of how the process of reading in itself is a form of authorship, as you edit together knowledge and opinions in your own mind as you read this or any other book.

This book also encourages you to continue such active dialogues with others by sharing your knowledge, experiences and work online. It is advisable to conduct further independent research into the themes, issues and concepts covered in this book, using the key words documented in your workbook to explore the indexes and chapters from further reading lists as a starting point.

Whether the outcome of the exercises is a film, installation or other body of work, the advantage for the animator-artist-filmmaker of being more active in responding to and getting inspiration from wider reading is that they can make references to other texts and concepts that are already known and understood and advance the message and meaning, especially in short films, much further and more quickly.

This form of cultural cross-referencing was termed by French philosopher Jacques Derrida (1930–2004) as intertextuality—how the narratives of completely different texts frequently borrow from and reference one another to create meaning. Intertextual references are commonly used in animated sitcoms or shows such as *The Simpsons* and *South Park*, which parody (make humorous references to) other television shows or films to make the audience laugh and advance the story within an episode.

This book has explored narrative and the human condition largely with reference to cultural thinking and forms of artistic expression from the age of the Enlightenment through to the modernist period. The concepts of intertexuality and cross-disciplinary practice extend into a whole other period or branch of cultural thinking and artistic expression known as post-modernism.

The scale of discussion needed on post-modernism requires a separate text. Useful starting points for research include the key words post-structuralism, appropriation, reproduction, hybridity, interdisciplinarity, anti-aesthetic, subversion and parody, as well as the art movement Pop Art and artist Andy Warhol, filmmaker Chris Marker, animator Frank Mouris and philosopher Julia Kristeva. A list of further reading for this and useful introductory texts relating to post-modernism can be found at the end of the chapter.

Hopefully the pedagogic (teaching) methods underpinning the exercises provided in this book will help you to develop a system of your own that enables you to combine your own experiences and research with your animation practice—making work that will continue to challenge you and others on your own personal creative journey into the unknown.

PULLING IT ALL
TOGETHER

FROM ANIMATED
SHORT TO
ESSAY FILM

CROSS-
DISCIPLINARY
PRACTICE

**READING AS
REWRITING &
INTERTEXTUALITY**

**FURTHER
READING**

KEY WORDS,
NAMES & WORKS

FURTHER READING

**Essay Film, Post-Structuralism
& Intertextuality in Film**

Corrigan, T. (2011) *The Essay Film:
From Montaigne, After Marker*,
Oxford University Press: Oxford

Stam, R., Burgoyne, R. & Flitterman-
Lewis, S. (2006) *New Vocabularies in
Film & Semiotics*, Routledge: London

**Post-Modernism and Relevant
Animation Texts**

Acton, M. (2004) *Learning to Look at
Modern Art*, Routledge: Abingdon

Cotte, O. (2006) *Secrets of Oscar
Winning Animation*, Focal Press:
Oxford

Wells, P. Hardstaff, J. (2008)
Re-imagining Animation,
AVA Publishing SA: London

Woods, T. (2009) *Beginning
Postmodernism*, Manchester
University Press: Manchester

KEY WORDS

Anti-Aesthetic
Usually an intentionally and consciously designed artefact or experience that investigates established tastes or conventions by challenging or contradicting them with often purposefully unpleasant alternative designs

Appropriation
To self-consciously and openly borrow and develop an idea

Cross-Disciplinary Practice
Where research and practices in two or more similar or distinct disciplines are common or shared, such as storyboarding in animation and film

Essay Film
In many ways an extension or alternative to the more expressive modes of documentary—a means of expressing personal experience, knowledge and opinions

Interdisciplinarity
Where research and practices in two or more distinct disciplines, such as fashion and architecture, come together to form totally new ideas and products separate from either discipline

Intertextuality
A form of cultural cross-referencing where the narratives of completely different texts frequently borrow from and reference one another to create meaning

Parody
To make humorous references to other television shows or films (for example), in order to make an audience laugh and advance the story within an episode

Pop Art
An art movement that challenged the boundaries between high art and the mass production of consumer culture

Postmodernism
A subsequent period or parallel branch to modernism, of cultural thinking and artistic expression defined by a range of concepts including post-structuralism

Post-Structuralism
A form of literary criticism that includes challenging structures and conventions of metanarratives (such as the formalist *Morphology of the Folk Tale* and structuralist use of binary opposites) and prioritizes the role of the reader over the author

Readerly Text
A linear, realistic text that requires a passive audience that accepts what is presented to them, such as the expository documentary mode

Reproduction
The recreation or simulation of an object or artefact

Subversion
The intention usually to undermine or expose something, often through humorous but disruptive methods

Writerly Text
A more abstract, subjective kind of text that requires an active response, such as the poetic documentary mode

PULLING IT ALL
TOGETHER

FROM ANIMATED
SHORT TO
ESSAY FILM

CROSS-
DISCIPLINARY
PRACTICE

READING AS
REWRITING &
INTERTEXTUALITY

FURTHER
READING

KEY WORDS,
NAMES & WORKS

KEY NAMES

Roland Barthes
Jacques Derrida
Julia Kristeva
Chris Marker
Frank Mouris
Dziga Vertov
Andy Warhol

KEY WORKS

Frank Film
Letter from Siberia
Man with a Movie Camera
Simpsons, The
South Park

APPENDIX

PICTURE CREDITS

Introduction
0.1: *The Lady in White* (2015) / © Michael Evans
0.2 *De Intus* (2010) / © Gavin Wrench
0.3: *Looming Marvellous* (2015) /
© April Slocombe

Chapter 1
1.1: Arthur Conan Doyle's story published in *The Strand Magazine*, London, 1892, illustrated by Sidney E. Paget. (Photo by Ann Ronan Pictures / Print Collector / Getty Images)
1.2: © 1937 Disney
1.3: Diane Diederich / Getty Images
1.4: PRANA-FILM/THE KOBAL COLLECTION
1.5: Film still of actor Gary Cooper in 'The Texan' for Paramount Pictures, 1930. (Photo by Archive Photos / Getty Images)
1.6–1.7: © Mark Collington
1.8: *The Love Letter* by Johannes Vermeer (c. 1669–70) / Courtesy of Rijksmuseum Amsterdam
1.9: *Going Equipped* © Aardman Animations Ltd 1989
1.10–1.13: © John Taber 2015
1.14: *The Entombment of Christ* by Fra Angelico (c. 1450) / Samuel H. Kress Collection / National Gallery of Art
1.15: *West Pier* (2001) / © Mark Collington
1.16: © Elora Aboua 2015
1.17: *The Nativity, Adoration of the Magi and Presentation in Temple*, triptych (c. 1470) / The Art Archive / Museo del Prado Madrid

Chapter 2
2.1: Photo by Fine Art Images / Heritage Images / Getty Images
2.2: Drawn by Gustave Doré, French artist, January 6, 1832–January 23, 1883; engraved by Pannemaker. From Charles Perrault's *Les Contes de Perrault / Perrault's Fairy Tales*; CP: French writer, January 12, 1628–May 16, 1703. (Photo by Culture Club / Getty Images)
2.3: Native American Indian totem pole in Stanley Park, Vancouver British Columbia.
Credit: Paul Giamou / Getty Images
2.4: © 1992 Disney
2.5: Photo by Alex Livesey; FIFA / FIFA via Getty Images
2.6: Still from *Laputa, Castle in the Sky* (1986) / Studio Ghibli / Tokuma Shoten / The Kobal Collection
2.7: *Mt Fuji Seen from Nakaharo* by Katsushika Hokusai (1760–1849) / The Art Archive / Victoria and Albert Museum London / V&A Images
2.8: Colliery Pit, Rhondda Heritage Park, Rhondda Valley, South Wales, United Kingdom, Europe / Credit: Billy Stock / robertharding / Getty Images
2.9: First Hindenburg Flight
2.10: Falkirk Wheel and Visitor Centre / Credit: Empato / Getty Images
2.11–2.12: *Peter & the Wolf* (2006) / © Breakthru Films
2.13: © Suzie Templeton
2.14: *Dog* (2001) / © Suzie Templeton
2.15: Still from *Ponyo* (2008) / Studio Ghibli / NTV / Dentsu / Toho / The Kobal Collection
2.16–2.17: © Museum of London
2.18: Sandstone pillars in mist, Zhangjiajie National Forest Park (UNESCO World Heritage Site), Hunan Province, China / Credit: Keren Su / Getty Images

Chapter 3
3.1: Viviana Gonzalez / Getty Images
3.2: Galaxy motion / Credit: Rob Atkins / Getty Images
3.3: Still from *The Good, the Bad and the Ugly* (1966) / PEA / The Kobal Collection
3.4: Abandoned horse carts in a town, Old Trail Town, Cody, Wyoming, USA / Credit: Glow Images, Inc. / Getty Images
3.5: Ghorfa near Ksar Haddada, Tataouine Governorate, Tunisia / Credit: De Agostini / Archivio J. Lange
3.6: Newspaper Rock, Canyonlands National Park / Credit: Franz Marc Frei
3.7: © 2010 Disney·Pixar
3.8–3.9: *Rapunzel* (2015) / © Noriko Okaku & Tom Salo
3.10: Still from *Modern Times* (1936) / Chaplin / United Artists / The Kobal Collection
3.11: © 2008 Disney·Pixar
3.12: Yawar Nazir / Getty Images
3.13: The Kobal Collection
3.14: Theatrical mask from the Dipylon of Athens, Greece. Greek civilization, 2nd century BC. Athens, Ethnikó Arheologikó Moussío (National Archaeological Museum). Photo by DeAgostini / Getty Images
3.15: A robot on top of a pile of discarded robot parts / Credit: Doug Armand / Getty Images
3.16: *Domesticated* (2015) / © Vaida Kereisyte
3.17: © Nick Smith 2014 / *Morpheus Rig* © Josh Burton
3.18: *Domesticated* (2015) / © Vaida Kereisyte
3.19: Africa, day and night, satellite image of the Earth / Credit: Science Photo Library—NASA / NOAA / Getty Images

Chapter 4

4.1: Still from title sequence of *Anatomy of a Murder* (1959) / Columbia / The Kobal Collection
4.2: Johann Gutenberg's (1400–1468) first printing press. Engraving published Mainz 1856. (Photo by Universal History Archive/UIG via Getty Images)
4.3: *Portrait of Albert Einstein*. Photo by Fred Stein Archive / Archive Photos / Getty Images
4.4: *An Experiment on a Bird in the Air Pump* by Joseph Wright of Derby (1768) / The Art Archive / DeA Picture Library
4.5: *Composition VIII* by Wassily Kandinsky (1923) / The Art Archive / The Solomon R. Guggenheim Foundation / Art Resource, NY / Solomon R. Guggenheim Museum, New York, Solomon R. Guggenheim Founding Collection, by gift
4.6: © Alice Barlow 2014
4.7: Shower killer in *Psycho* / Credit: Paramount Pictures / Handout / Getty Images
4.8: *The Bottle of Banyuls* by Juan Gris / Credit: Peter Will / Getty Images
4.9: *The Typewriter* (2003) / © Richard Haynes & Mikolaj Watt
4.10: *Death and the Mother* (1988) / © Ruth Lingford
4.11: Still from *'M'* (1931) / Nero / The Kobal Collection
4.12: *Zoi* (2013) / © Amanda Curl
4.13: *When the Day Breaks*, 1999 / National Film Board of Canada
4.14: © Michael Evans 2014
4.15: Shadow play puppet of Malaysia / Credit: Photography by Leo Li / Getty Images

Chapter 5

5.1: Second World War—kitchen is key to victory, eat less bread, propaganda poster / Credit: DEA / G. Nimatallah / Getty Images
5.2: Vintage war poster of Uncle Sam pointing / Credit: Barbara Singer / Getty Images
5.3: Still from *The Sinking of the Lusitania* (1918) / Universal / Jewel / The Kobal Collection
5.4: © Shelda Cohen 2010
5.5: Published in London in 1915 by the Parliamentary Recruiting Committee. Image by Bernard Partridge. Credit: Library of Congress—edited version © Science Faction / Getty Images
5.6: Dominique Faget / AFP / Getty Images
5.7: Three yellow cabs / Credit: Photography by Steve Kelley aka mudpig / Getty Images
5.8: Martin Dimitrov / Getty Images
5.9: Credit: Sam Edwards / Getty Images
5.10: Lost in a book / Credit: Image by Catherine MacBride / Getty Images
5.11: Arrangement of craft materials, tools and digital tablet on black wood / Credit: Westend61 / Getty Images
5.12: Husband Smelling Pot of Soup / Credit: GraphicaArtis / Getty Images
5.13: *Bath Time* circa 1890, advertisement for Pears' Soap / The Art Archive / Amoret Tanner Collection
5.14: Still from *Good Times* / Bud Yorkin / Norman Lear / Tandem / The Kobal Collection
5.15: Still from *Family Guy* / FOX TV / Seth Macfarlane / The Kobal Collection
5.16: Promotional image for *Lara Croft Tomb Raider: The Cradle of Life* (2003) / Paramount / The Kobal Collection
5.17: Promotional image from the 'Make Baobab Famous' campaign (2015) / © Aduna Ltd.
5.18: Production still for an animated viral for the 'Make Baobab Famous' campaign (2015) / © Emeka Uzoh
5.19: Close-up of God and Adam's hands / Credit: Stuart Dee / Getty Images

Chapter 6

6.1: Belgium History Waterloo Anniversary / Credit: John Thys / AFP / Getty Images
6.2: Still from *Persepolis* (2007) / 2.4.7. Films / The Kobal Collection
6.3: Still from *Waltz with Bashir* (2008) / Bridgit Folman Film Gang / The Kobal Collection
6.4: 1876, Europe Map, World Maps / Credit: Historic Map Works LLC / Getty Images
6.5: Mark Stevenson / Stocktrek Images
6.6: Eskimo medicine man exorcising evil spirits from a sick boy in Alaska, USA (between ca. 1900 and ca. 1930). (Photo by: Universal History Archive / UIG via Getty Images)
6.7–6.8: *Hysteria* (2001) / © Alys Scott-Hawkins
6.9–6.10: *Crying & Wanking* (2002) / © Alys Scott-Hawkins
6.11: *A Is for Autism* (1992) / © Tim Webb / Artist: Daniel Sellers
6.12: *Snack & Drink* (2000) / © 1999 Flat Black Films
6.13: *A Is for Autism* (1992) / © Tim Webb
6.14: *A Is for Autism* (1992) / © Tim Webb
6.15: *Test Strip* (2000) / © Mark Collington

Conclusion

7.1: © Mark Collington
7.2: Still from *Frank Film* (1973) / © Frank Mouris
7.3: © Mark Collington

INDEX

INDEX

INDEX

ACKNOWLEDGMENTS

This book is the result of many working relationships and life experiences that make up my own 'Writer's Journey' over the last twelve years. With limited space I apologize for breaking down acknowledgements into essentially name lists from stages in my career. Without further ado I would therefore like to thank the staff and alumni community from the Royal College of Art, where I completed my own postgraduate studies in animation (1999-2001): Joan Ashworth, Ruth Lingford, Jayne Pilling, Tim Webb and Tereza Stehlikova.

I would like to thank colleagues at the Arts University Bournemouth (2004-2006): Liam Scanlan, Peter Parr, Peter Symons, Paul Ward, Paul Hilton and Jon Turner; colleagues at the University of Bedfordshire (2006-2013): John Stephens, Alec Charles, Joanna Callaghan, Garry Layden, Viv Cherry, Noel Douglas, Beverley Bothwell, Rachel Gannon, Colin Davies and Gemma Marmalade; colleagues at The Cass Faculty, London Metropolitan University (2013-2016): Andrew Stone, Karen Smith, Charlotte Worthington, Peter Hewitt, Michelle Salamon, Ben Melville, Noriko Okaku, Janette Parris, Anne Markey, Jen Ng, Helen Mallinson, Nick Haeffner, Jeremy Collins, Michael Upton and Marcus Bowerman.

There are many other people who I should like to thank individually, including the numerous peer reviewers who helped shape and refine the text; the many animators, studios and industry partners who have supplied material and content for the book; as well as friends and colleagues at other universities for their encouragement and support. I cannot possibly mention them all by name. But for those whose names largely do not *at least* appear in the main text as direct contributors, or who were informal advisors on the content, I should like to thank: Paul Wells for his initial encouragement, Bella Honess Roe, Kim Charnley, Steve Henderson, Skwigly Magazine, Slurpy Studios, Louis Clichy, Max Hattler, Michael Flexer, Robin Kershaw, Meriel Jeater, Sean Waterman, Manoj Bhardwaj, Alison Persson, Sophie Capron, Enrica Sciandrone and Slavka Jovanovic.

Fundamentally this book is as much the product of the many undergraduates and post graduates whom I have had the privilege of working with. The list is endless, so I would simply like to thank them all! And of course I must thank the team at Bloomsbury for all their mentoring, support, encouragement and patience: Georgia Kennedy, James Piper, Renee Last. Chris Black at Lachina was also extremely helpful in managing this book's production.

I would also like to thank my father and mother who have always wholeheartedly supported my interests. Their own professions, as BBC producer and adult literacy tutor respectively, provided me with the media, research and literacy skills needed to make my way in the field of animation and academia in the fast pace of the twenty-first century.

But ultimately I would like to thank my wife for her absolute support in what has been a major undertaking for us both at the beginning of our marriage, whilst changing job, moving house and during two pregnancies. As a last word, in light of these factors I must therefore take sole responsibility for any inaccuracies or unintended misrepresentation in this text, which has had to compete with the sleepless nights and rewards of family life.

The publishers would like to thank Alec Charles, Eleanor Cowen, Harvey Deneroff, Mary Krell, Paul Taberham and Richard Yarhouse.